HUMANISM AND AM

Humanism and America is the first major study of the impact of the Renaissance and Renaissance humanism upon the English colonisation of America. The analysis is conducted through an interdisciplinary examination of a broad spectrum of writings on colonisation, ranging from the works of Thomas More to those of the Virginia Company. Andrew Fitzmaurice shows that English expansion was profoundly neo-classical in inspiration, and he excavates the distinctively humanist tradition that informed some central issues of colonisation: the motivations of wealth and profit, honour and glory; the nature of and possibilities for liberty; and the problems of just title, including the dispossession of native Americans. Dr Fitzmaurice presents a colonial tradition which, counter to received wisdom, is often hostile to profit, nervous of dispossession and desirous of liberty. Only in the final chapters does he chart the rise of an aggressive, acquisitive and possessive colonial ideology.

IDEAS IN CONTEXT

Edited by Quentin Skinner (*General Editor*), Lorraine Daston,
Dorothy Ross and James Tully

The books in this series will discuss the emergence of intellectual traditions and of related new disciplines. The procedures, aims and vocabularies that were generated will be set in the context of the alternatives available within the contemporary frameworks of ideas and institutions. Through detailed studies of the evolution of such traditions, and their modification by different audiences, it is hoped that a new picture will form of the development of ideas in their concrete contexts. By this means, artificial distinctions between the history of philosophy, of the various sciences, of society and politics, and of literature may be seen to dissolve.
The series is published with the support of the Exxon Foundation.

A list of books in the series will be found at the end of the volume.

HUMANISM AND AMERICA

An Intellectual History of English
Colonisation, 1500–1625

ANDREW FITZMAURICE

CAMBRIDGE
UNIVERSITY PRESS

CAMBRIDGE UNIVERSITY PRESS
Cambridge, New York, Melbourne, Madrid, Cape Town, Singapore, São Paulo

Cambridge University Press
The Edinburgh Building, Cambridge CB2 8RU, UK

Published in the United States of America by Cambridge University Press, New York

www.cambridge.org
Information on this title: www.cambridge.org/9780521822251

First published 2003
Reprinted 2004
This digitally printed version 2007

A catalogue record for this publication is available from the British Library

ISBN 978-0-521-82225-1 hardback
ISBN 978-0-521-03618-4 paperback

For my parents

Contents

Contents

Acknowledgements

This book has a history embracing more than ten years, in various characters, and has accordingly acquired some profound debts.

I have received generous support from St John's College, Cambridge, Churchill College, Cambridge, and also from the Cambridge Commonwealth Trust. Since arriving at Sydney University I have received invaluable guidance from Michael Jackson, Richard Waterhouse and Shane White.

Early versions of the chapters have been delivered in a number of conferences and seminars. In particular the Atlantic History Seminar in August 1997 at Harvard University was an invaluable forum in which to present ideas and I thank Bernard Bailyn for the opportunity to participate and for the inspiration which he and the other participants provided. My thanks also to the participants in *The touch of the real: A symposium hosting Stephen Greenblatt*, at the Humanities Research Centre, the Australian National University, June 1998. Stephen Greenblatt's generous suggestions were also greatly appreciated. I am grateful to the editors of *The Historical Journal, The Journal of the History of Ideas* and to Manchester University Press for permission to reproduce and revise previously published material.

More people than I can remember have aided in various ways. They include Richard Bourke, Martin Dzelzainis, Sam Glover, Mark Goldie, Neil Kenny, Andrew McRae, Jonathan Scott, John O. Ward and Iain Wright. Karen Kupperman and Anthony Pagden contributed greatly in advising on the direction the project should take. David Armitage has been untiring in his encouragement and unflinching in his intellectual generosity. My students have many times forced me to reconsider my convictions concerning some of the book's central arguments. I am indebted also to Richard Fisher at Cambridge University Press for his great patience. The anonymous readers for the Press have been particularly helpful in the final stages.

I have several special debts. Conal Condren set me on the path that led me here. He has tried to teach me to be more sceptical, as well as the best way to cook broad beans. Saliha Belmessous has read and commented on the manuscript more times than she would care to remember. She has tried to teach me to be less sceptical. I promise her never to mention the Virginia Company again, certainly not after 7 pm.

My greatest debt in the writing of this book is to Quentin Skinner. His support over the years is beyond praise. The example of his research and writing is surpassed only by his commitment in teaching – the two virtues are not always found in company.

At proof stage the text has been copy-edited with the greatest care by Hilary Scannell.

CHAPTER I

Introduction

And yet when these insatiably greedy and evil men have divided among themselves goods which would have sufficed for the entire people, how far they remain from the happiness of the Utopian Republic, which has abolished not only money but with it greed![1]

Thomas More's hostility to greed was characteristic of Renaissance humanism. The distinctive aspect of his discussion of greed in *Utopia* is that he invented a society free from this vice which he located, twenty-four years after Columbus' first voyage, in the New World. Was More alone in imagining the New World through humanism? Humanism was the dominant intellectual force of Renaissance Europe. In what way did it shape Europe's 'discovery' and conquest of the New World? My aim is to explore this question in relation to the English (or, more precisely, anglophone) understanding of America from More's generation, early in the sixteenth century, through to the demise of the Virginia Company in 1625.[2] Humanists were active in New World projects throughout Europe, but it was in England, I shall argue, that the humanist imagination dominated colonising projects.[3] Frequently, prominent English humanists – John Rastell, Thomas Smith, Philip Sidney, Humphrey Gilbert, Walter Ralegh – were at the forefront of colonisation. Many others who were prominent humanists (or patrons of humanists) – Richard Eden, John Florio, Dudley Digges, Henry Wriothesley – were also involved in the projects. We also find that many men of more humble birth, such as Captain John Smith, employed their education in the *studia humanitatis* as a tool of colonisation. But what in the humanist imagination drew these men to the New World? And why,

---

[1] Thomas More, *Utopia*, ed. George M. Logan and Robert M. Adams (Cambridge, 1989), p. 109.
[2] Our subject is anglophone because while dominated by the English, many of these projects involved Welsh, Scottish and Anglo-Irish interests. Moreover, Scottish, Welsh and Irish (resettling the Old English) colonies were projected. As we shall see, these projects all employed similar humanist tools.
[3] On humanism in European colonising projects, see Wolfgang Reinhard, ed., *Humanismus und Neue Welt* (Bonn, 1987). For humanist nervousness of conquest and war, see Robert P. Adams, *The better part of valor: More, Erasmus, Colet, and Vives, on humanism, war, and peace, 1496–1535* (Seattle, 1962).

more than in any other European country, did the first period of English colonisation assume the form of a humanist project?

Profit and possession are central to our understanding of the motives for European expansion.[4] These motives have great intuitive appeal. Greed, a desire that serves only itself, is a powerful explanation of human action, particularly actions that lead to the destruction of entire cultures, the death of millions and the dispossession of those who survive. It should come as no surprise, therefore, that Renaissance humanism furnished arguments of profit and possession for early English colonisers. The highest aim of humanism was glory, and what better way to achieve glory, promoters of colonies asked, than to conquer barbarian lands? While historians remain largely unaware of the impact of humanist culture on European expansion, it is clear that an understanding of that impact would support their central conclusions on the motives of profit and possession.[5]

What may cause surprise is that humanists were deeply sceptical of profit and nervous of foreign possessions at the same time that they saw both as possible sources of glory. These 'adventurers' were formed by the Platonic (and Ciceronian) dictum that 'man was not born himself alone'.[6] According to humanist moral philosophy, we are social animals and as such we have a duty to pursue the good of the community. This means putting self-interest to one side, which in turn demands the cultivation of virtue. Profit and luxury divert us from active participation in public life. The Roman cultural heritage (upon which humanism was built) showed that foreign possessions were one of the most likely sources of luxury and corruption. A variety of Roman sources, including the histories of Sallust and Tacitus, and works on oratory and moral philosophy (such as Cicero's *Brutus*), show that the luxury of Rome's colonies was believed to be a source of effeminate

---

[4] See Kenneth R. Andrews, *Trade, plunder and settlement: Maritime enterprise and the genesis of the British Empire* (Cambridge, 1984), p. 5; Jack P. Greene, *Pursuits of happiness* (Chapel Hill, 1988), p. 8; Wm Roger Louis, foreword to *The origins of empire*, ed. Nicholas Canny, vol. I of *The Oxford history of the British empire*, ed. Wm Roger Louis (Oxford, 1998), pp. x–xii. For more general accounts of the themes of profit and possession in colonisation, see Ania Loomba, *Colonialism/postcolonialism* (London, 1998) p. 2; Marc Ferro, *Colonisation: A global history*, trans. K. D. Prithipaul (London, 1997).

[5] Studies that have examined the role of humanism in English colonising projects include David B. Quinn, 'Renaissance influences in English colonisation', *Transactions of the Royal Historical Society*, 5th ser., 26 (1976), pp. 73–92; David B. Quinn, 'The colonial venture of Sir Thomas Smith in Ulster, 1571–1575', *The Historical Journal*, 28 (1985), pp. 261–78; G. J. R. Parry, 'Some early reactions to the three voyages of Martin Frobisher', *Parergon*, new ser., 6 (1988), pp. 149–61. Cf. Howard Mumford Jones, 'Origins of the English colonial idea in England', *Proceedings of the American Philosophical Society*, 85 (1942), pp. 448–65. On the impact of humanist geography on colonisation, see Lesley B. Cormack, *Charting an empire: Geography at the English universities, 1580–1620* (Chicago, 1997).

[6] Cicero, *On duties*, trans. and ed. M. T. Griffin and E. M. Atkins (Cambridge, 1991), pp. 9–10.

and 'Asiatic' influences and consequently the cause of a decline in virtue and the decline of the Republic. For some Romans, for example Cicero in *De officiis* (*On duties*), these problems of conquest reach further into a more general concern about the justice of empire, a concern that exceeds fears for the Republic and extends to the treatment of other peoples.

Drawing a parallel between the experience of Rome and their own encounters with the New World, humanists perceived colonisation with nervousness, anxiety and, sometimes, outright hostility. Indeed, through to the first quarter of the seventeenth century, these concerns overshadowed discussions of colonies. Profit and possession, it was repeatedly emphasised, were secondary aims or were denied to be aims at all. 'Beware my hearers', Alexander Whitaker declared in the first sentence of his 1613 report from the Chesapeake, 'to condemne riches.'[7] He echoes book 1 of *De officiis* in which Cicero, who for Renaissance humanists was pre-eminent among moral philosophers, states that 'nothing is more the mark of a mean and petty spirit than to love riches'.[8] Cicero's comment is made in the context of an argument in which even honour and glory are treated with scepticism and subordinated to justice. He mentions conquest as one of the pitfalls for the vices of greed and the excessive appetite for glory.[9] For early English would be colonisers, glory had to be separated from profit and allied to the exercise of virtues such as courage in death, temperance in subduing desire, justice in the treatment of native Americans and the pursuit of the ends of God, not Mammon. The mental world of the early modern English was not, of course, entirely inhabited by dead pagans. When colonisers argued for the pursuit of glory they usually placed the glory of God first. Religion complemented the humanist preoccupation with virtue and the scepticism of greed.

Underlying the humanist nervousness of profit is one of the principal factors dividing classical and early modern European culture from that of modern Europe. Following the rise of liberal individualism and the industrial revolution, selfishness and the profit motive came to be perceived as potentially positive social forces. Of course, selfishness may well have been

---

[7] Alexander Whitaker, *Good newes from Virginia* (London, 1613), p. 1.

[8] Cicero, *On duties*, I, 68. On the pre-eminent position of Cicero in Renaissance humanism, see Paul Oskar Kristeller, *Renaissance thought and its sources*, ed. Michael Mooney (New York, 1979), p. 29: 'The ancient writer who earned their highest admiration was Cicero. Renaissance humanism was an age of Ciceronianism in which the study and imitation of Cicero was a widespread concern'; Jerold E. Seigel, *Rhetoric and philosophy in Renaissance humanism* (Princeton, 1968); Quentin Skinner, *The foundations of modern political thought*, 2 vols. (Cambridge, 1978), I; Markku Peltonen, *Classical humanism and republicanism in English political thought, 1570–1640* (Cambridge, 1995).

[9] Cicero, *On duties*, I, 54–8 and II, 26–8.

as present in classical and neo-classical cultures as under twentieth-century capitalism. Why else would Cicero and Thomas More have spent so much energy writing against this vice? The difference between the cultures is that, under liberal individualism, selfishness is understood to be the engine of wealth and wealth is believed to be desirable, whereas in early modern culture both selfishness and wealth are perceived as threats to the fabric of the community.[10] Cicero, one of the most influential writers on self-interest, is at best ambivalent on the subject. He believes it is unrealistic or even dangerous not to consider questions of advantage (as some Stoics had argued), but he insists that honour and virtue must always prevail, even if honour demands death. This view came to be widely held in the Renaissance and early modern period. Of course, we must question whether such sentiments were genuine when applied to European conquest, and we shall come to this problem. It is clear, however, that America was first colonised by people who stated that a glorious death in pursuit of the desires of their god was preferable to dishonourable self-preservation. In the twenty-first century such people would be more likely to be described as terrorists than as the proto-capitalists that historians have discerned.[11] These self-described 'adventurers' would not, of course, recognise either category.

What was humanism? At about the same time that the New World was being 'discovered' by Europeans in the late fifteenth century, a new learning was becoming established in England. This was the *studia humanitatis*: the revival of the Greek and Roman disciplines of grammar, rhetoric, history, moral philosophy and poetry that had flourished in Italy for more than a century.[12] From the mid-fifteenth century the English, in common with northern Europeans in general, began adopting this new education system, greatly extending the existing medieval tradition of studying the classics. Through the course of the sixteenth century the *studia humanitatis* became entrenched in England, first in schools and then universities.[13] At the same

[10] See J. G. A Pocock, *The Machiavellian moment: Florentine political thought and the Atlantic republican tradition* (Princeton, 1975); Albert O. Hirschman, *The passions and the interests* (Princeton, 1977, with a foreword by Amartya Sen, 1997); Skinner, *The foundations of modern political thought*.

[11] On the proto-capitalism of early American colonisation, see S. M. Kingsbury, ed., *The records of the Virginia Company of London*, 4 vols. (Washington, 1906–35), I, pp. 12–15; Wesley F. Craven, *The dissolution of the Virginia Company* (Oxford, 1932), p. 24; Herbert L. Osgood, *The American colonies in the seventeenth century*, 3 vols. (first published 1904, reissued New York, 1930), I, pp. 68–71.

[12] On humanism and the *studia humanitatis*, see Kristeller, *Renaissance thought and its sources*, pp. 21–3.

[13] On school curricula, see T. W. Baldwin, *William Shakespere's small Latine and lesse Greeke*, 2 vols. (Urbana, 1944). On the universities, see Mark H. Curtis, *Oxford and Cambridge in transition 1558–1642* (Oxford, 1959). The best recent examination of humanism in English education is part 1 of Quentin Skinner, *Reason and rhetoric in the philosophy of Hobbes* (Cambridge, 1996).

time, numerous treatises were published outlining the education of boys in the *studia humanitatis*. Literate culture came increasingly to be dominated by this revolution in learning. Works within the disciplines of the *studia humanitatis* were produced following the classical models.

One of the fundamental distinctions made within humanist texts was the classical, characteristically Ciceronian, distinction between the contemplative and active life. The study of the classical disciplines was, according to this distinction, essential for the contemplative life. At times this understanding of contemplative life would reach a pessimism in which withdrawal was portrayed as the only alternative to participation in a corrupt society. In general, however, humanists, and particularly northern European humanists, maintained on the authority of Cicero that the contemplative life was a preparation for the active.[14] The skills of the *studia humanitatis*, and the wisdom, justice, courage and temperance that those disciplines were believed to impart, were to be employed in the active life. This meant that the classical disciplines would be a source of reflection for immediate political concerns. Classical and humanist texts were employed to reflect, for example, upon political and military ethics.[15] In an even more direct way, however, the humanist disciplines could be employed as the language or the medium of everyday life; the life, as Petrarch had put it, of the street.[16] Thus according to the humanistic understanding of the relation between the contemplative and active life, the study of the classical disciplines was to be employed, for example, in political life, military affairs, the law courts, in commerce and in religion.

Several studies have explored the role of the humanist disciplines in religious reform but, to a large degree, the study of Renaissance humanism has been confined to those pursuits humanists themselves would have regarded as contemplative. It is true that many contemplative pursuits reflected on the active life, and no humanist would have denied that any form of speech or writing was a kind of act. Nevertheless, humanists insisted on distinguishing levels of engagement with civic life. It is surprising to find, therefore, that our understanding of the use of the *studia humanitatis* in civic life is anecdotal. Our knowledge of the use of classical learning to understand the colonisation of the New World, which was perceived as an extension of the civic sphere, has likewise been anecdotal and yet, as I argue, the *studia humanitatis* was fundamental to that understanding.

[14] Skinner, *The foundations of modern political thought*, I, pp. 193–262.
[15] Anthony Grafton and Lisa Jardine, ' "Studied for action": how Gabriel Harvey read his Livy', *Past and Present*, 129 (1990).
[16] Seigel, *Rhetoric and philosophy in Renaissance humanism*.

The fear of corruption drove some humanists to oppose the foundation of colonies altogether. Those who did pursue colonisation did so because they found an outlet for the humanist passion for the *vita activa*, a means to exercise virtue in the foundation and conservation of a commonwealth – the highest calling of the active life. Moreover, when the promoters of colonies spoke of the glories of serving the commonwealth they did not always restrict their meaning to the English commonwealth. Their first duty was, of course, to their sovereign and to England. Frequently, however, the understanding of virtuous duties in the service of their sovereign extended to the foundation of new commonwealths. 'Commonwealth' was a translation of *res publica*, or republic. For the early modern English, it meant simply a coherent political body defined by mutual obligations.[17] A commonwealth could be a guild, a business, a parish, a town, a city, the state or, in this case, a colony. The creation of colonies could be represented as the creation of discrete commonwealths, separate from England but under the *imperium* of the crown. In 1610, for example, the Virginia Company advertised for 'men of most use and necessity, to the foundation of a Common-wealth'.[18]

The language of the *vita activa* was quasi-republican. This presented a problem. In the courtly world of northern Europe, the expression of Roman republican sentiment was limited. The possibilities for a life of virtuous action were even more limited. Humanists made great progress in reconciling much of the republican thought central to the *studia humanitatis* with princely societies.[19] England was commonly portrayed not simply as a monarchy but as a mixed constitution, a layered political structure that provided many opportunities for political participation for men and women of almost all estates.[20] Humanism, as we shall see, provided the ideological architecture for this constitution. But a tension between the values of the humanist education system, with its emphasis upon self-government, and Renaissance European culture persisted. The opportunity to establish new commonwealths provided a means of political expression both for those who had no desire to be in conflict with their monarch and for those (particularly as the conflict between monarch and Parliament deepened

[17] See, for example, Thomas Smith's definition of 'commonwealth' in Thomas Smith, *The commonwealth of England [De republica Anglorum]*, ed. L. Alston [London, 1583], (Cambridge, 1906), p. 10.

[18] *A true and sincere declaration of the purpose and ends of the plantation begun in Virginia* (London, 1610), pp. 25–6.

[19] Skinner, *Foundations of modern political thought*, I; Patrick Collinson, 'The monarchical republic of Queen Elizabeth I', *Bulletin of the John Rylands University Library of Manchester*, 69 (1987), pp. 394–424; Peltonen, *Classical humanism and republicanism in English political thought*.

[20] On the political participation of women, see Tim Harris, ed., *The politics of the excluded, c.1500–1850* (London, 2001). While they were involved in colonising, women did not directly participate in the promotion of colonies between 1500 and 1625.

under James I) who did seek political expression outside the confines of their society. In similar fashion others chose literary means to pursue the same ends.[21]

The humanist character of English colonisation can, therefore, in part be explained by tensions between the *studia humanitatis* and its reception into northern Europe. But why, as I argue, did humanism do more to shape the English understanding of the New World than that of other Europeans? The answer lies in part in the dependence by the English crown upon the grant of private patents for establishing colonies. It is true that all European colonisation began in this way. Christopher Columbus was licensed by the Spanish crown to establish colonies, as were the conquistadors (even if retrospectively). Similarly, in 1541 Francis I of France granted the right to colonise to Jean François de laRoque de Roberval, just as in 1578 Elizabeth I granted the first English patent for colonising in America to Humphrey Gilbert. As silver and gold were plundered in huge quantities from Mexico and Peru, the Spanish crown moved quickly to exercise close military, political and financial control over its New World possessions. It had little need to persuade anyone to provide support for the conquests (except, of course, on the question of justice). By contrast, in the period with which we are concerned, English colonising projects were persistently unsuccessful. They consumed rather than produced resources. As a consequence, the crown provided legal support but otherwise kept colonial matters at arm's length. The success or failure of the enterprises rested entirely on the ability of private interests to raise capital and personnel. The colonising attempts of the French Huguenots were the most striking European parallel with the model of English colonisation. The Huguenot projects were also licensed to private interests and enlisted men of humanist education in their support. Those men, as we see in ch. 2, included a number of English humanists, such as Richard Eden, who gained employment with their French co-religionists and subsequently came to prominence in the promotion of English colonies. Such was the common identification of English and Huguenot colonisation that joint projects were planned. However, the massacre of Saint Bartholomew's Day in 1572 and its aftermath limited further French Protestant involvement in the New World, and in 1627 Huguenots were officially banned from venturing to the New World by Cardinal de Richelieu.[22]

---

[21] See David Norbrook, *Writing the English republic: Poetry, rhetoric and politics, 1627–1660* (Cambridge, 1999), and David Norbrook, 'Lucan, Thomas May, and the creation of a republican literary culture', in Kevin Sharpe and Peter Lake, eds., *Culture and politics in early Stuart England* (London, 1994).

[22] For the ban, see 'Article XVII de la charte de la compagnie des Cent-Associés', *Mercure de France*, XIV, 245, cited in Pierre Clément, *Lettres, instructions et mémoires de Colbert* (Paris, Imprimerie

Falling back upon their wits and their education the English would be colonisers appreciated that an enormous persuasive project would be required to gain the necessary support. The creation of private colonising grants corresponded with the peak of the *studia humanitatis* in England. This new intellectual world was fundamentally rhetorical in character. At the heart of humanism was a belief that the moral world was contingent and that all political action, or indeed, all social relations, rested upon moral persuasion. As his model of 'deliberative', or political, rhetoric the English humanist Thomas Wilson used an example from Erasmus of 'An epistle to persuade a young gentleman to marriage'.[23] Rhetoric was, accordingly, a central discipline of the *studia humanitatis*. It was thus to the *studia humanitatis* that the promoters of colonies turned to convince their audiences to part with their purses and, if necessary, with their lives. 'If losse of life befall you by this service', argued Robert Johnson in *The new life of Virginea*, 'yet in this case too, wee doubt not but you are resolved with constant courage.'[24]

It is often argued that the private grants to European colonisers reflected a medieval and feudal mental world.[25] The position of the conqueror resembled that of the feudal lord. This argument is perhaps true of the Spanish conquistadors, who could understand their actions as an extension of the reconquista or, like Columbus, the crusades. It is also true that Ciceronian values could be reconciled with feudal England.[26] It is difficult, however, to fit a feudal image upon English colonising enterprises in which the language of self-representation concerned the rewards of virtuous political action, a language of the classical commonwealth and of the city.[27] We shall see that Walter Ralegh appealed to both traditions, but as silver and gold proved elusive, the English rejected the possibility of emulating the conquistadors.[28]

Impériale, 1865), tome 3, vol. II, p. 404. On Huguenot colonising projects, see Frank Lestringant, *Le Huguenot et le Sauvage. L'Amérique et la controverse coloniale en France au temps des guerres de religion, 1555–1589* (Paris, 1990).

[23] Thomas Wilson, *The art of rhetoric*, ed. Peter E. Medine (Pennsylvania, 1994), p. 79.

[24] Robert Johnson, *The new life of Virginea* (London, 1612), sigs. D4r–v.

[25] See, for example, Francis Jennings, *The invasion of America: Indians, colonialism, and the cant of conquest* (New York, 1975), pp. 3–5.

[26] See Stephen Alford, *The early Elizabethan polity: William Cecil and the British succession crisis 1558–1569* (Cambridge, 1998).

[27] This is not to say that civic language was employed exclusively in cities. It was a language also used for the parish 'commonwealth'. On the parish as republic, see Mark Goldie, 'The unacknowledged republic: officeholding in early modern England', in Harris, *The politics of the excluded, c.1500–1850*.

[28] See also Anthony Pagden, *Lords of all the world: Ideologies of empire in Spain, Britain and France c.1500–c.1800* (New Haven, 1995).

We can say, therefore, that humanism provided the tools of persuasion necessary for the projects to gain support. But we can go further than that. We must remember that the prospective colonies were represented as new commonwealths. For the humanist imagination, persuasion, or oratory, was fundamental to the foundation of a new commonwealth. When humanists questioned the origins of political society, the answer was not merely that it lay in a natural sociability (which was certainly not assumed in the opening of Cicero's *De inventione*) but an act of persuasion. According to Cicero, 'there was a time when men wandered at large in the fields', but a man of great eloquence 'transformed them from wild savages into a kind and gentle folk'.[29] Humanists attempting to establish colonies seized upon the idea that oratory was necessary to establish new commonwealths; indeed it is through this idea that they understood the process of gaining support for their projects. The emphasis upon persuasion reflected the understanding that the colonies were new commonwealths and simultaneously complemented the necessity of raising private support. Promoting the enterprises had a double imperative: first, the practical necessity of raising finance and personnel for private projects; and secondly, what we might call the 'imaginative' understanding of that first process, namely, the performance of oratory in the foundation of new commonwealths. This imaginative, ideological, dimension was no less practical than the first. For humanists, nothing could be more practical than the performance of an act in the foundation of a commonwealth.

One consequence of this understanding of the relation between oratory, or promotion, and the foundation of commonwealths, or colonies, was that the English produced more literature promoting colonisation in this period than any other European country. Through to the demise of the Virginia Company, numerous tracts and pamphlets in particular, but also histories, verse and plays, were produced debating the virtues of colonisation. This literature was composed by a wide a variety of authors from noble to humble birth, by authors who never set foot in America, by others who participated in voyages, and by many who lived in the New World. In this book, I will be concerned with the whole range of these texts because they all participated in the oratorical foundation of the commonwealths.[30]

---

[29] Cicero, *De inventione*, trans. H. M. Hubbell (London, 1949), I, 2.
[30] Cf. David Beers Quinn, *New American world: A documentary history of North America to 1612*, 5 vols. (London, 1979), V, p. 233. Quinn excludes some material from his documentary history: 'no examples . . . of the sermons preached to potential subscribers are given' because 'they are long-winded and of intermittent interest'.

The presence of civic, quasi-republican, thought in early English colonisation brings us to the myths concerning the origins of American liberty. From Thomas Jefferson to the patriotic American historians of the early twentieth century, early American colonisation was seen as the foundation of American liberty.[31] Since the 1930s, this understanding has been overturned. It has been argued that early colonisation was devoid of political content.[32] The driving force was commerce. The story of the foundation of liberty has become a story of the foundation of capitalism and individualism. Certainly, as I will argue, this emphasis upon commerce is misplaced. Moreover, a language of citizenship does appear to have been employed in early American colonising projects. It was, however, a citizenship conceived in terms of duties and not the rights-based citizenship valued by the patriotic historians.

It is true that studies of the transmission of civic thought in early modern Europe have, since the 1970s, described a movement from Florence to the English republic to the American revolution which gave little attention to the intervening periods.[33] Indeed, the standard accounts held that England was devoid of republican thought prior to the civil wars.[34] Recent studies have shown, however, a widespread consciousness of quasi-republican thought in the Tudor and early Stuart periods.[35] This consciousness prevailed despite the limitations placed upon political participation by the culture of the court. This was a time, as Patrick Collinson has said, when citizens were cloaked as subjects.[36]

The *studia humanitatis* were, of course, heuristic. Ancient texts could be read in a variety of ways to support a variety of political interests from

---

[31] Alexander Brown, *English politics in early Virginian history* (first published 1901, reissued New York, 1968), pp. 11–13; E. D. Neill, *The English colonisation of America during the seventeenth century* (London, 1871); Charles Mills Gayley, *Shakespeare and the founders of liberty in America* (New York, 1917).

[32] Andrews, *Trade, plunder and settlement*, p. 5; Edmund S. Morgan, *American slavery, American freedom* (New York, 1975), pp. 44–5, 95, 118; Greene, *Pursuits of happiness*, p. 8; Jack P. Greene, *Peripheries and center: Constitutional development in the extended polities of the British empire and the United States 1607–1788* (Athens, Ga., 1986).

[33] See, for example, Pocock, *The Machiavellian moment*.

[34] Blair Worden, 'English republicanism', in J. H. Burns and Mark Goldie, eds., *The Cambridge history of political thought, 1450–1700* (Cambridge, 1991), p. 445; J. P. Sommerville, *Politics and ideology in England, 1603–1640* (London, 1986), p. 86, n.1 'civic humanism was buried if not dead before the English civil war'; see also pp. 57–8.

[35] Collinson, 'The monarchical republic of Queen Elizabeth I', pp. 394–424; Peltonen, *Classical humanism and republicanism in English political thought*; Skinner, *Reason and rhetoric in the philosophy of Hobbes*; Andrew Fitzmaurice, 'The civic solution to the crisis of English colonisation, 1609–1625', *The Historical Journal*, 42, 1 (1999), pp. 25–51; Goldie, 'The unacknowledged republic'.

[36] Patrick Collinson, *De republica Anglorum: or, history with the politics put back*. Inaugural lecture delivered 9 November 1989 (Cambridge University Press).

republicanism to absolute rule. The same authority, as we shall see, could be employed to support contradictory positions. Tacitus could be read as nostalgic for a lost civic virtue or as a guide for the corrupt courtier. Cicero could be read as an advocate of the life of citizenship and action. But Cicero with Seneca could also be seen to support contemplation and withdrawal from the corrupt world.

Crucially, however, the foundation of new commonwealths in America could not be pursued purely through study and contemplation. The projects demanded, and attracted, those who were committed to the highest ideals of the Ciceronian conception of the active life. Sir William Alexander (a Scot) struck the familiar theme of virtuous action rewarded by glory: 'Where was ever Ambition baited with greater hopes than here, or where ever had Vertue so large a field to reape the fruits of Glory.'[37] The projects attracted, therefore, those most in sympathy with quasi-republican ideals of citizenship even though many participants, such as Alexander, could never be described as republicans. These sympathies are abundantly evident in the language employed in promoting the new commonwealths. The early modern English tracts promoting colonies prove to be one of the most sustained and vigorous humanist discussions of the best form of government produced prior to the civil wars. While it is, of course, true that revolution was not the aim of the colonisers, we may still say that the republican tradition which developed following the English civil wars and the American revolution had far greater depth than has been recognised.

It is important to emphasise that humanist thought was neither coherent nor stable. Humanists pursuing colonisation were writing within multiple contexts and attempting to respond simultaneously to pressures from those different spheres. Over the period with which we are concerned, for example, the Ciceronian optimism of the early Renaissance gave way to the pressures of the wars of religion and saw the emergence of a more jaundiced view of the political world. Moreover, promoters of colonies were not dealing only with the European context for their ideology; their convictions were constantly tested by the realities of colonial experience, although that experience did not always lead them to the conclusions we might expect. As I show in ch. 2, English would be colonisers of the sixteenth century generally argued for what can be characterised as a Ciceronian humanist balance of honour and profit in the pursuit of glory. Profit, they argued, was a legitimate aim if it was subordinate to the pursuit of honourable and

---

[37] Sir William Alexander, *An encouragement to colonies* (London, 1624), p. 42.

pious ends. Those who failed in their enterprises, as Edward Haies, the humanist tutor turned ship's captain, argued, were being punished by God for thinking too much of their own advantage. In ch. 3 we see that the experience of repeated and disastrous failure caused a revision of this ideology. Against a backdrop of Elizabethan colonising failures and an inauspicious start on the Chesapeake, many Virginia Company promoters dismissed the pursuit of profit altogether and denied any intention to dispossess the 'Powhatans'. Here experience encouraged the humanist scepticism of profit and foreign possessions and produced an almost Stoic zeal. These sentiments were shared equally by the hired pens writing for the Company in London and by the participants in the colony such as Alexander Whitaker. In this sense it can be difficult to distinguish at this early point of American colonisation between the ideology of 'paper empires' and that of the colonisers.[38]

To privilege direct experience in the colonies is to some degree anachronistic. The distinctions between these various accounts of colonisation – measured by the distance from the 'action' – are more precious to modern historians than they were to early modern Europeans. Certainly, the claim to have experience held as much rhetorical force for early modern audiences as it has in the twenty-first century. As I have said, however, humanist culture placed great emphasis upon the power of speech (including printing) as a form of action. Understood in this context, those who wrote to promote the colony, even those without 'first hand' experience, cannot be dismissed merely as an 'intelligentsia' or as marginal to the enterprise – they were believed to be central to the act of colonising.

In at least one very important case, however, experience in the colony did underpin a major shift in the Jacobean ideology of colonisation: in the writings of Captain John Smith. Although only in Virginia for a short period, Smith was one of the first colonisers to distance himself from the attitudes of the metropolis, a more familiar story later in the colonial period.[39] In ch. 6, I show that Smith reacted violently against the Virginia Company's concern with behaving justly toward the 'Powhatans'. In doing so, he appealed to deeply Machiavellian notions on the necessity of fear and

---

[38] Recent studies emphasise that colonisation creates a gap between the ideology of metropolitan propagandists and that of colonists engaged with a new environment and new peoples, see Jennings, *The invasion of America*; Karen Kupperman, *Settling with the Indians* (London, 1980); James Axtell, *The invasion within: The contest of cultures in colonial North America* (Oxford, 1981); Richard White, *The middle ground* (Cambridge, 1991); Karen Kupperman, *Indians and English: Facing off in early America* (Ithaca, 2000).

[39] See Jennings, *The invasion of America*; Kupperman, *Settling with the Indians*; Axtell, *The invasion within*; White, *The middle ground*; Kupperman, *Indians and English*.

violence as political instruments.[40] Again, Smith's ideological turn reveals a relationship between thought and experience that is not simply one way. Machiavellian and Tacitist thought were particularly fashionable in Jacobean England and Smith was clearly responding to that context. On the other hand, it was his dealings with the Powhatans that provided Smith with the opportunity to employ the instrument of Machiavellian critique. The colonial experience must therefore be considered part of the context that facilitated the reception of Machiavellian thought in England. The experience of Irish colonisation provided similar opportunities for the emergence of Machiavellian thought. The view advanced here is that the experience of colonisation shaped the thought of the protagonists: that the *studia humanitatis* were a tool for solving problems in the world of experience. The view presented is also, given that humanism provided terms in which colonisation was understood, that the foundation of colonies was a means through which humanists could pursue their moral and political values.

The question arises of whether it is possible to appeal to fear and violence as necessary instruments of politics without being labelled 'Machiavellian'. We could also ask whether a commitment to the primacy of honour over advantage must be labelled 'Ciceronian'. It is true that such political dispositions are often reified by intellectual historians. For the purposes of this book it is necessary only to observe that the authors we consider possessed certain distinctive attitudes, or conventional sentiments, to a field of related political values, including glory, honour, virtue, duty, corruption, profit or advantage, possession, fear, violence and persuasion. These attitudes were central to their plans to establish colonies; these were the terms of much of the political discourse of this culture. The conventions of this linguistic system were recognised and exploited by its participants. It was a convention of sixteenth-century political discourse, for example, that rulers should seek to be loved rather than feared. In this context, the argument that rulers should employ fear was recognisably an attempt to alter political discourse. It need hardly be added that this argument was popularised by Machiavelli. Terms such as 'Machiavellian' and 'Ciceronian' are merely the shorthand of the period. It should be stressed that a statement advocating the use of fear, to remain with the example, could hardly be made in this linguistic

---

[40] Machiavelli had also expressed anxieties over expansion. He acknowledged the conflict between empire and liberty but concluded that the loss of liberty was inevitable. It is preferable, he argued, to lose liberty in the pursuit of empire and greatness than to lose liberty without having achieved greatness. See David Armitage, *The ideological origins of the British empire* (Cambridge, 2000), ch. 5.

environment in a way that was innocent of the conventions of debates over political leadership.

What, it will be asked, could writers of Classical and Renaissance central and northern Italy have to do with a series of enterprises lasting more than one hundred years in which the people of an island archipelago on the western boundary of Europe crossed the Atlantic? The answer, as I have suggested, lies in the attraction of the problems that the New World ventures provoked for men educated in the *studia humanitatis*. But it is possible to pursue the question further. The colonisation of the New World involved a large cross-section of English society, from leaders such as Ralegh to ships' crews, soldiers, artisans and common labourers. I have noted that leaders of the enterprises were frequently leaders of humanism in England – but to what extent did this ideology penetrate through the social orders? Are we concerned here simply with the mental world of an elite? Intellectual histories offer few leads here because the great majority of intellectual history is still concerned with the most highly educated portion of early modern society. Moreover, with a few notable exceptions, historians of colonisation have neglected intellectual history.[41] At a more general level, as Mark Goldie has observed, intellectual and social history have been slow to draw upon each other.[42] This problem is particularly evident when the fields deal with the same subject such as political participation. Intellectual history has pointed to the existence of an ideology of civic participation in early modern Europe. Social historians have shown that participation was pervasive through the orders. Little has been done to demonstrate what links, if any, existed between these two facts. Was the humanist ideology of participation employed widely throughout the orders, or was it the preserve of a highly educated elite? Historians of popular culture have alerted us to the fact that the elites of early modern Europe participated in supposedly 'popular' forms of culture.[43] People of humble origin also have been shown to have participated in supposedly 'elite' culture. Indeed, recent studies of popular culture call into question the dichotomy between popular and elite employed in Peter Burke's seminal study of European popular culture.[44]

---

[41] Notable exceptions are Anthony Pagden, *The fall of natural man: The American Indian and the origins of comparative ethnology* (Cambridge, 1978); James Tully, *An approach to political philosophy: Locke in contexts* (Cambridge, 1993); Pagden, *Lords of all the world*; and Armitage, *The ideological origins of the British empire*.

[42] Goldie, 'The unacknowledged republic', p. 154.

[43] Peter Burke, *Popular culture in early modern Europe* (London, 1978); Keith Wrightson, *English society 1580–1680* (London, 1980).

[44] Tim Harris, 'Problematising popular culture', in Tim Harris, ed., *Popular culture in England, c.1500–1850* (London, 1995), pp. 1–27; Jonathan Barry, 'Literacy and literature in popular culture: reading and writing in historical perspective', in Harris, *Popular culture*, pp. 69–94.

Certainly, this dichotomy is difficult to maintain when we examine the mental world of the different orders involved in colonisation. Men from the yeomanry, such as the soldier Captain John Smith or the sea captain and fisherman Richard Whitbourne, employed the same range of humanistic values to discuss colonies as their social superiors. Literacy was not confined to an elite or even to the large number of the 'middling sort' who had access to a grammar-school education. But who were the audience of these men who wrote about colonies and could that audience include even those who were not literate?

Their audience was diverse: the authors explicitly addressed themselves to those who could support the ventures 'in purse' and those who would adventure 'in person'. They addressed themselves to the nobility, the gentry, merchants, all of whom could provide support in purse but who also adventured in person, remembering that in early colonies such Roanoke and Jamestown gentlemen were far more numerous than in England.[45] The promoters also addressed the 'lower sort' who could adventure in person. Would the humanistic mental world of the authors have furnished persuasive arguments with such an audience? Several possibilities present themselves. The first is that the notion that humanist values could have universal appeal was simply the self-delusion of an elite. We must remember, however, that the authors did not exclusively belong to an elite. Furthermore, we will see that they possessed a keen rhetorical awareness that different arguments were appropriate to different social orders. They contained these differences within a tension between the motives of honour and profit, within, that is, the tensions of humanist ideology (with honour urged upon the 'better sort' and a compromise urged upon the 'lower sort'). Second, we must concede that, given that the tracts promoting colonies were attempting to persuade their audience, the audience necessarily did not agree with all that was said in those tracts, for otherwise persuasion would not have been required. All persuasion, according to a humanistic understanding, rested upon bringing something unfamiliar together with something familiar. In this case, however, the unfamiliar idea was to make a commitment to the New World in purse or person; the more familiar values were the terms of the humanist moral philosophy in which that proposition was presented.

A third possible reaction to the humanistic content of the promotion tracts was for the audience to have internalised and reprocessed the humanistic conventions in terms of their needs and circumstances in the fashion

---

[45] On gentlemen in the colonies, see Kupperman, *Settling with the Indians*, p. 17.

of Carlo Ginsburg's Menocchio, although evidence for this is difficult to find.[46] Such accommodation would appear to be inevitable and was even, as I shall argue in ch. 4, encouraged by the necessities of persuasion. The possibility for reinterpretation was limited, however, by the very practical nature of humanist moral thought, by the need, that is, for a degree of consensus on the terms of political discourse. Here we come to the final and most important point. When we study the writings of figures such as Machiavelli or Montaigne, as intellectual historians are wont to do, we may believe that humanism was confined to the mental world of an elite. It is easily forgotten that in its medieval origins (from the *dictatores*) and in everyday life the *studia humanitatis* were concerned with practical matters and their adherents constantly emphasised the practical character of their movement.[47] Office-holding was not restricted to monarch and councillors. Early modern England offered a multitude of political offices at the levels of parish, town and county.[48] The city of Exeter, for example, 'had mayor, alderman, councillors, stewards, receiver, recorder, clerk, serjeants, constables, scavengers, swordbearer, porters, watchmen, and wardens of the poor, the bridges and shambles'.[49] The majority of these positions were unpaid, although their responsibilities could be onerous. Eligibility for the lower offices extended to all householders, who included men in such occupations as bricklayers, blacksmiths, tanners, bakers, glovers, butchers, soapboilers and turners. The lower orders had some say, as Thomas Smith argued, in the destiny of the ship upon which they were passengers. Discussion of the nature and aims of government was not possible without some consensus upon the weights and measures of political life. The language of good government was furnished by the *studia humanitatis*. At its heart, the humanist language of government was a language of duty. Debate could centre upon a whole spectrum of social duties, from those of the sovereign down to the duties of husbandmen (as Thomas Smith again pointed out). These debates invoked a whole field of humanist conventions on virtue and corruption.

But how could the lower orders come to understand Ciceronian moral philosophy? The majority of the lower orders could not read. It has been

---

[46] Carlo Ginsburg, *The cheese and the worms: The cosmos of a sixteenth century miller*, trans. John and Anne Tedeschi (London, 1980).

[47] Seigel, *Rhetoric and philosophy in Renaissance humanism*; Skinner, *The foundations of modern political thought*, I.

[48] Collinson, 'The monarchical republic of Queen Elizabeth I'; Peltonen, *Classical humanism and republicanism in English political thought*; Conal Condren, *The language of politics in seventeenth century England* (London, 1994).

[49] Goldie, 'The unacknowledged republic', p. 161.

estimated, for example, that before the middle of the seventeenth century more than half of the rural men holding the office of constable were illiterate.[50] Moreover, it is hard to imagine a literate labourer returning home at night from a day in the fields to read Cicero by candlelight. Ideas, however, were not the prisoners of books. There were a number of bridges between the literate and non-literate worlds through which the lower sort would have been involved in the humanist language of good government. Participation and office-holding in parish and town assemblies were perhaps the primary basis for the development of this common language of government but the reformation of religion was also central to that process.

One of the principal aims of the Reformation was to make scripture accessible. In accordance with this desire, Erasmus and Melanchthon reformed the sermon. Preachers were instructed to use the tools of the *studia humanitatis* to make sermons persuasive and moving. Classical rhetoric, which embodied Ciceronian moral philosophy, was to be used to that end.[51] The moral content of sermons shifted away from abstract doctrine to the praise of God's actions and his works, especially man, in a humanist moral vocabulary. Merely through weekly attendance at church, all orders could find themselves exposed to humanist moral values. Moreover, the reform of the sermon had particular importance for the introduction of humanist values into the discussion of the New World because the sermon, as we shall see, was one of the favoured instruments for promoting the voyages.

There were other ways, also, in which the 'common sort' were exposed to humanist moral philosophy. The reading of texts to both literate and illiterate audiences was common practice, and these texts were not always ballads, chapbooks, almanacs and jestbooks. The promoters of colonies repeatedly emphasised that their texts should be read to the 'common sort'. This ambition was expressed by John Rastell, writing about one of the first English colonial projects in 1520, through to Richard Eburne writing in 1624, the closing year of this study. Rastell declared his desire to reach 'men of meane estate/ Whiche nothynge but englyshe can understande'.[52] The Privy Council, to give another example, ordered that copies of Richard Whitbourne's *A discovery and discourse of Newfoundland* should 'bee

---

[50] *Ibid.*, p. 163.
[51] John W. O'Malley, 'Content and rhetorical forms in sixteenth century preaching', in James J. Murphy, ed., *Renaissance eloquence* (Berkeley, 1983), pp. 242–4; Debora Shuger, *Sacred rhetoric: The Christian grand style in the English Renaissance* (Princeton, 1988); Skinner, *Reason and rhetoric in the philosophy of Hobbes*, pp. 66–7.
[52] John Rastell, *A new interlude and mery of the nature of the four elements*, in *Three Rastell plays*, ed. Richard Axton (Cambridge, 1979), p. 31.

distributed' throughout the 'parishes of the Kingdon'.[53] Similarly, Richard Eburne repeatedly emphasised that his *Plaine pathway to plantations* was written for the 'common and meaner sort', and yet, as we shall see, the work was no exception from the humanist discourse of promoting colonies. He intended that his book should be read to his chosen audience: 'And now, that I may revert my speech to you, my countrymen and friends – you, I say, of the meaner sort... be pleased, I pray you, to peruse, that is, *to read and cause to be read to you* over and over, this book which I have written to you and for you.'[54] Ideology can also be absorbed without reading or hearing texts. In the late twentieth and early twenty-first centuries a person may oppose state ownership of production without having read Milton Friedman. Or we may support state ownership without having read Marx or Keynes. It is very difficult to hold either position without entering liberal or socialist discourses, regardless of our level of literacy or learning. Humanism provided a language of government that was no less pervasive in the Renaissance. Histories of humanism and intellectual history in general tend to be culturally top heavy in part simply because the less literate have left fewer records of their mental world.[55] The textual remains we examine in this book were frequently intended for audiences across cultural boundaries. This did not mean that every audience and every member of every audience necessarily agreed with what is often called the 'propaganda' of those texts. Frustratingly, there is very little evidence of how audiences responded to the arguments of the promotional tracts.[56] We shall examine, however, satires of the promotional tracts that reveal a vigorous dialogue over the proposed colonies. Importantly, while those satires dispute the aims of the colonial projects, they conduct that dispute within a moral vocabulary shared with the promoters. While the audience of the promotional literature may not have shared the aims of the promoters, they did share the same moral universe. Indeed, it is the leverage of that familiar moral language, as I have said, that the promoters had to employ if they were to be successful with their proposals.

We are not simply dealing with the internalisation of elite culture at a popular level. The language of government, while necessarily held in common, could be employed to a variety of ends. Authors promoting colonies recognised this reality when they distinguished different audiences and

---

[53] Gillian T. Cell, ed., *Newfoundland discovered* (London, 1982), p. 101.

[54] Richard Eburne, *A plaine pathway to plantations* (London, 1624), ed. Louis B. Wright (Ithaca, 1962), p. 10, my emphasis.

[55] Harris, 'Problematising popular culture'; Barry, 'Literacy and literature in popular culture'.

[56] There are, for example, very few marginal comments on the surviving texts.

urged different balances of honour and profit upon those audiences. Moreover, the language of good government was very much a civic language: that is, a language both of citizenship and of the city. As a language of citizenship it included the landed gentry (in so far as the gentry perceived their political participation in terms of citizenship), but as a language appropriate to cities it was perhaps more useful for the emerging middle classes than the aristocracy.[57] Similarly, the ascetic aspect of humanism, the scepticism of luxury, was more fitting to puritan thrift than to the aristocracy.[58]

Was the humanist ambivalence over profit a cynical cloak over a genuinely avaricious design? Cynicism has been attributed to the colonisers on those occasions when historians have confronted evidence confounding a straightforward commercial understanding of the enterprises.[59] When the *studia humanitatis* are understood to be heuristic, whether the promoters of colonies and their audiences believed what they wrote becomes of secondary importance. Certainly we shall see that humanism, like religion, could be and was employed opportunistically, or even cynically, but the designs of the cynics were no less serious for that. Indeed, cynicism is a mechanism through which political argument responds to its context: it is an acknowledgement of the boundaries of legitimate political discourse. We shall also see that the promoters of colonies cautioned against greed precisely because they understood that it was a motive for adventuring and could corrupt the enterprises. Equally, however, civic values were used by those authors who did in fact travel to America to account for why they were prepared to risk their lives, a risk underlined by the very high mortality rates. In the spectrum between these points humanism provided the terms in which the actions of colonisation were understood.

---

[57] On the political discourse of cities, see Condren, *The language of politics in seventeenth century England*. On humanist values and city government, see also Peltonen, *Classical humanism and republicanism in English political thought*; and Collinson, 'The monarchical republic of Queen Elizabeth I'.

[58] On the thrift of the middling sort, see Peter Earle, *The making of the English middle class* (London, 1989); Harris, 'Problematising popular culture', p. 18.

[59] See, for example, Quinn, *New American world*, V, p. 233, dismissing the seriousness of the Virginia Company's promotional sermons; Andrews, *Trade, plunder and settlement*, p. 320; and Francis Barker and Peter Hulme, 'Nymphs and reapers heavily vanish: the discursive con-texts of *The Tempest*', in John Drakakis, ed., *Alternative Shakespeares* (London, 1985), p. 200.

CHAPTER 2

The moral philosophy of Tudor colonisation

This chapter will examine the moral philosophy that framed discussions of English colonial projects in their first hundred years. That moral philosophy was characterised by two impulses. On the one hand, the projects were promoted as a duty, a means for the citizen to employ his virtues in the pursuit of an active life. Virtue was needed to hold the citizen to the pursuit of the common good and to keep him from using his position to serve his own selfish interests.[1] The active life was framed in the context of the foundation of new commonwealths and so offered the glory, honour and profit that were portrayed as the reward of virtuous public service. On the other hand, this impulse to the active life was constrained by the fear of corruption. The profit which could be generated by colonies could also divert men from virtue and threaten the commonwealth through the creation of an 'Asiatic' and effeminate wealth and luxury.

This tension was central to Roman and humanist moral philosophy. Cicero's *De officiis* was one of the more optimistic representations of the possibilities of the active life. He stressed that the basis of citizenship was the employment of the virtues in political participation. But anxiety about corruption is also central for Cicero. He emphasises that the four cardinal virtues (wisdom, justice, courage and temperance) are necessary for the citizen to place private profit below the common good, and he is acutely sensitive to the possible conflict between these ends. This anxiety over corruption was developed by Roman moralists and historians including Sallust, Juvenal, Tacitus, Seneca and Quintilian. For these writers, corruption – manifested as wealth, 'Asiatic' luxury and the loss of martial virtues – is the cause of the decay of the commonwealth and the rise of tyranny.

[1] In Roman and neo-Roman moral philosophy a good citizen was always represented as a man, a *vir virtutis* or *bonus homo*. Masculinity and virility were important elements of virtue, just as femininity was perceived an element of corruption.

TUDOR MORAL PHILOSOPHY: THE *VITA ACTIVA* AND CORRUPTION

These themes were enthusiastically revived by humanist authors. The humanists of northern Europe, and England in particular, placed great stress upon the necessity of an active life to maintain the commonwealth in good health. The tensions between the active and contemplative life are central to More's *Utopia* in which he decides in favour of the former.[2] The imperative for an active life was stated boldly by Thomas Starkey in his *Dialogue*:

> You know right well, Master Pole, that to this all men are born and of nature brought forth: to commune such gifts as be to them given, each one to the profit of other, in perfect civility, and not to live their own pleasure and profit.[3]

Northern humanists, however, had to contend with the problems posed by a theory of citizenship adapted to a monarchical society. For many, the solution lay in exhorting the qualities of republican citizenship – the observance of the virtues in the performance of public duty – from the prince and a select number of 'governors'. This was the approach adopted by Elyot in *The boke named the governor* and by Erasmus in *The Christian prince*.[4] Even this mirror-for-princes literature, however, allowed some role for the concept of citizenship in admitting the role of counsellors (a necessary admission given that this was precisely the role adopted by the authors in writing, particularly when, as we shall see in ch. 4, humanists possessed a complex understanding of the relationship between rhetoric – even the rhetoric of display – and action).

Many other authors confronted the conflict between princely government and the possibilities for citizenship suggested by the revival of classical learning. These writers described the English constitution as mixed and thereby accommodated the tension. As we have seen in ch. 1, this description was based upon the various levels of participatory government from Parliament through county, city and town councils down to the 9,700 parish councils in seventeenth-century England and Wales.[5] Just at the level of the parish the number of office-holders in any year would have numbered several tens of thousands, given that each parish demanded that several positions be filled. It has been estimated that up to half of adult males would

[2] Quentin Skinner, *The foundations of modern political thought*, 2 vols. (Cambridge, 1978), I, p. 218.
[3] Cited in *ibid.*, p. 219.   [4] *Ibid.*, pp. 229 and 231.
[5] See Mark Goldie, 'The unacknowledged republic: officeholding in early modern England', in Tim Harris, ed., *The politics of the excluded, c.1500–1850* (London, 2001), p. 161.

serve in public office in any decade.[6] Positions were filled by election and rotation. Office-holding was 'remarkably' socially extensive and included yeoman, artisans and shopkeepers.[7] Prominent among works that claimed England possessed a mixed constitution were Thomas Smith's *De republica Anglorum* (1583) and the work attributed to him, *A discourse of the commonweal of this realm of England* (1581). Smith's account of moral philosophy also merits our attention because he was, as we shall see, a seminal promoter of English colonies. In *De republica* Smith insists that all commonwealths are 'mixed', with power residing in different measures with a monarch, an aristocracy and the 'multitude'.[8] Given his assertion, later in the same work, that 'the most high and absolute power of the realme of Englande, consisteth in the Parliament', he apparently believed the commonwealth of England to be one in which the mixture of power was weighted toward the multitude.[9] Smith followed this conviction by addressing his work not to the 'governors' or court but to a broad audience, including not only the gentry but also the yeomanry. Accordingly, he wrote his political treatises in the vernacular.

Smith was not unaware of the possible tensions between civic thought and courtly society. In the preface to the *Discourse of the commonweal*, he notes that he will address questions of the commonwealth even though he is not a member of the King's Council.[10] Yet he is, he retorts, a member of the commonwealth and has as much interest in its health as a passenger on a ship in danger of wreck, even though that passenger may not be the captain. Smith insists that the 'gifts of wit be so divers' that even wise princes cannot hold all the knowledge necessary to the government of the commonwealth.[11] He therefore extends the role of counsel not merely to the gentry but by introducing into his dialogue (and addressing through his work) 'members of every estate' including 'merchantmen, husbandmen and artificers'.[12] This approach is frequently represented as 'radical' by contrast with those writers who restricted their advice to princes. Recent research on the scope of early modern political participation, and on the proliferation of quasi-republican thought, indicates that Smith employed his classical learning to reconcile

---

[6] *Ibid.*, p. 163. See also Valerie Pearl, *London and the outbreak of the Puritan revolution* (Oxford, 1961), ch. 2; and Ian Archer, *The pursuit of stability: Social relations in Elizabethan London* (Cambridge, 1991).

[7] Goldie, 'The unacknowledged republic', p. 163.

[8] Thomas Smith, *The commonwealth of England [De republica Anglorum]*, [London, 1583], ed. L. Alston (Cambridge, 1906), pp. 11–14.

[9] *Ibid.*, book 2, ch. 1.

[10] Thomas Smith, *A discourse of the commonweal of this realm of England* [London, 1581], ed. Mary Dewar (Charlottesville, 1969), p. 11.

[11] *Ibid.*, pp. 11–12.   [12] *Ibid.*, pp. 12–13.

monarchical society with the reality of citizenship. Moreover, in the *Discourse of the commonweal*, Smith is not concerned simply with matters of moral philosophy but with employing moral philosophy to address the most pressing practical problems of the day. The apparently radical nature of his thought was also an indirect consequence of his attempt to apply humanist moral philosophy to practical issues. This conjunction of practical problems and moral philosophy – which was, in fact, central to the humanist conception of the *vita activa* – is also found in the humanist-inspired colonial enterprises of the sixteenth century, of which Smith, as we shall see, was a pioneer.

While the scope of Smith's moral philosophy can no longer be regarded as radical, its content was certainly commonplace. He addressed the problems of enclosure, inflation and religious discord. While his answers were innovative, his tools were familiar. He stressed the need to pursue an active life employing the classical commonplace (with marginal notes to Cicero and Plato) that 'man was not born for himself alone'.[13] He emphasised the need for the virtues in conducting that life and defended the role of education in cultivating those virtues.[14] He observed that there were too few learned men employed in counsel, noting (as had More in *Utopia*) that those who participate in public life are 'put to trouble'. But he condemned those who restrict themselves to a contemplative life.[15] Citing Cicero, he insisted that action and industry must be rewarded with honour and profit.[16]

English humanists were no less anxious about the threats to citizenship than they were enthusiastic about the possibilities of virtuous action. Their account of the causes of corruption closely followed their Roman models. Thomas More denounced the luxury and idleness of the nobility. Elyot invoked the authority of Cicero to criticise those who preferred their 'particular commodity' to the 'state of the public weal'.[17] Smith again followed these models. In his discussion of enclosures, he noted the force of self-interest and argued that the problem could not be resolved until the desire for profit was brought in line with the common good.[18] He was deeply concerned by the corrupting force of 'lucre', despairing at the growth in luxury that threatens 'utter desolation for the Commonweal'.[19] Apparently drawing upon Sallust and Juvenal for this account, Smith observed that 'like excesses, as well in apparel as in fare, were used in Rome a little before the decline of the Empire, so as wise men have thought it was the occasion of the decay thereof'.[20] In England, the corresponding loss of martial virtues

---

[13] *Ibid.*, p. 16.   [14] *Ibid.*, pp. 16–17 and 23–7.   [15] *Ibid.*, pp. 32–3.   [16] *Ibid.*, pp. 58–9.
[17] Cited in Skinner, *The foundations of modern of political thought*, I, p. 223.
[18] Smith, *Discourse of the commonweal*, pp. 50–3, 119–20; see also p. 125 arguing for 'public weal' over 'private liberties'.
[19] *Ibid.*, pp. 119–20 and 81–3.   [20] *Ibid.*, p. 83.

'make our men clean effeminate and without strength'.[21] He lamented the time when men 'rode carrying good spears in their hands instead of white rods which they carry now more like ladies or gentlemen'.[22]

The problem of corruption was not confined to the nobility or the gentry. Luxury permeated through the whole society, even to the servingman who would now wear clothes more fit, in times past, to a 'prince or great lord'.[23] Similarly, the loss of martial virtue was particularly problematic among 'our servingman and yeoman' who 'we reckon here in England our chief strength'.[24] There is no question that Smith saw corruption amongst these lower orders as a threat to civic virtue. It is true that, in *De republica*, Smith described servingmen as 'the fourth sort of men which do not rule'; 'these have no voice or authoritie in our common wealth'. He noted, however, that they had some civic responsibilities, that they were even eligible for certain parish offices, and he anticipated some expansion in their role:

And in villages they be commonly made Churchwardens, alecunners, and manie times Constables, which office toucheth more the common wealth, and at the first was not imployed uppon such and lowe and base persons.[25]

Yeomen, however, were not included among those 'men which do not rule'; indeed, they were said to 'have the greatest charge and doings in the commonwealth'.[26] Yeomen, he observed, were generally farmers.[27] In the *Discourse of the commonweal*, Smith adopted the Ciceronian position that the 'ploughing' of 'husbandmen' is the most noble of occupations: 'the occupation was had so honorable among the Romans that one was taken from holding the plow to consul of Rome, who, after his year ended, thought no scorn to resort to the same feat again'.[28] Playing on the humanist theme of the nature of true nobility, he lamented 'how much it is vilified that this nobility reputes them but as villeins, peasants, or slaves... that I marvel much there is any... will occupy the feat of husbandry at all'.[29] Accordingly in *De republica*, Smith reminded his audience that yeomen 'are they which olde Cato calleth *Aratores* and *optimos cives in Republica*: and such as the writers of common wealthes praise to have manie in it'.[30]

The tension between the *vita activa* and corruption was not simply transferred to colonial designs by the humanist promoters of those projects. The potential to construct the foundation of colonies as the foundation of new commonwealths provided a particularly attractive sphere in which

---

[21] *Ibid.*, p. 83.   [22] *Ibid.*, p. 82–3.   [23] *Ibid.*, pp. 81–2.   [24] *Ibid.*, p. 83.
[25] Smith, *De republica*, p. 46.   [26] *Ibid.*, p. 42.   [27] *Ibid.*, pp. 42–3.
[28] Smith, *Discourse of the commonweal*, p. 120.   [29] *Ibid.*, p. 120.
[30] Smith, *De republica*, p. 43.

humanists could exercise the *vita activa* and its associated virtues. But these same humanists, and their critics, were also mindful that it was precisely that colonial sphere which could pose the greatest dangers of corruption. As Smith notes, Roman historians had shown that it was the wealth and 'Asiatic' luxury generated by Rome's colonies and conquests that had corroded the civic spirit of its citizens. By contrast, humanists were conscious that the Spartans had maintained the strength of their commonwealth by refusing opportunities for expansion. For the humanist colonial projects to succeed, therefore, it was going to be necessary to be particularly vigilant against the commonly held causes of corruption – wealth, luxury and idleness – to be vigilant, that is, against the projected colonies producing such corruptive influences.

ALEXANDER BARCLAY'S SCEPTICISM

English involvement in the New World almost certainly predated the 'discovery' of the continent by Columbus. As English adventurers were later eager to observe, Columbus had first approached Henry VII before turning to Isobel and Ferdinand. It is also probable that, from at least ten years prior to Columbus' trans-Atlantic voyage, Bristol fisherman had travelled to the rich Newfoundland fishing grounds but that they were not anxious to publicise their find to potential rivals.[31] With a patent from Henry VII, the Venetian John Cabot successfully crossed the Atlantic on his second attempt in 1497.[32] Over the next ten years, several more attempts were initiated from Bristol to explore the 'New Lands'.[33] None of these efforts produced much publicity. It is striking, therefore, given the relationship we shall see which developed between humanism and New World projects, that it was the successful voyage of Sebastian Cabot in 1508–9 which would generate the greatest publicity for New World adventures in England in this period. Certainly Cabot's voyage was acknowledged for his achievement in having explored a great extent of the east coast of the northern continent of America. But it is also notable that Cabot desired to and knew how to promote his efforts. He would remark that he had left Venice for England having only first mastered the classics.[34] After his early voyage, Cabot spent the following thirty-six years in Seville training pilots.[35] It is remarkable, then, to find him in England from 1548 to 1557 returned to the centre, as we shall see, of a humanistically inspired revival of interest in the New

---

[31] David B. Quinn, *England and the discovery of America 1481–1620* (London, 1974), pp. 9 and 16–17.
[32] *Ibid.*, pp. 136–7.   [33] *Ibid.*, pp. 137–8.   [34] *Ibid.*, p. 133.   [35] *Ibid.*, pp. 133 and 145.

World after many years of what has been described as indifference on the question.

Indifference is not, however, the right term for the English failure to emulate the great activity of the Spaniards in the New World in the first decades of the sixteenth century. It is true that in this period the English government was deeply concerned by European and domestic matters. It was too stretched to follow the kind of state-sponsored colonial effort seen in Spain. That did not preclude, however, the private projects that the English would later attempt. In the year of Sebastian Cabot's voyage, the first reference to the New World in a book printed in England provides some insight into the subsequent inactivity of the English. The work contained no celebration of the success of Cabot's voyage. It was an English translation, or rather adaption, by Alexander Barclay, of Sebastian Brandt's *Ship of fools*.[36] Brandt was one of the leading humanists of his generation in Europe.[37] In the *Ship of fools*, he employed satire, much in the style of Juvenal, who was one of his models, to attack the vices and corruption of the times.[38] He was innovative in his use of vernacular and appeal to a popular audience. Barclay, while probably born in Scotland, was one of the leading humanists of England.[39] He published the first English translation of Sallust, choosing the *Jugurthine war*, in which Sallust attributed responsibility for Rome's decline to the link between empire and the venality of the nobility.[40] The ship of Barclay's *Ship of fools* is the ship of the commonwealth, about which Smith would later write with such optimism. By contrast, Barclay's perspective is bleak, although he published with the explicit hope of provoking reform through holding up a 'bright Myrrour' to the vices of his readers.[41] In the commonwealth described by Barclay, 'Vertue hath no rewarde', men 'love and worshyp ryches so fervently' that 'he that is ryche hath gretter reverence/ Than he that hath sadnes wysdom and scyence.'[42] He similarly attacked 'sothly slouth and wretched Idleness' observing that 'whyle Rome was gyven to labour and dylygence/ They won Cartago' but 'when the romaynes were voyde of care and payne/ Of batayle and labour, and other besynes/ They gave theyr bodyes to slouth

---

[36] On Barclay's adaption, see John Parker, *Books to build an empire* (Amsterdam, 1965), p. 18; Quinn, *England and the discovery of America*, p. 169.

[37] Skinner, *The foundations of modern political thought*, II, pp. 27–8.

[38] On Brandt's use of Juvenal, see Alexander Barclay, *The ship of fools* ed. T. H. Jamieson, 2 vols. (Edinburgh, 1874, reprinted New York, 1966), I, p. xiii.

[39] *Ibid.*, I, pp. xxv–xxx; and David Armitage, 'Literature and empire', in Nicholas Canny, ed., *The origins of empire*, vol. I of *The Oxford history of the British empire*, ed. Wm Roger Louis (Oxford, 1998), p. 111.

[40] On the translation of Sallust, see Barclay, *The ship of fools*, I, pp. lxxvi–lxxvii.

[41] *Ibid.*, pp. 17 and 2.   [42] *Ibid.*, p. 12.

and ydelness'.[43] They lost their martial virtues having 'no warre to exercyse their myght', they 'lost theyr force, theyr might and strength' and 'theyr hye couragyousness' until 'utterly they loste theyr glorious name'.[44] Indeed, Barclay repeatedly emphasised that, through such sloth and covetousness, 'the worthy Romayns lost theyr name'.[45]

Brandt had attacked the foolish vanity of those who attempt to develop knowledge of 'dyvers contrees and regyons', observing that new discoveries constantly prove that such knowledge is flawed.[46] Prominent among such vanities was the discovery of the 'new fonde londe' of 'Ferdynandus that late was kynge of spayne'.[47] If such knowledge was vain, so much more was the effort expended to gain it. Brandt and Barclay ranked these efforts with the greed, idleness and profligacy which corrupt the commonwealth. Stressing the point and moving beyond translation, Barclay suggested that 'people that labour the worlde to mesure' should 'Knowe first your self, that knowledge is most sure'.[48] It is that knowledge, a wisdom synonymous with virtue and with good government, which the Romans lost as they allowed themselves to be corrupted by the spoils of their foreign possessions.

The implication of Barclay's comment was that the labour of the Spanish was, at best, vain. The contrast between this English perspective and the Spanish conquest is striking. The Reformation would draw much of its attack upon the vices of the church from the humanist language of corruption. The success of Brandt's attack was seminal to that conjunction between humanism and Reformation. In his condemnation of folly in the *Ship of fools*, Barclay reserved his greatest venom for the corruption of the church. The strength of the Reformation in England through the sixteenth century, and the corresponding strength of a humanist language of corruption which competed with a humanist preoccupation with glory, undoubtedly contributed to the difficulties encountered by England in following the Spanish path to the New World. As the first mention in print of the 'new fonde londe', Barclay's text anticipated the English mood toward the New World for the following fifty years. The ramifications of his use of satire reached even further. For Juvenal satire had been the means of revealing a lost civic virtue. His humanist imitators seized upon the same moral potential in the genre. As we shall see, opponents of New World colonisation, anxious about the potential for corruption, would employ satire to attack the enterprises for more than a hundred years after Barclay. In passages that have sometimes puzzled historians, promoters of the

---

[43] *Ibid.*, II, pp. 186 and 187. [44] *Ibid.*, II, p. 187. [45] *Ibid.*, I, p. 32. [46] *Ibid.*, II, p. 23. [47] *Ibid.*, II, pp. 25–6. [48] *Ibid.*, p. 27.

colonies would accordingly frequently reserve their strongest vituperation for 'satirists'.

This humanist scepticism of the New World as a possible source of corruption was not entirely absent from the greatest work of early sixteenth-century English humanism, Thomas More's *Utopia*, published only seven years after Barclay's *Ship of fools*. To some degree the New World was merely a convenient theatre for More to stage his imaginary commonwealth. He was careful, however, to exploit his knowledge of New World voyages and geography, stressing, for example, that Hythloday was one of the twenty-four men whom Amerigo Vespucci left behind on his fourth voyage.[49] Significantly, More used the New World to describe a commonwealth with which he could reproach the European corruption of greed, wealth, luxury and idleness. Like Barclay, More presented a mirror for his readers. Rather, however, than imagining the New World as a source of corrupting vanity or wealth, he recognised that the only commonwealth in the New World that would not be a threat to Europe, or European virtues, would be one that was vigilant against corruption. While equally sensitive to the possibility of corruption, More's inversion of the significance of the new lands made it possible to imagine virtuous commonwealths in that world which would present an instructive ideal for Europeans. For humanists, therefore, More presented the idea of virtuous action as a possible reconciliation between the new discoveries and the Roman anxiety over the 'Asiatic', or luxurious and effeminate, influences of foreign lands. In so doing, he established a model for future humanist projects for the foundation of real commonwealths in the New World.

JOHN RASTELL'S APOLOGY

Bristol fishermen continued to ply their way to the summer fishing grounds off Newfoundland, but it would be More's son-in-law, John Rastell, who would revive interest in making 'buyldynge and habytacion' in the 'new landes'.[50] Rastell was a member of More's humanist circle.[51] When, by 1610, Rastell had established a printing press, More's *Life* of Pico della Mirandolla was one of the first works he printed.[52] The records of a case brought to

---

[49] Thomas More, *Utopia* ed. George M. Logan and Robert M. Adams (Cambridge, 1989), p. 10.
[50] John Rastell, *A new interlude and mery of the nature of the four elements*, in *Three Rastell plays*, ed. Richard Axton (Cambridge, 1979), p. 49.
[51] See *ibid.*, pp. 1–10, and A. W. Reed, *Early Tudor drama* (London, 1926).
[52] His connection with prominent humanists was also revealed in the marriage of his daughter to John Heywood. Heywood's treatise *Gentleness and nobility*, which was one of the earliest English

the Court of Requests in November 1519 reveal that Rastell attempted 'a viage unto the new found land' in 1517.[53] There is uncertain evidence that the enterprise may have been sponsored by Sebastian Cabot, then employed training pilots in Seville. Cabot made an appearance in England at this time.[54] Certainly Rastell appears to have developed a considerable geographical knowledge.[55] With the assistance of Sir Thomas Sperte, 'one of Henry's leading master mariners', Rastell chartered two vessels, the *Barbara* and the *Mary Barking*.[56] The records of the Court of Requests reveal that Rastell's voyage failed for the simple reason that the mariners he employed could not agree with him about the ends of the enterprise.

The mariners, led by John Ravyn, the owner of the *Mary Barking*, argued that a voyage to the new found land would bring no profit, whereas the provisions for which Rastell had paid one hundred pounds could be profitably traded in Bordeaux. They 'exhorted' Rastell to change his objective but he was unmoved by their arguments. Clearly, while he hoped for profit in the New World, this was not his chief motivation. This dispute slowed the progress of the ships as the crews found various excuses to delay by bringing the vessels to port in their progress around the south of England. The captain of the *Mary Barking*, who was apparently unsympathetic to Rastell, was locked in his cabin when his ship reached Cork. Threatened by what was effectively mutiny, Rastell abandoned the voyage at Waterford in Ireland whereupon the crew sailed the two ships to Bordeaux, sold the provisions and divided the profit among themselves. This episode was, as we shall see, but the first of many in which New World colonial ventures were frustrated by the desires of ships' crews who were concerned with more profitable aims.

While spending the following year in Ireland, Rastell wrote his play *A new interlude and mery of the nature of the four elements*.[57] He printed this work on his own press in 1520. As adventurer, author and publisher, Rastell underlines the great emphasis that humanists placed on promoting their ventures, an emphasis itself that we shall see was informed by the humanist understanding of rhetoric as action. Rastell's play also reflected his humanistic preoccupations in other ways. He stated that the ambition of the

---

presentations of the humanist theme of virtue as true nobility, was also printed by Rastell. See Quentin Skinner, 'Political philosophy', in *The Cambridge history of Renaissance philosophy*, ed. C. B. Schmitt and Quentin Skinner (Cambridge, 1988), p. 447; and *Three Rastell plays*, pp. 1 and 3.

[53] Reed, *Early Tudor drama*, p. 189, where a full transcript of the case and its account of the voyage is also printed at appendix 1, pp. 187–201.

[54] *Ibid.*, pp. 187–8. Cf. *Three Rastell plays*, p. 5 and Quinn, *England and the discovery of America*, pp. 144–5.

[55] *Three Rastell plays*, p. 5.   [56] Reed, *Early Tudor drama*, p. 187.   [57] *Three Rastell plays*, p. 10.

work was to emulate the 'works excellent' of the 'grekys' and 'romaynes' but to do so 'in our englyshe tongue'. He aimed to satisfy the humanist sentiment that learning be brought to a large audience and to practical ends, to reach 'dyvers pregnaunt wyttes . . . as well of noble men as of meane estate/ Whiche nothynge but englyshe can understande'.[58] Rastell presented a central theme of Roman moral philosophy as central to his own play, namely the necessity of placing virtue and the common good above private profit: 'For all clerkys afferme that that man presysely,/ Whiche studyeth for his owne welth pryncypally,/ Of God shall deserve but lytyll rewarde,/ Except he the commyn welth somewhat regarde'.[59] He endorsed the Ciceronian conception of the active life arguing that 'every man' must labour not only for his 'owne necessary lyvynge' but 'for the welth of his neyhbour also', echoing the Platonic dictum that 'man was not born for himself alone'.[60] He lamented the corruption of these values observing that he 'that for common welth bysyly/ Studyeth and laboryth . . . men count him but a daw'.[61] The cause of this corruption, as for the Roman moralists, is riches: 'he that is ryche is everywhere honouryd'.[62] The consequence is the decay of the commonwealth as those 'labouryng all their lyffys' for nothing but to 'bringe ryches to their owne possession' disregard their 'neybours distruccion'.[63]

This moral philosophy frames the action of the play in which 'Humanity' is tutored by 'Studious Desire' and 'Experience', on the one hand, and tempted by 'Sensual Appetite' and 'Ignorance' on the other. Expounding on cosmography, Experience recounts that 'within this twenty yeare,/ West-warde be founde new landes'.[64] He suggests 'Great ryches' might be found there, but indicates that the highest aim of such an enterprise must be 'an honourable thynge/ Bothe to the realme and to the knynge'.[65] Experience laments that 'englyshe men' have not taken 'possessyon' of those lands. He then recounts Rastell's own recent failure 'Some men of this countrey went,/ By the kynges noble consent,/ It for to serche to that entente/ And could not be brought therto'. The corruption of the 'maryners', manifest as dissimulation and selfish desire, was the cause of this failure:

> But they that were the venteres
> Have cause to curse their maryners,
> Fals of promys and dissemblers,
> That falsly them betrayed,
> Which wolde take no paine to saile farther

---

[58] *Ibid.*, p. 31.   [59] *Ibid.*, p. 32.   [60] *Ibid.*   [61] *Ibid.*   [62] *Ibid.*
[63] *Ibid.*,   [64] *Ibid.*, p. 49.   [65] *Ibid.*, p. 50.

Than their owne lyst and pleasure.
Wherfore that vyage and dyvers other
Suche kaytyffes have distroyed.[66]

Given this diagnosis of his failure, it is not surprising that Rastell should have insisted, at the opening of the play, upon the necessity of using vernacular to ensure the moral education of men of 'meane estate'. Clearly in his experience, the vices of such men, as much as the gentry or nobility, were capable of frustrating projects intended for the common good, in which success depended upon the participants exercising virtue above 'their ownne lyst and pleasure'. Rastell believed that these lower orders should be instructed in moral philosophy.

There was some agreement, then, between critics such as Barclay, who were anxious that civic virtue could be corrupted by foreign ventures, and those such as Rastell, who supported colonising but were vigilant against the motivation of profit. These anxieties contributed to the apparent lack of interest in the New World through the remainder of Henry's reign, even while Spanish, Portuguese and French interest was exploding. Those voyages that were made in this period, such as that by John Rut in 1527, had the discovery of a passage to Asia as the primary motive or were concerned with fishing.[67] An exception was the voyage led by Richard Hore with two ships in 1536. Hore's voyage mirrored the division of gentry and merchant interest in the New World.[68] One of his ships was clearly sent with the purpose of making some profit from the Newfoundland fisheries, and this end was successfully attained. The passengers of the second ship, the *Trinity*, were 'many gentlemen of the innes of court, and of Chancerie, and divers other good worship' including John Rastell's son, John.[69] This ship succeeded in crossing the Atlantic but it became stranded on the coast of Labrador. The gentlemen suffered such 'extreme famine' that they began to 'eate one another'.[70] Providence brought a well-provisioned French ship into the same bay and the English were saved only through becoming 'masters of the same' and 'changing ships'.[71] There was no material here for a humanistic celebration of glorious deeds and the episode would appear only to have provided support for the sceptics convinced of the folly of such an enterprise. It is particularly striking that the adventurers did not attempt to justify their actions by arguing for expedience above honour,

---

[66] *Ibid.*, p. 49.   [67] Quinn, *England and the discovery of America*, p. 171.
[68] On Hore's voyage, see Richard Hakluyt, *The principal navigations, voiages and discoveries of the English nation* (London, 1589), pp. 517–19; and Quinn, *England and the discovery of America*, pp. 182–9.
[69] Hakluyt, *Principal navigations*, p. 517.   [70] *Ibid.*, p. 518.   [71] *Ibid.*

as their successors could one hundred years later (see ch. 6). The resort to self-preservation was perceived as a failure.

(see ch. 6)

RICHARD EDEN'S PROJECTIONS

Through the reigns of Edward and Mary and in the early years of the reign of Elizabeth, there was a steadily growing interest in England in the possibilities of colonisation. That interest was clearly in part prompted by the country's growing economic problems: inflation, the loss of cloth markets and increase in enclosures. It was believed that colonisation could provide new markets and siphon off the perceived excess in the population. The interest in colonies as a solution to such problems was predominantly located around a small number of humanist figures with close personal and intellectual ties. For those humanists, however, colonies were not merely the means of employing their education as an instrument to solve economic problems. The problems and the prospect of establishing new commonwealths were seized as an opportunity to articulate a distinctive moral vision.

In the reigns of Edward and Mary, it is perhaps not surprising that the subject of colonisation would be brought to public notice through a comparison with the great strides taken by the Spanish. In 1553 Richard Eden published *A treatise of the newe India*, translated into English out of Sebastian Munster's *Cosmographia*. In 1555, he published a translation of Peter Martyr's *Decades of the new world* and Gonzalo Fernández de Oviedo's *Summario*.[72] In the substantial prefaces to these works, Eden exhorted Englishmen to emulate Spanish achievements (with due care for Spanish sensibilities). He did so through a demonstration of the full potential of a humanist education. His pedigree in the *studia humanitatis* was impeccable. He had been a student of Thomas Smith at Cambridge in the ten years he spent there between 1535 and 1544.[73] Eden described his teacher as 'the floure of the University of Cambridge'. He was still using Smith as a referee some thirty years later, with Smith testifying to his 'erudition'.[74] Leaving university, Eden was employed at court and possibly as the private secretary of Sir William Cecil.[75]

From this modest position, Eden developed a friendship with Sebastian Cabot when Cabot returned to England in 1548. With the support of the

---

[72] On Eden's publications, see Edward Arber, ed., *The first three English books on America* (Birmingham, 1885); Franklin T. McCann, *English discovery of America to 1585* (New York, 1952), pp. 112–19; Parker, *Books to build an empire*, pp. 36–54.
[73] Arber, *The first three English books on America*, pp. xxxvii and xlv.
[74] *Ibid.*, p. xlv.   [75] *Ibid.*, pp. xxvii–xxviii.

duke of Northumberland, Cabot led a group of merchants interested in the prospect of overseas expansion. Eden's link with Cabot was prompted not simply by a similar interest in the prospects of trade and colonisation but by the service he could bring to those ends through the employment of his humanistic skills. His first work promoting English expansion was dedicated to Northumberland and coincided with the first exploratory voyage of Cabot's company.[76] The work was published one month before Edward's death, when Eden was aware that he would soon be ruled by a Catholic monarch with close ties to Spain.[77] While canvassing possible voyages and, implicitly, possible colonies, Eden observed that the Spanish 'Eagle' had 'so spled his winges' in the New World that it would be difficult to establish a colony there without giving 'offence'.[78] He claimed to be 'loth to lay an egge, wherof other men might hatch a serpent', but he was prepared to comment that the Spanish possessions in America were 'yet not in every place' with the obvious implication that he was encouraging English colonisation in those areas of America unoccupied by Spain.[79]

Mary was on the throne and her marriage to Philip concluded when, in 1555, Eden published his translation of Martyr's *Decades*, dedicated to the new king and queen. His sensitivity to Spanish claims to possession over the New World was now even greater. He stated that the English must emulate Spain in the most flattering terms for Spain and he attacked English critics of Philip, declaring 'stoope England stoope, and learne to knowe thy lorde and master'.[80] Eden nevertheless made a forceful appeal for action albeit obliquely through praise of Spanish conquests. His flattery and sensitivity did not spare him from being charged with heresy and being deposed from his position in Mary's government later that year.[81]

Through his subsequent employment, Eden may have retrospectively justified the charges made against him. Shortly after his translation of Martyr, a French attempt was made to establish a colony in Brazil under the leadership of the Chevalier Nicholas Durand de Villegaignon. The enterprise included a large contingent of Protestants.[82] In 1562 Eden entered the service of the French Huguenot leader Jean de Ferrières, Vidame of Chartres, who was visiting England in an attempt to enlist Elizabeth's support for Huguenots in the civil war. It was at this time that Huguenot plans to establish a colony in the New World reached their peak. A Huguenot colony was established in Florida in 1562. As Jean Ribault, one of the leaders of that colony, returned through England in 1563, further interest was

---

[76] Parker, *Books to build an empire*, p. 37–8.　　[77] *Ibid.*, p. 40.
[78] Arber, *The first three English books on America*, p. 9.　　[79] *Ibid.*, p. 9.
[80] *Ibid.*, p. 52.　　[81] *Ibid.*, pp. xxxix–xl.　　[82] *Ibid.*, p. xliv.

stimulated in colonial projects. A joint English and Huguenot project was planned by Ribault and Thomas Stukley to reoccupy the Florida colony.[83] A further plan to occupy the site was developed by Richard Hawkins the following year. The circles in which Eden now moved were concerned with pan-Protestant prospects for colonisation and not simply those of England. Throughout this period, Eden continued his work of translating texts that would support colonial enterprises. He also, through his ten-year service with the Vidame, associated closely with other promoters of colonial projects, including Peter Martyr and André Thevet.

The ideology Eden favoured for these enterprises had been clear even during the period of his guarded support for the foundation of English colonies under the reign of Mary. The appeal of colonies, to his humanistic reasoning, was the opportunity they provided for a man to exercise his higher faculties in service for the commonwealth, and to be rewarded with honour and glory. In the *Decades*, Eden opens the preface to the reader with the observation that 'the moste famous oratoure and learned Phylosopher Marcus Tullius Cicero' pointed out to us 'howe farre the dignitie of mans nature, excelleth the condition of brute beastes'.[84] Beasts are 'ruled altogether by sense', they think of nothing but 'beastely appetites' and their own 'felicitie'. Warming to this humanistic theme, he continued: 'The mynde of man' is of a 'more noble nature.' The mind of man 'taketh pleasure' in devising 'sume honest thynge' which leaves a memory of his 'immortal nature' and encourages his successors in such 'commendable' acts. From this statement that virtue is the quality that distinguishes man as man, Eden declared that virtue flourishes most when exercised through the *vita activa*. Virtue flourishes, he argued, in acts performed for our fellow man or for the commonwealth. 'Cicero', he declared, again leaving no doubt about his intellectual debts, 'Cicero defineth trewe glory to bee a fame of many and greate dessertes eyther towarde owre citzens, owr countrey, or towarde all man kynde.'[85] Honour and glory were the reward for these services to the commonwealth: 'the ancient Romans and Greekes gave such glorye' to those who 'well deserved of the common welthe' that they created statues 'made to their lykenesse' which also succeeded in provoking others to the 'emulation of their vertues'.[86] This description of the glory which rewards public acts served as Eden's frame for his translation of Martyr. He instructed the reader that conquests by Spain in 'late dayes' in the 'newe worlde' were precisely such 'desertes' and that the glory of the Spanish may

---

[83] Humphrey Gilbert, *The voyages and colonising enterprises of Sir Humphrey Gilbert*, ed. David B. Quinn, 2 vols. (Cambridge, 1940), I, p. 5.
[84] Arber, *The first three English books on America*, p. 49. [85] *Ibid.*, p. 49. [86] *Ibid.*, p. 59.

be compared to 'goddes made of men'.[87] But Eden was no less clear that he wanted these virtuous public acts of the Spanish to provoke his English readers to emulate the same. Indeed, that was his reason for publicising these glorious deeds. For Eden, the foundation of colonies in the New World would be an opportunity for his humanistically educated readers to pursue the *vita activa*. His vision of the opportunities for glory provided by colonisation was in direct contrast with Barclay's humanistic anxieties over corruption.

THOMAS SMITH AND IRELAND

Eden had not produced 'the first piece of sustained argument for colonisation to be published in England'.[88] That honour would belong to his former tutor Sir Thomas Smith.[89] Given the leading role taken by previous generations of humanists in addressing the question of colonisation, it is appropriate that one of the leading 'commonwealthmen' of the mid-sixteenth century should have produced the first direct consideration of establishing an English colony and should have done so, as we shall see, in the context of a specific colonial venture. The object of Smith's interest was not America but Ireland. That the same humanist imagination was brought to the problem of Irish colonisation is consistent with the similar Elizabethan and Jacobean perceptions of the two spheres.[90] Moreover, the colonial projects in America and Ireland were themselves entangled. Many of the actors in one would, as we shall see, play central roles in the other. A basis for these links were the common humanist ambitions for both colonial projects. For these reasons, Smith's seminal contribution to Irish colonisation, as Quinn argued, is important to any consideration of the development of American colonisation projects.[91]

In the years following Eden's publications of the 1550s, Englishmen continued to refrain from concrete involvement in colonial projects, watching Huguenot attempts from the sidelines. The closest they came were the joint plans of Ribault and Stukley and the plan of Hawkins to occupy the Florida site, both in the early 1560s.[92] In 1565, Sir Henry Sidney was

---

[87] *Ibid.*, pp. 49–50.

[88] David Beers Quinn, 'Sir Thomas Smith (1513–1517) and the beginnings of English colonial theory', *Proceedings of the American Philosophical Society*, 4 (1945), p. 550.

[89] In 1565, Smith's library contained Eden's *Decades* and his translation of Martin Cortez's *Art of navigation* which included a tribute to his former tutor; see Quinn, 'Sir Thomas Smith', p. 545.

[90] On common perceptions of Ireland and America, see Nicholas Canny, 'The ideology of English colonisation: from Ireland to America', *The William and Mary Quarterly*, 30 (1973), pp. 575–98.

[91] Quinn, 'Sir Thomas Smith', p. 543.   [92] *Humphrey Gilbert*, I, p. 5.

appointed Lord Deputy of Ireland at a time of growing concern with the need to subject the Irish.[93] Sidney advocated the foundation of colonies, through private licence, as the means to achieve this aim.[94] Rebellion in Munster in 1569 limited short-term colonising projects to the north. Three patents were granted in 1571 for colonies to be established in Ulster. One of the patentees was Sir Thomas Smith, who had petitioned the Queen for a grant in the Ards in the spring or summer of 1571.[95] He entered into the venture with his son, Thomas Smith junior, who was to take day to day responsibility for the project including leadership of the colony once it was established. The Smiths moved quickly with preparations. They had outlined a plan for conquest and occupation and assembled a force of 700–800 prospective colonists at Liverpool by May 1572.[96] When news of this expedition reached Ireland, fear of further rebellion led the English authorities to delay the Smiths. Three months later, the force crossed to the Ards but it had been reduced to approximately 100 by various desertions. Despite armed resistance, the colony survived a hard winter. The following year, Smith junior's Irish household servants killed him and the venture effectively collapsed. In 1574 and 1575, Sir Thomas Smith attempted a further expedition that again fragmented.

Smith launched an 'intense propaganda drive' to attract subscribers and personnel for his colony.[97] His efforts underlined the links between humanism, print and colonisation that had been evident since the projects of Cabot and Rastell. As we shall see, while Eden had portrayed print as the epideictic means of presenting models of virtue for subsequent generations to emulate, Smith understood his publications explicitly in terms of rhetorical deliberation, or exhortation. When apparently reproached by William Cecil, Lord Burghley and the Privy Council for the damage that his pamphlets had caused in relations with the Irish, Smith responded that he had no means 'to compel' investment or personnel to support the colony: 'nothing was left but persuasion, either by words or writing and writing goes further'.[98] The main platform of Smith's promotion was the publication of a pamphlet probably written by his son under his supervision and entitled *A letter sent by I.B. gentleman unto his very frende Master R.C. esquire, wherin is conteined a large discourse of the peopling & inhabiting the cuntrie called the Ardes* (London, 1572).[99]

In content, Smith's pamphlet presented a moral philosophy familiar not only from his student Eden but also to be articulated later in *A discourse*

---

[93] Quinn, 'Sir Thomas Smith', pp. 543–4.   [94] *Ibid.*, p. 544.   [95] *Ibid.*, p. 548.
[96] *Ibid.*   [97] *Ibid.*, pp. 548 and 550.   [98] *Ibid.*, p. 551.
[99] On the promotional efforts associated with this enterprise, see *ibid.*, pp. 550–1.

on the commonweal and *De republica Anglorum*. As in these works of moral philosophy applied to practical problems, in *A letter* Smith insisted upon the duty to pursue the *vita activa* and upon the centrality of that duty in political life. Participation in the colony, he argued, was the 'most honorable service that can bee in our times done for England'.[100] The principal virtue required for this service was 'noble courage' and, in reward, participants would be 'crowned with garlands of honour and fame'.[101] It would be a 'most honourable and profitable voyage'.[102]

Most striking was Smith's employment of a Roman and Machiavellian concept of martial citizenship. The chief preoccupation of the pamphlet was to set out his desire that as far as possible, each colonist would be a citizen soldier 'to the ende the Souldiours should be the more vigilant'.[103] In a distinctly Machiavellian tone, he argued that if the soldiers also possessed land, a family and a livelihood in the colony, they would be most concerned about the security of the new commonwealth:

> As for having the Queens ayde and garrison, I have good hope it shall not need for sith the every Souldiour is made Mayster and owner of his land, to him and to his heires for ever, will he not think you look as well and as carefully to that, as hee would if hee had six pence sterling a day of the Queens Maiestie... Now if he keepe and defende this, hee is a Gentlemen, a man of livelyhode and of enheritaunce... if he lose it, he loseth his owne inheritaunce, and hindreth his posteritie.[104]

Here Smith anticipated the requirement of civic duty from a broad spectrum of social classes which he later sought in *A discourse of the commonweal* and *De republica Anglorum*. The quasi-republican design ensured that each colonist would be responsible for maintaining the security and common good of the commonwealth. The colonists' vigilance was guaranteed by their share in the enterprise. Smith's proposal was not as carefully or thoroughly articulated as the Machiavellian treatises that addressed the problems of Ireland in the 1590s, written by Richard Beacon, William Herbert and Edmund Spenser.[105] What Smith revealed, however, is that those later

---

[100] [Thomas Smith], *A letter sent by I.B. gentleman unto his very frende Master R.C. esquire, wherin is conteined a large discourse of the peopling & inhabiting the cuntrie called the Ardes* (London, 1572), sig. Giiv.

[101] *Ibid.*, sigs. F3v–F4v. See also in sig. F4v, 'Be of good courage therefore, and resolve yourselfe to be a partaker with him in person.'

[102] *Ibid.*, sig. Hiir.   [103] *Ibid.*, sig. Ciir.   [104] *Ibid.*, sigs. Ciir–Ciiv.

[105] On these works, see Markku Peltonen, *Classical humanism and republicanism in English political thought, 1570–1640* (Cambridge, 1995), pp. 73–102; Sidney Anglo, 'A Machiavellian solution to the Irish problem: Richard Beacon's Solon his follie (1594)', in Edward Chancey and Peter Mack, eds., *England and the continental renaissance: Essays in honour of J. B. Trapp* (Woodbridge, 1990); Lisa

works were not profoundly 'radical': they were introduced into an ideological climate in which Machiavellian thought had been employed to address the problems of Ireland since the first colonies were sponsored under Henry Sidney more than twenty years earlier.[106]

While presenting colonisation as a duty of the *vita activa*, an avenue of virtue, rewarded with honour and glory, both Smith and Eden were acutely conscious of the possible corruption of the enterprises. The problems against which they warned were precisely those raised by opponents of colonies. Both warned against idleness, effeminacy and luxury. Eden reproached English 'slothfulness' and warned his countrymen against their addiction to 'soft beds'.[107] Echoing the Roman anxiety over 'Asiatic' luxury (remembering that Eden translated Sallust), he warned against the 'barbarous ostentation and superfluous riches' of the east.[108] Smith similarly cautioned that his colony 'requireth rather lasting and warm clothes than gorgeous and deere garmentes'.[109]

Both men also warned against the corrupting desire for profit. Directly addressing merchants, Eden condemned the 'desire to get riches', asking how much more could be achieved by the commonwealth if the same efforts were put to virtuous rather than bestial ends. 'This covetousness', he concluded, 'is to be reproved.'[110] Smith also lamented that men are 'more moved by peculiar gain: than of respect they have to common profite' and he acknowledged that this intemperance was a threat to the commonweal.[111] As in the *Discourse of the commonweal*, he was careful, however, also to acknowledge that this desire was a reality of political life. Profit posed no problem if it was not pursued to the exclusion of the common good: 'they shall have their peculiar portions in that fruitfull soile'.[112] Here Smith again revealed the breadth of audience to whom he was appealing – he does not try to force lofty motives upon self-interested men.[113]

Jardine, 'Mastering the uncouth: Gabriel Harvey, Edmund Spenser and the English experience in Ireland', in John Henry and Sarah Hutton, eds., *New perspectives on Renaissance thought* (London, 1990).

[106] Cf. Peltonen, *Classical humanism and republicanism in English political thought*, pp. 74–6; Jardine, 'Mastering the uncouth', p. 73.

[107] Richard Eden, *The decades of the newe worlde or west India* (London, 1555), p. 55 and Richard Eden, *A treatyse of the newe India* (London, 1553), both reprinted in Edward Arber, *The first three English books on America*, p. 6.

[108] Eden, *The decades of the newe worlde*, p. 49.   [109] [Smith], *A letter*, sig. Fiv.

[110] Eden, *The decades of the newe worlde*, pp. 58–9.   [111] [Smith], *A letter*, sig. Dir.   [112] *Ibid*.

[113] Cf. Steven Pincus, 'Neither Machiavellian moment nor possessive individualism', *American Historical Review*, June 1998, on the reconciliation of virtue with commerce following the civil war. The moral arguments revealed by Pincus to be employed in a merchant literature were in fact readily accessible to school students reading Cicero's and Quintilian's rhetorical works throughout

'How say you now', he concludes, 'have I not set forth to you another Eutopia?'[114]

HUMPHREY GILBERT'S PROJECTS

Links between Irish and American colonisation were not only ideological. The ideological parallels between the two spheres of interest facilitated many adventurers in slipping from designs concerning one to the other. Humphrey Gilbert was the first English adventurer to fill that role. To both enterprises he brought his passion for the *studia humanitatis*. He was noted by contemporaries for his learning. John Hooker observed in Holinshed's *Chronicles* that Gilbert was 'adorned with learning and knowledge...and could notablie discourse anie matter in question...with the noble, wise and learned'.[115] Indeed, according to Hooker, he first gained favour with Queen Elizabeth on account of the 'ornament' of his learning and not for his military accomplishments.[116] His commitment to the *studia humanitatis* was revealed in his projection from 1570 of a new university to be established in London: an academy for the Queen's wards with a humanist curriculum.[117]

Gilbert is believed to have been educated at Eton in the early 1650s at the time that Sir Thomas Smith was provost and there is a suggestion that he may have served in Smith's household.[118] When in 1562 Elizabeth intervened in the French civil war on the side of the Huguenots, Gilbert was commissioned to raise a force to join the attempted occupation of the Havre (which Eden had joined with the Vidame of Chartres). It has been suggested that Gilbert's interest in colonisation was stimulated by the twelve months he spent in Huguenot territory, and that he would have met Eden and Thévet in le Havre. No doubt such direct links with Smith and Eden could play a part, but of greater importance in shaping the aspirations of these men was the humanistic culture in which they were immersed.

---

the Renaissance. Quintilian recommends that the orator should avoid urging high motives to a base audience (Quintilian, *Institutio oratoria*, trans. H. E. Butler, 4 vols. (London, 1920–22), III, xiii, 38–9). Indeed, this decorum of argument with audience is fundamental to the character of Renaissance humanism.

[114] [Smith], *A letter*, sig. Eir.   [115] *Humphrey Gilbert*, II, p. 433.

[116] *Ibid.*, p. 432. Cf. Nicholas Canny, *The Elizabethan conquest of Ireland: A pattern established, 1565–76* (London, 1976), pp. 101–3; Jardine, 'Mastering the uncouth', p. 74.

[117] [Sir Humphrey Gilbert,] 'The erection of an achademy in London for educacion of her Majesties Wardes' (c.1570), in F. J. Furnivall, ed., *Queene Elizabethes achademy, a booke of precedence, &c.* (London, 1869).

[118] *Humphrey Gilbert*, I, pp. 2–3.

On his return to England, Gilbert became involved in plans to discover a north-west or north-east passage to Asia. He composed a treatise on this subject in 1566 that included a proposal for establishing a colony in America.[119] His plans to follow up on the proposal were blocked, however, by the Muscovy Company.[120] Gilbert was then drawn into Sidney's project to colonise Ireland. In the four years he spent in Ireland between 1566 and 1570, he was effective and brutal in quashing resistance (for which he was knighted). Like Smith, he was less successful in advancing the cause of occupation.[121] Gilbert was certainly well acquainted with Smith in 1571, the year Smith's *A letter* promoting his colony was published. It was in that year that Smith, Gilbert, Cecil and Leicester entered into a partnership financing an alchemy venture. Gabriel Harvey, an eminent humanist, also recorded that at this time he was present at a debate, in which Gilbert participated, at Smith's house on the subject of Livy's histories.[122]

In the following years, Gilbert was active first in military ventures in the Netherlands and later in managing his own estates. The poet George Gascoigne visited his house in the winter of 1575–6 demanding to know 'howe he spent his time in this loytering vacation from martial strategemes'. It appears that Gilbert had turned to more contemplative pursuits. He took Gascoigne 'up into his Studie, and there showed me sundrie profitable and verie commendable exercises, which he had perfected painefully with his owne penne'.[123] In true humanist spirit, however, this study and withdrawal was a preparation for further action. One of the 'exercises' that Gilbert probably showed Gascoigne was his plan for the foundation of a third university.[124] It would appear that another of these exercises was Gilbert's *Discourse* of 1566 planning the discovery of a north-west passage and an American colony, to which he had been making changes. Following the close links between humanism and colonial plans in preceding generations, these two projects were clearly complementary. To Gilbert's humanistically trained mind, plans for colonisation would be perceived as an extension of humanist learning.

Gascoigne possessed a humanist education and had distinguished himself as a poet. He had also participated in the military ventures in the Netherlands at the time of Gilbert's command there.[125] He became drawn into Gilbert's plans, editing and writing an introduction to the *Discourse*

[119] *A discourse of a discovery for a new passage to Cataia*, not published until 1576, see *Humphrey Gilbert*, I, p. 8.
[120] *Ibid.*, pp. 10–11. [121] *Ibid.*, pp. 12–18. [122] Jardine, 'Mastering the uncouth', pp. 73–4.
[123] *Humphrey Gilbert*, I, p. 27. [124] *Ibid.*, pp. 27–8; Armitage, 'Literature and empire', p. 108.
[125] C. T. Prouty, *George Gascoigne: Elizabethan courtier, soldier and poet* (New York, 1942).

and then publishing it in 1576.[126] He revealed his concern with both learning and action when he concluded the introduction to this work: 'From my lodging where I march amongst the Muses for lacke of exercise in martiall exploytes.'[127] The adventurer Michael Lok would later imply in a letter that this publication was directed by Gilbert.[128] The treatise appears to have established a platform for Gilbert's initiation of plans, the following year, for a voyage to the new lands.[129] In part these plans were linked to privateering against Spain that had been particularly active with growing anti-Spanish sentiment in court, and with the success of Drake's 1572–3 Caribbean voyage. The plan to establish a colony may have been intended also in part to hide the interest in privateering from the Spanish ambassador at the same time as providing a base from which to launch such actions. Opinions as to precisely where Gilbert planned to establish the colony varied among his contemporaries from Newfoundland in the north to the new lands of terra australis in the south.[130]

Francis Walsingham, the Secretary of State, had long been interested in the possibilities of colonisation and favoured Gilbert's project.[131] In 1578, Gilbert was granted the first letters patent by the English crown to establish a colony in the New World. Although his patent did not clarify his destination, he was given the power

to discover...such remote and heathen and barbarous landes...not actually possessed of any Christian prince...And the same to have hould occupie and enjoye...all the soyle of such landes.[132]

This patent included the power to grant tenures and was to expire after six years. Through the course of 1578, Gilbert prepared an expeditionary force of eleven ships and 500 men. Among the subscribers was his half-brother Walter Ralegh, who financed and commanded at least one ship, the *Falcon*.[133] This fleet never crossed the Atlantic. It fragmented through disorganisation and indiscipline, the attractions of piracy and the distraction of James Fitzmaurice's rebellion in Ireland. Both the Privy Council and the High Court of Admirality pursued Gilbert for compensation owed to French and Spanish ships that had been spoiled.[134]

---

[126] *Humphrey Gilbert*, I, p. 29. Any further participation by Gascoigne in the plans was prevented by his death the following year.

[127] *Ibid.*, p. 133.   [128] *Ibid.*, p. 30 n. 4.

[129] Gascoigne's publication was also designed to promote Frobisher's voyage to discover a north-west passage undertaken a couple of months after its publication. In 1571 Frobisher met Gilbert and claimed that his plans were influenced by him; see Parker, *Books to build an empire*, pp. 65–6.

[130] *Humphrey Gilbert*, I, pp. 38–9.   [131] *Ibid.*, p. 35.   [132] *Ibid.*, pp. 188–9.   [133] *Ibid.*, p. 44.

[134] For documents relating to the aftermath of this first voyage, see *ibid.*, pp. 219–37.

Gilbert and Ralegh found that the fleet simply had not 'according to appointment followed' them.[135] Gilbert's problem was similar to that to which Rastell had attributed his failure. Privateering and trading were profitable, colonising voyages were not. The humanists who promoted colonisation warned against profit, but apparently ships' crews frequently were not moved by these arguments. The crews' lack of interest in colonising, however, serves to reveal the degree to which those ventures were understood in terms of an ideology that was distinctive from the language of the merchant, in so far as that language was one of profit and self-interest. Promoters often distinguished between gentry and merchant audiences. As we shall see, however, the distinction between gentry and merchants in terms of education and values was not always clear. Humanist arguments of virtue were frequently employed by or addressed to merchants.

Gilbert had invested much of his estate in this venture and was now, according to his own account, 'forside to gadge and sell my wyffes clothes from her backe'.[136] His hopes were revived by the 1581 Act of Obedience. In 1570, Elizabeth had been excommunicated by the pope and, over the following twenty years, tension with Spain escalated. English Catholics came under increasing pressure to conform. The Act of Obedience dramatically increased fines for recusancy (not attending Church of England services) from one shilling per service to twenty pounds a month, and the hearing of mass became punishable by imprisonment.[137] Many Catholics now seized upon the plans for a colony as a means of escaping these draconian laws, and the crown offered them tacit support if they first paid their fines.[138] Gilbert assigned $5\frac{1}{2}$ million acres of land to two Catholics, Sir George Peckham and Sir Thomas Gerard, for which he received a substantial but unknown sum.[139] Under this agreement Gilbert's powers were delegated to Peckham and Gerard, including the power for them to make further assignments of their own land for others interested in adventuring. In panic, the Spanish ambassador to England, Don Bernadino Mendoza, reported to Philip II that many Catholics did indeed appear to be interested in planting. It seemed that Spain's missionary ambitions in England could be thwarted if all the Catholics left. Mendoza issued a threat through the priests that any English Catholics settled in the New World would have their throats cut and confirmed in July 1582 that the threat had apparently

---

[135] *Ibid.*, p. 236.   [136] *Ibid.*, pp. 49 and 54.
[137] Quinn, *England and the discovery of America*, p. 365; *Humphrey Gilbert*, I, p. 71.
[138] *Ibid.*, p. 72.
[139] *Ibid.*, pp. 57 and 243; Quinn, *England and the discovery of America*, pp. 371 and 375–6.

succeeded in stemming Catholic support for the project.[140] It is not surprising, therefore, to find Gilbert granting a further 3 million acres in July 1582 to Philip Sidney, the prominent courtier and humanist (and the son of Henry Sidney, whose Irish colonial projects Gilbert had served).

Gilbert finally succeeded in launching a further expedition in June 1583 with the departure of five vessels.[141] This expedition represented the interests of the principal subscribers instead of, as originally planned, the different parties attempting their own separate colonies. The five vessels were badly provisioned and so made for Newfoundland where they could requisition salted fish from the summer cod fishing fleets.[142] Gilbert landed in the harbour of St John's claiming possession of the land within 200 leagues, consistent with his patent.[143] The captains of two of the vessels announced they were returning to England. The remaining three ships set off south down the coast but when one was wrecked a decision was made on 31 August to return to England.[144] In a storm at night nine days later the lights went out on the smaller vessel, the *Squirrel*, on which Gilbert was travelling and he was not seen again.[145] Fittingly, Gilbert's last recorded act was to read aloud, sitting in the stern of the *Squirrel*, either from More's *Utopia* or Cicero's *Tusculan disputations* as his ship was 'oppressed by the waves'. He called across to Edward Haies' ship, 'We are as neere to heaven by sea as by land', no doubt to the great consolation of his crew.[146]

A series of publications promoting American colonisation followed in the years after Gascoigne's edition of Gilbert's *Discourse* in 1576 through to Gilbert's death in 1583. His plans were not the sole focus of those publications but they were the principal focus for discussions of colonisation in the period. Indeed, the two characteristics which distinguish these pamphlets are first, that they are vitally interested in contemporary colonisation plans and are motivated by immediate and practical concerns with establishing colonies; and second, that they are produced by authors with strong humanist credentials. Frequently they are linked to many of the most prominent humanists of the period. As we will see in ch. 4, these ties were produced by a humanist understanding that speaking and publishing were forms of action that were crucial to achieving political ends. We have seen this point suggested by Eden's claim that the central purpose of his work was to

---

[140] *Humphrey Gilbert*, I, p. 279. Cf. Patricia Seed, *Ceremonies of possession in Europe's conquest of the New World 1492–1640* (Cambridge, 1995), arguing that European colonial projects were distinguished along national lines.

[141] *Humphrey Gilbert* I, p. 83.   [142] *Ibid.*, pp. 84 and 86.

[143] *Ibid.*, p. 86.   [144] *Ibid.*, p. 88.   [145] *Ibid.*, p. 89.

[146] *Ibid.*, II, p. 420. On the issue of whether Gilbert was reading from More or Cicero, see Armitage, 'Literature and empire', pp. 107–8.

spur good actions. Many humanists would go further and represent their publications as central acts in the ventures. First, we must consider the links between the enterprise, the promotional pamphlets and the humanist credentials of the authors before turning to the moral content of those publications through which the venture was understood.

A new edition of Richard Eden's *Decades* was published in 1577.[147] Eden had died in 1576 while the work was in preparation, so the edition appeared under the editorial guidance of Richard Willes, who also contributed substantially to the narratives.[148] Willes was sufficiently prominent in the *studia humanitatis* to have been professor of rhetoric at the university of Perugia until 1572.[149] He explicitly acknowledged the link between his publication and Frobisher's voyage but also adopted Gilbert's arguments in the *Discourse*.[150] In 1577, Gilbert began to consult one of the most learned men of his time, John Dee, on questions relating to his ventures, and in that year, Dee's *Art of navigation* was published.[151] The treatise promoted American colonisation amongst other projects. Dee would play an active role in Gilbert's plans in the following years, producing maps favourable to investment and delivering opinions on the legality of the proposed colony to reassure the Catholic group troubled by the hostility of the Spanish. For these services, he was rewarded with an assignment of land from Gilbert in 1580 and, for his legal opinion, he was probably granted 100,000 acres of land by Peckham and Gerard in 1582.[152]

In 1578, the poet Thomas Churchyard published treatises arguing the cause of English colonisation in general, and supporting Frobisher's and Gilbert's ventures in particular.[153] He dedicated one of the volumes to Dr Thomas Wilson, a member of the Privy Council, and author of the most successful Ciceronian rhetoric to be published in English in the sixteenth and seventeenth centuries. It was not the only occasion on which tracts promoting colonisation were to be dedicated to Wilson. Again in 1581, the merchant Thomas Nicholas made the same dedication to Wilson, now Secretary of State, in his translation of Agustin de Zarate's *Discovery and conquest of Peru*.[154] Earlier in 1578, Nicholas had also argued strongly for

[147] Under the title *A history of travayle in the West and East Indies.*
[148] E. G. R. Taylor, ed., *Tudor Geography, 1485–1583* (London, 1930), pp. 38–9.
[149] Parker, *Books to build an empire*, p. 77; Taylor, *Tudor geography*, p. 38.
[150] Parker, *Books to build an empire*, p. 79.
[151] *Humphrey Gilbert*, I, p. 33. See also William H. Sherman, *John Dee: The politics of reading and writing in the Renaissance* (Amherst, 1995), p. 102.
[152] *Humphrey Gilbert*, I, pp. 52 and 64.
[153] Parker, *Books to build an empire*, pp. 81–2; Quinn, *England and the discovery of America*, p. 217.
[154] Parker, *Books to build an empire*, p. 107.

English colonisation in America when he produced a translation of Lopez de Gomara's history of Spanish conquest.[155]

Gilbert's plans received further impetus from the publication, in 1580, of John Florio's translation of the narrative of Jacques Cartier's voyages (which had been conducted in the same part of the New World with which he was now concerned). Florio was an Italian Protestant, and a teacher of languages at Oxford, recognised for his mastery of the *studia humanitatis*, known for his Italian–English dictionary and later renowned for his translation of Montaigne's *Essaies*.[156] His translation of Cartier included a preface spelling out the lesson that colonies would be necessary if England was to emulate the prosperity of the Spaniards.

Florio's translation appeared to have been sponsored on Gilbert's behalf by Richard Hakluyt.[157] With his older cousin of the same name, Hakluyt would become recognised as foremost among Elizabethan promoters of an American colony. Hakluyt the elder had written *Notes on colonisation* in 1578 for Gilbert's voyage of that year.[158] The younger Hakluyt promoted Gilbert's third voyage in a treatise, *Divers voyages*, published in 1582. This seminal work was dedicated to Philip Sidney, now one of the major interests in the venture.[159]

The moral value of verse was appreciated by one of the more notable humanists in Gilbert's company, Stephen Parmenius. Parmenius was a Hungarian Protestant humanist tutoring at Oxford and, in a reflection of Gilbert's humanist priorities, he was employed to accompany the voyage with the title of 'voyage orator'. His role would be to celebrate and promote the venture: 'to record in the Latin tongue, the gests and things worthy of remembrance, happening in this discoverie, to the honour of our nation, the same being adorned with the eloquent stile of this Orator and rare Poet of our time'.[160] The humanist emphasis upon Latin was realised in Parmenius' publication of a commendation of the voyage in Latin verse before embarking. His opportunity further to fulfil this role was curtailed as he drowned with Gilbert when the *Squirrel* foundered off the coast of Newfoundland.

Two of the most learned of the pamphlets promoting Gilbert's plans would come from two men, George Peckham and Edward Haies, deeply involved in the enterprise. Peckham was the son of George Peckham who

[155] *Ibid.*, p. 87. [156] *Ibid.*, pp. 105–6, and 125 n. 14. [157] *Ibid.*, p. 105.
[158] Richard Hakluyt the Elder and Richard Hakluyt, *The original writings and correspondence of the two Richard Hakluyts*, ed. E. G. R. Taylor, 2 vols. (London, 1935), I, pp. 116–22.
[159] Parker, *Books to build an empire*, p. 109.
[160] Edward Haies, *A report of the voyage*, in Hakluyt, *Principal navigations*, pp. 692–7.

held the largest assignment of land under Gilbert's patent. His tract appeared in 1583 when Gilbert was apparently lost and all efforts to establish a colony had failed. And yet at this moment a new partnership between Philip Sidney and Peckham's father was established to raise capital for a new attempt to establish a colony. Peckham's tract was anticipating those new designs even as it accounted for the recent failure. Moreover, the book was intended to have a direct influence upon the realisation of his plans. When Peckham senior pressed the Merchant Adventurers of Exeter to support his new plans he sent his agent to address the merchants. The agent presented not only the letters patent 'for the assurance' of the adventurers, but also 'a booke towching the discription and order of the saide pretended voyage' to persuade his audience.[161] The book was the *True report* written by Peckham.

Edward Haies left King's College, Cambridge, in the early 1570s to act as a tutor to the sons of Sir Thomas Hoby, translator of Castiglione's *The courtier*, a position one might assume that would only be filled by a person who had impressed with his mastery of the classics. He remained in this employment at least until 1578 when he subscribed to Gilbert's first expedition, probably with his merchant father's money.[162] In 1582, Haies had turned from tutoring the *studia humanitatis* to finance and captain a ship in Gilbert's last voyage. His account of the voyage the following year did not appear in print until it was published by Hakluyt in 1589. While Haies, like Gilbert, was prepared to invest his inheritance in the venture we shall see that he thought profit should not be the principal motive, and his personal experience supported that conviction. As Quinn observes, 'at the end of the period he is a poorer man', and yet Haies would continue to be involved in colonising projects for more than another twenty years.[163]

Eden's humanist conviction that publishing was necessary to provoke virtuous action remained fundamental to the way in which these authors understood their purpose in writing. In his preface to Gilbert's *Discourse*, Gascoigne expressed the same understanding. 'Every man', argues Gascoigne, who 'hath a reasonable disposition to the attaining of anie vertue... will confesse, that we are... bounde to encourage and commend the industrie of diligent, as to dispraise and punish slouth or abuse of the negligent.'[164] For Gascoigne, as for Eden, the health of the commonwealth was dependent upon this order, this decorum between the praise and exhortation of virtue and the condemnation of vice:

---

[161] *Humphrey Gilbert*, I, p. 92.   [162] Quinn, *England and the discovery of America*, p. 230.
[163] *Ibid.*, p. 230.   [164] *Humphrey Gilbert*, I, p. 129.

For if princes doe not aswell rewarde and cherish the well deserving subjecte, as their Judges and Magistrates are readie to correct the offendour, the Common Wealth might then quickly be deprived both of the one and the other: I meane that as fast as the sword of Justice should weede out the one, so fast the scourg of ingratitude woulde chase out the other. And so thereby their dominions might (in the end) become naked and altogether unfurnished.[165]

It is not, however, the prince's duty alone to maintain the order of the commonwealth through these means. Gascoigne repeatedly emphasises that his motive in publishing is 'to highly prayse the noble minde and courage' of Gilbert, to set his virtue 'in the sunshine'.[166]

THE MORAL PHILOSOPHY OF GILBERT'S PROJECTS

We also find again that the enterprise in which these authors believe themselves to be playing such a central role is conceived in terms of the *vita activa* or, as Gasgoigne put it, the 'public performance, of a common dutie'.[167] The performance of such duties was again to be expected from all men, not merely the prince or nobility. 'The desire to advance the honour of our Countrie', argued Hakluyt in *Divers voyages*, 'ought to be in every good man.'[168] The ends of this public duty are glory, honour and profit, the conventional ends of Ciceronian moral philosophy, and the means to the successful attainment of those ends is the exercise of virtue. Thomas Churchyard wrote that Gilbert performed his first voyage: 'For Countreys wealth, for private gayne,/ or glory'.[169] Here Churchyard draws an important humanist distinction between public and private profit. Profit in a private commercial sense is certainly one aim of the adventurers. But profit is more frequently used in a non-commercial sense that concerns the commonwealth and not the individual, and refers to an array of motivations based upon expedience and strategic and political advantage. Following a Ciceronian position, promoters in general insist that all senses of profit or expedience are to be subordinate to virtue and honour.

Peckham provides the clearest statement of the tension between these ends of moral philosophy as they bear upon the adventurers. In the *True report*, he presents the recent voyage by Gilbert in terms of the conflict between honour and profit, *honestas* and *utilitas*. He recounts a story from

---

[165] *Ibid.*, I, pp. 129–30.   [166] *Ibid.*, pp. 131 and 133.   [167] *Ibid.*, I, p. 133.
[168] Richard Hakluyt, *Divers voyages*, in *The original writings and correspondence of the two Richard Hakluyts*, I, p. 175.
[169] Churchyard, 'A matter touching the journey of Sir Humphrey Gilbert', in *Humphrey Gilbert*, I, p. 217.

Plutarch. Themistocles 'had invented a device' for the Athenian 'common-wealth very profitable'. Aristides then 'made relation to the Citizens, that the stratageme . . . was a profitable practice for the commonwealth but it was dishonest'. The Athenians accordingly did 'condemn it, preferring honest and upright dealing before profit'.[170] It is crucial to this story that Peckham endorsed the customary Ciceronian position that expedience, or profit, is desirable, but it must be secondary to honesty.[171] While it may have been dangerous for English Catholics ever to suggest otherwise in public, the sentiment was shared equally by Protestant promoters of Gilbert's patent. When Peckham turned to consider the Athenians' debate in the light of his own plans, he found a balance between the ends of *honestas* and *utilitas*:

By occasion of this History, I drew myselfe into a more deepe consideration, of this late undertaken voyage, whether it were as well pleasing to almightie God, as profitable to men: as lawful as it seem honourable: as well grateful to the Savages, as gainful to the Christians. And upon mature deliberation, I found the action to be honest and profitable.[172]

Peckham repeatedly emphasised the context in which the moral dilemma facing the Athenians was debated, namely that it was in deliberations over the best course for the 'commonwealth'. For Ciceronian humanists, the language of the active life, virtue, honour and profit was fundamental to the conduct of politics, that is, to the business of the commonwealth. It is for this reason that this language was believed to be central to establishing colonies in the New World. Humanist promoters of colonies in the New World imagined themselves to be establishing new commonwealths. Accordingly, Peckham argued that his purpose in America was the creation of a 'well governed common wealth'.[173]

Peckham was careful to allay fears of corruption that critics, such as Barclay, had raised. With his humanist mentality, such anxieties would easily follow upon his ambitions for foreign possessions. But his caution would also have been provoked by continued strong scepticism of colonis-ing projects. In discussing Gilbert's *Discourse*, Thomas Churchyard com-mented 'Well, I admitte that many maie mislike this travail, and shewe many perswasions for the maintenance of their disliking.'[174] Yet he con-cluded with the hope that the *Discourse* would cause them to 'hold their peace' and cease their 'murmuryng'.[175]

[170] George Peckham, *A true report of the late discoveries . . . by Sir Humphrey Gilbert*, reprinted in Hakluyt, *Principal navigations*, p. 703.
[171] Cicero, *De officiis*.   [172] Peckham, *A true Report*, p. 703.
[173] Peckham, *A true report*, in *Humphrey Gilbert*, p. 468.   [174] *Humphrey Gilbert*, I, p. 168.
[175] *Ibid.* On opposition, see also George Gascoigne, *Discourse*, in *Humphrey Gilbert*, I, pp. 131 and 133.

It is as a result of this vulnerability to critics that the tracts promoting Gilbert's patent were as much concerned with corruption as they were with glory. Gascoigne stressed that Gilbert embraced the martial virtues and rejected luxury, he was 'more respecting the publique profit that might ensue by this Discoverie, then the delicate life of a Courtier'. He, accordingly, 'had prepared his owne bodie to abide the malice of the windes and waves'.[176] In a trope popular with promoters, Gascoigne had turned from the threat of luxury and corruption from foreign conquests to a comparison with the life of a courtier in England. Stephen Parmenius employed the same reversal in his embarkation poem for Gilbert's last voyage, expressing the hope that 'There [in the New World] a man's value will not be measured by birth, nor the people's liberty crushed by riches.'[177] Here, Parmenius appealed to two supposedly radical arguments of humanist republicanism. First, that virtue is the only true nobility. And, secondly, he explicitly endorses the idea that wealth diverts men from the pursuit of liberty. His views on colonisation had been shaped by his friend, Hakluyt, who explored the theme of the corrupting power of wealth in greater depth in the preface to *Divers voyages*, dedicated to Philip Sidney. According to Hakluyt, 'Certes, if hitherto in our own discoveries we had not been led with a preposterous desire of seeking rather gaine then God's glorie, I assure myself that our labours had taken better effecte.'[178] Corruption accounts for past failures. Hakluyt expects that profit should not, therefore, be the motivation for future enterprises: 'I trust that now being taught by their manifold losses, our men will take a more godly course, and use some part of their goodes to his glory.'[179] Consistent, however, with a Ciceronian moral philosophy, Hakluyt simply elevates glory above profit. He does not exclude profit as a motivation altogether, and he suggests that 'covetousness' and 'avarice' displayed by the Spaniards and Portuguese may even serve the ends of God.

This imbalance between honour and profit is tipped even further following the failure of Gilbert's voyage. It is in the light of this failure that Peckham made his strong plea against expedience. But an even greater anxiety about the role of profit in corrupting the enterprise was expressed by Haies, who captained the only ship to survive the last leg of the voyage. In Haies' report, the image of Gilbert as the embodiment of martial virtue is dramatically revised. The failure has to be explained and responsibility is tied to Gilbert, particularly to his intemperance, and to the corruption of

---

[176] *Humphrey Gilbert*, I, p. 131.   [177] Cited in Parker, *Books to build an empire*, p. 111.

[178] Hakluyt, *Divers voyages*, in *The original writings and correspondence of the two Richard Hakuyts*, I, p. 178. cf. Canny, 'The origins of empire: an introduction', in Canny, *The origins of empire*, pp. 4–5.

[179] Hakluyt, *Divers voyages*.

his design. Gilbert was, in fact, a flawed man, according to Haies. He acknowledged his 'manifold virtues' but argued that they were insufficient to maintain his 'good fortune', given what apparently were also his manifold vices. Haies blamed Gilbert's 'temerity' (a moral redescription of the cardinal virtue of courage), his 'presumption' and 'intemperate humours'.[180] Moreover, Haies argued, the design of Gilbert's enterprise was at fault, the adventurers had sought 'rather gain than glory'.[181] Gilbert's voyage had shown that this was 'an action doubtlesse not to be intermedled with base purposes... which doth excite Gods heavy judgements in the end'.[182] Haies provided an example for this argument and once again we find that the profits offered by piracy had diverted the crew of one of the vessels from the glorious ends of the enterprise. According to Haies, this act of piracy by the crew of the *Swallow* met with God's judgement: 'God had determined their ruine', their death, that is, when the vessel was wrecked on the Newfoundland coast.[183] If plans to establish a colony 'proceed of ambition or avarice' they will not 'have confidence of Gods protection'. 'Otherwise', he argued, 'if his motives be derived from a heroycall mind, preferring chiefly the honour of God' then the venture will succeed.[184]

WALTER RALEGH'S PROJECTS

George Peckham's plans to establish a colony were curtailed by his imprisonment for 'catholic activities' but Philip Sidney was still writing of his colonising ambitions in July 1584.[185] The plans of both, however, would have been altered by the renewal of Gilbert's patent in the name of his half-brother, Walter Ralegh, on 25 March 1584. Ralegh had participated in Gilbert's first voyage and invested in the last. He now turned the focus of interest further south on the American coast, in more temperate latitudes and in closer range of Caribbean privateering. It may accordingly have been a concern about Spanish sensitivities that limited printed promotion of Ralegh's preparations. It was, however, in this year that Hakluyt composed his manuscript for private circulation which has been given the title *Discourse of western planting*, written 'at the request and direction' of Ralegh.[186] David Armitage has argued that we can read Hakluyt's humanist

---

[180] Haies, *A report of the voyage*, in Hakluyt, *Principal navigations*, pp. 696–7.
[181] Cited in Mary Fuller, *Voyages in print: English travel to America 1576–1624* (Cambridge, 1995), p. 12.
[182] Haies, *A report of the voyage*, in *Humphrey Gilbert*, II, p. 389.
[183] *Ibid.*, pp. 399–400, 409, and 413.   [184] *Ibid.*, pp. 386–7.   [185] *Humphrey Gilbert*, I, pp. 93–4.
[186] Hakluyt, *Discourse of western planting*, in *The original writings and correspondence of the two Richard Hakluyts*, II, p. 211. Hakluyt's title for the manuscript was 'A particular discourse concerninge the

'Analysis' of Aristotle's *Politics*, written in 1583, as a companion to the *Discourse on western planting*.[187] It is a persuasive argument; the 'Analysis' is a work deeply concerned with the best form of a commonwealth or, as Hakluyt translated book VII, 'De optima Republica'.[188] When we consider, as I argue, that the tracts promoting colonisation were an extended discourse on the best form of a commonwealth, it is clear that Hakluyt's translation of Aristotle could play a complementary role in that discussion. Hakluyt backed his written efforts by seeking to participate in the projected voyage. He apparently failed in this desire only through a lack of finance.[189]

A colony of 108 men was established on Roanoke Island in April 1585 and was re-established in 1587 with 117 men, women and children under the leadership of John White. In a response to the difficulties encountered, Hakluyt published two translations in 1587: namely, an edition of Peter Martyr's *Decades*, and René de Goulaine de Laudonnière's account of the unsuccessful French attempt in the 1560s to establish a colony in Florida. He dedicated both works to Ralegh and stated his hope that the translations might help in avoiding the errors of the French.[190] Even as colonising prospects declined with the diversion of naval resources to combat the Spanish Armada, a full account of the Roanoke colony appeared the following year written by the respected mathematician and scientist Thomas Harriot, who had been a member of the first settlement. This treatise was illustrated with drawings by John White and republished in 1590 in Theodore De Bry's *America*. Harriot and White would continue to be employed by Ralegh through the 1590s on his plantation in Ireland, and Harriot was further consulted about colonisation in America in the 1600s.[191] In 1589, Hakluyt published the first edition of his *Principal navigations*, a massive documentary history of all the English voyages of discovery and plans for colonies. The work was dedicated to Sir Francis Walsingham, the principal sponsor of colonising plans within the government since Gilbert had secured his patent. It further publicised Ralegh's plans and,

---

greate necessitie and manifolde comodyties that are like to growe to this Realme of Englande by the Westerne discoveries lately attempted'.

[187] Armitage, *The ideological origins of the British empire*, pp. 72–6.

[188] *Ibid.* On Hakluyt's 'Analysis' see also James B. McConica, 'Humanism and Aristotle in Tudor Oxford', *English Historical Review*, 94 (1979), p. 315; Charles B. Schmitt, *John Case and Aristotelianism in Renaissance England* (Kingston Ont., 1983), pp. 41–5, 52–8; Lawrence V. Ryan, 'Richard Hakluyt's voyage into Aristotle', *Sixteenth Century Journal*, 12 (1981), pp. 73–83.

[189] George Bruner Parks, *Richard Hakluyt and the English voyages* (New York, 1961), p. 106.

[190] Hakluyt, *Epistle dedicatory*, in *The original writings and correspondence of the two Richard Hakluyts*, II, p. 372.

[191] W. A. Wallace, 'John White, Thomas Harriot and Walter Ralegh in Ireland', Durham Thomas Harriot seminar occasional papers (Durham, 1985).

in the same year, Hakluyt was made an assignee of Ralegh's Virginia patent.

The Roanoke colonists were effectively abandoned as conflict with Spain prevented the dispatch of relief ships until 1590, when the colony was found to be uninhabited. In the same year, Jose de Acosta's *Moral and natural history of the Indies* was published in Spain. Acosta described an undiscovered city of riches in South America, named El Dorado by the Spanish. Ralegh was quickly familiar with the work. His publicist, Hariot, wrote to the Secretary of State, Sir Robert Cecil, in July 1596 'Concerning El Dorado which hath been showed your Honor out of the Spanish book of Acosta'.[192] Hariot was writing to justify what had been Ralegh's new focus since the failure in Roanoke (although Ralegh did not concede the complete loss of Roanoke because a condition of his patent was the continued maintenance of a colony in America).

Ralegh sailed with five ships to Guiana in February 1595, in search of El Dorado. Upon his return he composed and published perhaps the most eloquent defence yet made for establishing an American colony: *The discoverie of the large, rich and bewtiful empyre of Guiana*. This work ran to three editions in 1596.[193] Hariot's entreaty to Cecil reveals that Ralegh was still trying to make his case when he sent Lawrence Keymis, one of his captains, on a second voyage to Guiana in January 1596. Keymis returned in June and immediately published a second treatise promoting Ralegh's designs. Ralegh's eloquence failed to attract support for the Guiana scheme. War with Spain continued and maritime resources were channelled into privateering through the second half of the decade. In this climate, further schemes for colonisation did not materialise and, with one major exception, there were correspondingly no treatises promoting colonies published in this period. The exception was the second edition of Hakluyt's *Principal navigations*, published in three volumes from 1598 to 1600.

A small colony, or trading post, was established in Guiana in 1604 and folded two years later. It had evolved out of privateering actions and, probably for that reason, it produced no promotional material.[194] In the new century, the profits from privateering began to contract as Spain withdrew from the seas and took greater protective measures. Interest in colonies was rekindled and the focus again moved north from the Caribbean. In 1602, Ralegh sent two ships in exploration of North America and, in the same

---

[192] Parks, *Hakluyt*, pp. 137–8. On the myth of El Dorado see the analysis of Neil L. Whitehead, 'Introduction' to Walter Ralegh, *The discoverie of the large, rich and bewtiful empyre of Guiana* [London, 1596], ed. Neil L. Whitehead (Manchester, 1997).

[193] Parker, *Books to build an empire*, p. 149.   [194] *Ibid.*, p. 193.

year, Bartholomew Gosnold and Bartholomew Gilbert attempted to establish a settlement on Cuttyhawk Island (south of present Massachusetts). The attempt lasted only a month but one of the participants, John Brereton, educated at Gonville and Caius College, Cambridge, published a treatise promoting the foundation of a colony in the area. The work was published in two editions and included a contribution from Edward Haies, who was possibly also the editor.[195] Brereton dedicated the treatise to Ralegh whose permission had not been sought either for Gosnold's voyage and settlement or for Brereton's projected settlement.

THE MORAL PHILOSOPHY OF RALEGH'S PROJECTS

In the works published in support of Ralegh's Roanoke venture, we again find that the dual ends of glory and profit were presented as the ends of the enterprise. As Hariot observed, the aim of the adventurers was 'the honour and benefit of our nation beside the particular profit'.[196] There was a marked shift, however, to arguments for colonies based upon expedience. This shift reflected the priorities of Ralegh and Hakluyt, his chief publicist. In support of the end of profit, the promoters presented detailed accounts of the commodities offered by Virginia. The greater part of both Hariot's *True report* and Hakluyt's *Western planting* are absorbed by this question. In his dedication of Laudonnière, Hakluyt claims that the 'sondrie men entring into these discoveries propose unto themselves severall ends'. Some, he continues, 'seeke authoritie and places of commandment, others experience by seeing of the worlde', but 'the most part worldly and transitorie gaine, & that often times by dishonest and unlawfull meanes'. He certainly does not speak approvingly of these motives but nor does he dismiss them, leaving open the possibility, as he had argued in the *Divers voyages*, that God's glory can be served by dishonourable men. Only 'the fewest number', he concludes, pursue 'the glory of God'.[197] Although here he is specifically referring to the evangelical aims of the enterprise (and so ignoring other possible sources of glory), he argued in his dedication to the edition of

---

[195] Quinn, *England and the discovery of America*, pp. 383, 405 and 416. Several other reconnaissance voyages were made from England to the north coast of America in 1602, 1603 and again in 1605 but they produced little in terms of promotional literature. Presumably the intention was to acquire material and knowledge rather than to establish a colony, so that neither finance nor personnel were immediate problems. See Parks, *Hakluyt*, p. 203.

[196] Thomas Harriot, *A brief and true report of the new found land of Virginia* (London, 1588), in Hakluyt, *Principal navigations*, p. 747.

[197] Hakluyt, *Epistle dedicatory*, in *The original writings and correspondence of the two Richard Hakluyts*, II, pp. 375–6.

Martyr that 'no greater glory can be handed down' than that which would arise from the foundation of a colony, rescuing 'your heroic enterprises from the vasty maw of oblivion'.[198]

Anxieties about corruption had not been suppressed. Substantial opposition to colonies continued. Hakluyt urged Ralegh 'do not let the envenomed shafts of your enemies and rivals trouble you, who like Aesop's dog will neither themselves enjoy the present opportunity, nor allow others to do so'.[199] There was also criticism from within the enterprise. John White, the governor of Ralegh's second Roanoke colony, complained bitterly of the same problems which had beset Rastell and Gilbert: that ships' companies put their self-interest above that of the new commonwealths. White had left the colony and his family in 1587 to raise more supplies in England, only to be trapped there for the next four years due to the requisitioning of all ships for the conflict with the Spanish Armada and its aftermath. He finally gained passage with three ships bound for the West Indies to trade. The ships had been released by the government provided that they guaranteed the passage of White and his supplies. The commanders broke this bond, refusing to provide space for White's supplies and then, according to White, making only cursory efforts, which failed, to contact the colony. The problem according to White, who wrote in 1593 from Ralegh's plantation in Ireland, was that 'both Governors, Masters, and sailers' were 'regarding very smally the good of their countreymen'; they rather 'wholly disposed themselves to seeke after purchase & spoiles'.[200] Again here, we find the expectation, also found in Thomas Smith, that the virtue of seeking the common good above private profit should be practised by all members of the commonwealth.

For these reasons Hariot, who accompanied White both to the first Roanoke colony and in Ralegh's plantation of Ireland, warned against the threat of luxury. He declared that colonies are not for those accustomed to 'soft beds'.[201] Similarly, Hakluyt devoted the first chapter of *Western planting* to denouncing those who pursued wealth, above all, when the glory of God must not be the 'laste worke but rather the principall and chefe of all

[198] *Ibid.*, p. 369.

[199] *Ibid.*, p. 368. On opposition to colonies, see also Hakluyt's discussion of 'A question of the adversary', namely 'howe many Infidells have beene by us converted?', to which he conceded 'I was not able to name any one Infidell by them [Ribault, Frobisher, Drake and Fenton] converted'; Hakluyt, *Western planting*, in *The original writings and correspondence of the two Richard Hakluyts*, II, p. 217.

[200] John White, *Letter*, in *The original writings and correspondence of the two Richard Hakluyts*, II, p. 416.

[201] Thomas Hariot, *A brief and true report of the new found land of Virginia* (London, 1588), sig. A4v.

others'.[202] Not troubled by coherence, he argues that English adventurers should seek neither profit nor luxury 'proposing unto ourselves in this action not filthie lucre nor vaine ostentation'.[203] It comes as no surprise, therefore, that Hakluyt would, by contrast, describe Ralegh's Roanoke colony as the foundation of a new Sparta: a commonwealth, that is, which had rejected not only the corruption of luxury, but had also understood that empire would be the cause of a luxurious and effeminate commonwealth.

When he turned his attention to the conquest of Guiana, Ralegh brought the emphasis upon profit, found in the promotion of Roanoke, to a new height. Whereas his ambition in Roanoke had been to establish a colony, historians have observed that, in Guiana, Ralegh sought conquest and modelled himself on the Spanish conquistadors.[204] With White as governor, Ralegh had sought to transplant a community of men and women on to the island, rather than merely establish a military post. By contrast, in Guiana, Ralegh sought gold. In an argument resonant of the 'new humanism' of Lipsius, Ralegh claimed that the greatness of states was based upon wealth (not corrupted by it as Sallust had argued).[205] Gold and riches, according to Ralegh, were the basis of Spain's greatness:

> if we now consider of the actions both of Charles the fifte, who had the Maydenhead of Peru, & the aboundant treasures of Atabalipa, together with the affaires of the Spanish King now living, what territories he hath purchased, what he hath added to the actes of his predecessors, how many kingdomes he hath indangered, how many armies, he hath & doth maintaine... we shall find these abilities rise not from the trades of sackes, and Civill Oranges... It is his Indian Golde that indaungereth and disturbeth all the nations of Europe.[206]

'The empyre of Guiana, he argued, 'hath more abundance of Golde than any part of Peru', and specifically 'Manoa, the emperiall Citie of Guiana which the Spanyardes cal el Dorado', to be found in the upper reaches of the Orinoco river, far exceeds 'any of the world' for 'riches.'[207] His argument was echoed by his lieutenant, Keymis, who published his account of the second voyage to Guiana in the same year. Keymis, too, held out the promise

---

[202] Hakluyt, *Western planting*, in *The orginal writings and correspondence of the two Richard Hakluyts*, II, p. 215.

[203] *Ibid.*, p. 216.

[204] Anthony Pagden, *Lords of all the world: Ideologies of empire in Spain, Britain and France c.1500–c.1800* (New Haven, 1995), pp. 67–8.

[205] On wealth and greatness in the work of Lipsius, see Richard Tuck, *Philosophy and government 1572–1651* (Cambridge, 1993), p. 61.

[206] Ralegh, *Guiana*, [London, 1596], sig. q3v.

[207] Ralegh, *Guiana*, ed. Whitehead, p. 10. See also pp. 93–4.

of 'gold mines'.[208] The 'conquest' of El Dorado was essential if England wished to rival Spain in greatness.[209] Indeed, here Ralegh appears to be at one with the humanism of Lipsius. It is gold and neither liberty nor virtue which is the basis of greatness.

Ralegh's ambitions in Guiana have frequently been represented as hopelessly fanciful, both in his desire to re-enact the feats of the conquistadors and in his belief in a golden city. Recent historical anthropology suggests that his belief in El Dorado was not simply a fantasy.[210] Similarly, his interest in conquest was less backward looking than based upon a concern with the finance of states which was itself borne out of the most vigorous intellectual currents of his time. His design was a synthesis of his knowledge of the most topical political philosophy and his reading of the most recent cosmography (particularly his reading of Acosta's *Moral and natural history* which had only been published in Spain in 1590).[211]

It is important to note that the profit which Ralegh claimed to pursue was common profit or the common good; it was not private profit or commercial profit. Indeed, he provided a full account of the classical sense of *utilitas*, or expedience, in his argument for profit. Profit, according to Ralegh, includes not simply material goods but, more importantly, the political power and influence that they can buy. When English promoters of colonies argue for the profit of their projects, it is this classical sense of expedience that they employ. Ralegh differs only in his understanding of such profit as the basis of greatness.

In the central argument of the *Discovery*, Ralegh is, however, thoroughly Ciceronian. The work, as he observes, is an apology, or defence, of his actions. As such, he argues not merely for the common good but repeatedly stresses that he has pursued the common good to the neglect of his own personal and selfish interests. This claim is the main subject of the preface to the work and he returns continually to the theme through to the conclusion. Like Gilbert before him, he claimed to have been impoverished by his enterprise. Yet, throughout, he had not been deterred by these sacrifices, seeking only the good of his prince and country:

From my selfe I have deserved no thankes, for I am returned a begger, and withered, but that I might have bettred my poore estate, it shall appeare by the following discourse, if I had not respected her Maiesties future honour and riches.[212]

---

[208] Lawrence Keymis, *A relation of the second voyage to Guiana* (London, 1596), sig. E3r.
[209] Ralegh, *Guiana*, ed. Whitehead, p. 91.
[210] Whitehead, Introduction to Ralegh, *Guiana*.
[211] On Ralegh and Hariot's reading of Acosta, see Parks, *Hakluyt*, pp. 137–8.
[212] Ralegh *Guiana* [London, 1596], sig. A3v.

While emphasising the importance of wealth, therefore, more than any promoter of colonies before him, Ralegh continued the emphasis that virtue would be the means to attain that end.

In this chapter we have examined the principal plans for American colonisation in sixteenth-century England. Two salient features emerge. The first is well known: all these projects ultimately ended in failure and often disaster. The second has not previously been widely understood or systematically examined: the ideological content of those projects was dominated by humanism. Humanism shaped colonisation in characteristic ways. The highest aim of the projects was honour and glory. It was consistently argued that expedience, and profit, should be subordinated to honour and the common good. Moreover, opponents of New World adventures employed the same humanist ideology. It is clear that this humanist critique of colonisation contributed to the perceived slowness of the English in following the Spanish example of colonisation. It might be thought that the first of our salient facts would undermine the second; that is, we might expect that the consistent failure of colonising enterprises would cast doubt on the efficacy of the tools of the *studia humanitatis* for colonisation. The result, we might conclude, would be the emergence of an ideology that was more robust on questions of expedience and profit. In his flirtation with the 'new humanism', this appears to have been the direction in which Ralegh was headed. His failures, however, were even more spectacular than those of his predecessors. As we shall see, therefore, rather than retreating from their humanist understanding of colonisation, Jacobean colonisers would conclude that the problems of colonisation arose from *insufficient* attention to the dangers of expansion underlined by neo-Roman thought. With few, although important, exceptions, they would argue that even greater care had to be given to the pre-eminence of honour and they would exhibit an even greater scepticism of expedience.

CHAPTER 3

The moral philosophy of Jacobean colonisation

The history of English colonisation to the beginning of the reign of James I was one of failure. Under James, a colony was established in the Chesapeake that would prove more resilient than its forerunners, but no less prone to disaster. The hopes for profit raised by Elizabethan promoters of colonies had proved false. Jamestown promised no greater returns. In its first ten years the colony produced no profits. In the following ten years, through to the dissolution of the Virginia Company, private tobacco plantations delivered profits to individual adventurers. The Virginia Company, which controlled the colony, never made a profit. Against this background, particularly with the spectacular Elizabethan failures in mind, the Virginia Company promoters never presented profit as the principal motivation for colonising. In the Jacobean period, promoters were no longer prepared to test the credulity of their audiences, and they turned away from Ralegh's dreams of riches. While still employing the language of Ciceronian moral philosophy, they augmented the argument of honour and diminished profit and expedience. The experience of failure produced a decisive turn in the ideology of Jacobean colonisation. The promoters of Jacobean colonies were increasingly deeply committed to a neo-Roman and quasi-republican scepticism of profit as a threat to the pursuit of civic action. They were committed, accordingly, to the primacy of virtue as the motive and guide for political life. I will analyse this commitment in this chapter, first, through a brief outline of the experience of the Virginia Company; secondly, through an examination of the humanist background of many of the central figures in the Virginia Company; and finally, through an analysis of the promotional literature sponsored by the Company.

THE VIRGINIA COMPANY

With the death of Elizabeth and the accession of James VI of Scotland to the English throne in 1603, peace with Spain was pursued and the Spanish war drew to a close. Privateering had dominated English maritime resources for fifteen years, but its scope was now limited. Those interests which had since 1602 been exploring the coast of North America coalesced to seek a patent to establish a colony in the region (replacing the patent of Ralegh, who was now in prison). On 10 April 1606 a patent was granted to colonise the east coast of North America between 34 and 45 degrees latitude. This patent was secured by two groups, one representing London, and the other west country, interests. The former was responsible for colonies in the southern part of the grant, and the Plymouth- and Bristol-based interests were to be concerned with the north.

These two groups were themselves composed of various nobility and gentry, merchant and military interests. Adventurers from the nobility included Henry Wriothesley, earl of Southampton, who had aided Gosnold's voyage in 1602 and George Weymouth's in 1605.[1] Southampton became a member of the Virginia Council in 1609. Seven of the eight men named in the initial patent of 1606 were soldiers. Among these was Ralegh Gilbert, son of Sir Humphrey and nephew of Sir Walter Ralegh.[2] The merchant interests included many members of the Levant and East India Companies, including Sir Thomas Smith, who would act as treasurer for both the East India and Virginia Companies.

In January 1607 three ships under the command of Christopher Newport sailed for the Chesapeake to establish a colony under the charter of the London Company. The colony suffered numerous hardships in its first years, including disease, conflict with the Algonquin peoples, faction and starvation. Of the 104 colonists established in Jamestown on 26 April 1607 only 38 were still alive in January 1608 when the first supply ship arrived. With no improvement in the colony's situation, a new patent was sought in 1609, greatly expanding public participation in the enterprise, a move significant for corresponding with the civic turn in the promotion of the colony.[3] The council was expanded and further stocks in the Company were sold. In 1612, facing continuing problems and difficulty raising further finance, the Company charter was again reformed. Stockholding was expanded and stockholders were granted greater control over the company through the institution of quarterly courts that would attract up to 200 members.[4] A weekly court of council representatives together with fifteen Company members was also established.

---

[1] See George Bruner Parks, *Richard Hakluyt and the English voyages* (New York, 1961), p. 203.

[2] *Ibid.*, p. 204. The eighth was Hakluyt, who would subsequently have little to do with the Chesapeake colony.

[3] David Beers Quinn, ed., *New American world: A documentary history of North America to 1612*, 5 vols. (London, 1979), V, pp. 191 and 205–12.

[4] Wesley F. Craven, *The dissolution of the Virginia Company* (Oxford, 1932), pp. 30–1.

Through its first years, the colony was unable to produce enough food for its own subsistence. It was heavily subsidised both by the London company and by the 'Powhatans'. Until 1614 the organisation of production had been largely controlled by the Company. Plantations were on Company land. Servants indentured to the Company worked for their keep and for land grants when their service was complete. These grants began in 1614, and when in 1616 the Company was unable to pay dividends, further grants of land were provided to stockholders. The colonist John Rolfe had sent the first shipment of tobacco from his private grant in 1614. The planting of tobacco rapidly accelerated on the private plantations and came to dominate the colonial economy. Having limited finances, the Company increasingly withdrew from direct involvement in planting but a 'magazine', a sub-company created by the merchants within the Virginia Company, led by Thomas Smith, was established to supply the tobacco planters with goods and to transport their crop. While both planters and the magazine made profits, the Company still did not return profits to its investors.

A division between the gentry and merchant members of the Company developed. The gentry interests, led by Sir Edwin Sandys and Southampton, were concerned that the Company was being exploited by the merchants for the ends of the magazine. The magazine was also believed to be exploiting the colonists (many of whom supported the gentry complaint). In 1619 the gentry faction gained the votes they needed to overturn the rule of the merchants and gain control of the Company.[5] Owing to his combativeness in Parliament, Edwin Sandys was barred from the position of treasurer in 1620. But members of Sandys' faction, Southampton and Nicholas and John Ferrar, were elected to the positions of treasurer, deputy and secretary. This new regime attempted to raise capital in order to establish more direct Company control over planting. The magazine was also first restricted and then dissolved. These attempts to stem perceived corruption met with limited success. A realignment of factions within the Company resulted in a petition to the crown to dissolve it. James obliged in 1624. The intention was that a new Company should be re-established. Instead, the death of James saw Charles I establish direct crown control over the colony in 1625.

While seemingly lurching from one disaster to the next, the Virginia Company and its colony dwarfed all previous English attempts at

---

[5] Their success required the support of the faction of Robert Rich, second earl of Warwick in 1619, who fell out with Smith, see *ibid.*, pp. 83–6.

colonisation. Financially, the Company's enterprise was minor compared to trading ventures such as those of the East India Company. In its entire history, the Virginia Company raised approximately 36,000 pounds through its joint stock (although this does not include other sources such as its lottery).[6] In a similar period, the East India Company raised 2 million pounds. But the Virginia Company, as we shall see, was not an essentially commercial enterprise, and historians have erred in attempting to evaluate it according to commercial standards. While levels of investment were low, the scope of the company's support was remarkably broad. As Theodore Rabb has shown, that support was particularly strong among the gentry. The Company attracted 560 gentry stockholders – including more than half the parliamentarians of the period – a greater level of participation than any previous colonial enterprise.[7] Rabb has argued that this gentry involvement, while public spirited, reveals a growing interest in commerce among the gentry in early modern England.[8] Rather, it reflects the deep ties between humanistic education and colonising projects. Moreover, it is widely acknowledged that, in Renaissance Europe, wealthy merchant families were frequently no less exposed to humanistic ideals than were the nobility.[9] And it is clear that merchants, notably Sir Thomas Smith and his son-in-law Robert Johnson, who were deeply involved in the Virginia Company, did not understand their involvement in the same terms as their other, more profitable, activities. Johnson, as we shall see, was insistent in his elevation of honour over expedience as the basis of the enterprise. Smith repeatedly revealed a different sensibility in his role as treasurer with the East India Company, on the one hand, and as treasurer of the Virginia Company on the other. While he was prepared, for example, to relinquish his position to Sandys' gentry faction in the Virginia Company, he would not countenance the possibility when presented with the same challenge from Sandys in the East India Company.[10]

---

[6] Robert Brenner, *Merchants and revolution: Commercial change, political conflict, and London's overseas traders, 1550–1653* (Cambridge, 1993), p. 97.

[7] Theodore K. Rabb, *Enterprise and empire: Merchant and gentry investment in the expansion of England, 1575–1630* (Cambridge, Mass., 1967), p. 93.

[8] See *ibid.*; and Theodore K. Rabb, *Jacobean gentleman: Sir Edwin Sandys, 1561–1629* (Princeton, 1998), ch. 12.

[9] See, for example, Anthony Grafton, *New worlds, ancient texts: The power of tradition and the shock of discovery* (New York, 1992), pp. 61–8 on Goro Dati.

[10] See Rabb, *Jacobean gentleman*, ch. 12. Brenner, *Merchants and revolution*, fails to account for this point. Judged by Brenner's measure, as a commercial enterprise, the Virginia Company makes no sense. For this reason, Rabb is correct to stress that the level of gentry involvement, and not the level of gentry finance, reveals much about the character of the enterprise.

THE PARTICIPANTS

From its foundation the Virginia Company attracted many of the greatest Jacobean patrons of learning. The participation of these men within the Company and their links with learning have been well documented and the accounts do not require great repetition.[11] The names of the patrons included William, Lord Cavendish, Henry Rainsford, William Herbert, the earl of Pembroke, Sir Edward Sackville, later fourth earl of Dorset, Fulke Greville, Lord Brooke (who had been involved in his cousin Philip Sidney's colonising project of 1585) and Sir Robert Sidney, later second earl of Leicester. These men were patrons of poets, playwrights, artists and composers, including such figures as Michael Drayton, John Donne, Ben Jonson, George Chapman, William Shakespeare and Thomas Hobbes. Many of these clients, as we shall see, would address the problems of the Virginian colony. The most prominent of these patrons of learning in his involvement in the Virginia Company was Henry Wriothesley, the earl of Southampton, to whom Shakespeare's *Venus and Adonis* was dedicated. In addition to his membership of the Council from 1609, Southampton became treasurer in 1618.

The Virginia Company also attracted the participation of many of the leading men of learning of the period, including Sir Edward Coke, the Chief Justice and proponent of common law, John Selden, Christopher Brooke, a prominent poet, Sir Henry Neville, who published an edition of *Chrysostom* in 1614, a characteristically humanist act,[12] John Hoskins, Dudley Digges, who displayed 'a remarkable proficiency in the ancient languages and a mastery of humanistic skills'[13] and Edwin Sandys. Many of these men were parliamentary leaders and were in conflict with the crown. Hoskins, for example, was imprisoned for his vocal opposition to the king in the 1614 Parliament; Selden was imprisoned for his opposition to prerogative rule in 1621; and Sandys also was arrested.[14] Edwin Sandys was the most notable of those within the Company who combined their learning with an active parliamentary career. He was tutored by Richard Hooker at Oxford and subsequently financed the publication of Hooker's

[11] On the links between learning and the Virginia Company, see Charles Mills Gayley, *Shakespeare and the founders of liberty in America* (New York, 1917); Alexander Brown, *Genesis of the United States*, 2 vols. (reprinted New York, 1964), II; Noel Malcolm, 'Hobbes, Sandys, and the Virginia Company', *The Historical Journal*, 24 (1981).

[12] On *Chrysostom*, see Paul Oskar Kristeller *Renaissance thought and its sources*, ed. Michael Mooney (New York, 1979), p. 73.

[13] Richard Tuck, *Philosophy and government 1572–1651* (Cambridge, 1993), p. 205.

[14] On Sandys' arrest, see Rabb, *Jacobean gentleman*, pp. 260–4.

Laws of ecclesiastical polity. He published *A relation of the state of religion*, a work which was 'learned and meticulous to a fault'.[15] Sandys then became a leader, with Digges and Coke, of the parliamentary argument for the limitation of prerogative rule. Since Thomas Jefferson, a patriotic tradition of American history has found the origins of liberty in the interest many Jacobean parliamentarians held simultaneously in the Virginia Company and in resistance to 'absolute rule' in Parliament. The claim has been discredited since the 1930s, but I shall argue that it deserves reconsideration in the light of the civic language employed by the humanists promoting the colony.

The links between the Company and London literary and humanist circles are vividly illustrated by the interests of members of the 'Mitre Club'. The club was a regular gathering of twelve poets and writers at the Mitre Inn. At least nine of those members were closely associated with the Virginia Company and four were members of its council. The members of the council were Sir Robert Phelips, also known for his opposition to the crown in Parliament;[16] Richard Martin who was an 'undertaker' in the *Virginian maske* performed at the marriage of Princess Elizabeth; Sir Henry Neville (see above); and Christopher Brook, himself a published poet, whose work included an elegy on the death of Prince Henry in whom many of the hopes for the future patronage of the Virginia Company had rested. Notably, the club included the poet John Donne who sought to become secretary of the Virginia Company in 1609 and later delivered and published a sermon promoting the Company.[17]

The delivery and publication of sermons was one of the principal means through which the Company sought promotion. Many of the leading churchmen of the day were involved in the activities of the Company, along with many of middling rank. In addition to Donne, they included Daniel Price, chaplain to Prince Henry, Richard Crakanthorpe, William Crashaw, fellow of St John's College, Cambridge, Thomas Morton, dean of Gloucester and later bishop of Durham, Richard Hakluyt, who was one of the eight named in the initial patent, Samuel Purchas and his patron George Abbot, the bishop of London (from 1611 archbishop of Canterbury). When, during the crisis of 1608–9, the Company sought to save the enterprise through expanding public involvement, they initiated a promotional campaign that for its sheer volume was unequalled in previous colonial

---

[15] *Ibid.*, p. 21.
[16] On Phelips' opposition in Parliament, see Brown, *Genesis*, p. 966; Tuck, *Philosophy and government*, p. 119; Gayley, *Shakespeare*, p. 27.
[17] On the other members of the Mitre Club, see Gayley, *Shakespeare*.

enterprises. The delivery and publication of sermons was the basis of that campaign. In the first months of 1609, eight orations promoting the imperilled colony were delivered in England. One was a speech by Alderman Robert Johnson to members of the Company. The other seven speeches were sermons. Three were sermons at Paul's Crosse: by Richard Crakanthorpe on 24 March; George Benson on 7 May; and Daniel Price on 25 May. William Symonds delivered his sermon *Virginia* in Whitechapel on 15 April, and Robert Gray's sermon *A good speed to Virginia* was also delivered in April. The seventh was a sermon by Thomas Morton, dean of Gloucester, who discussed the lawfulness of colonising. The eighth (and ninth, if counted as two) was Robert Tynley's *Two learned sermons*. Each of these orations was printed the same year, with the exception of Morton's sermon, which has not survived, and Benson's, which appeared the following year. Many more sermons promoting the colony would follow, through to the dissolution of the Company, including printed works by Crashaw, Donne and Purchas. Moreover, preachers would continue to play a central role in the promotion of the Company in general. Crashaw and William Symonds, for example, edited promotional material, and Samuel Purchas produced his monumental *Hakluytus posthumus* in this context. Preachers would also produce promotional tracts that were not sermons. Alexander Whitaker, for example, was preacher in the colony and he was the son of the former master of St John's College, Cambridge. He published the optimistically entitled *Good newes from Virginia* shortly before drowning in the Chesapeake.

These links between the clergy and colonisation were not new. The clergy had always held prominent positions in the promotion of English colonial projects. The Reverend Richard Hakluyt, for example, was the foremost Elizabethan promoter of American colonies. While Hakluyt withdrew into retirement, this relationship with the clergy was augmented throughout the Company's turbulent existence.

The Company's reliance upon promotion also continued. In 1610, the colony slid further into despair and three further publications appeared, two being official statements by the Company. In 1612 the Company charter was reformed, and that year and the following year saw the publication of a further five treatises promoting the colony. With the first successful tobacco crop in 1614 and some stabilisation in the colony, there was less demand upon the use of print to raise participation. Moreover, with the encouragement of private plantations and the withdrawal of the Company into the business of the supply magazine, the pressure on Company finances eased. The pressure to publish returned, however, when Thomas Smith's administration was substituted by the gentry faction led by Sandys and Southampton. The new administration believed that the common good of the colony was being neglected and it is for this reason they sought to re-establish control over the colony. This policy demanded greater public participation and more money. The 1620s correspondingly saw a new battery of publications including three Company tracts, and works by John Donne, Patrick Copland and Samuel Purchas.[18] The dissolution of the Company buried these attempts just as they were being initiated.

Why, then, did the Virginia Company employ propaganda more than any previous colonial enterprise, and why did the sermon hold the central position in this promotional design? The answer to both questions, as we shall see in ch. 4, lies in the education of the leaders and promoters of the colony in the *studia humanitatis*, and particularly in classical rhetoric, and in the centrality of that education in the business of the foundation of a commonwealth. Oratory, as we shall see, was believed to constitute the central act in the foundation of a commonwealth. Following the reforms of Erasmus and Melanchthon, the sermon was composed according to the conventions of classical rhetoric. Given the limitations placed upon public oratory in the courtly societies of northern Europe, this reform of the sermon provided a context within which the humanist vision of the political power of rhetoric could be implemented. The sermons delivered in support of the Virginia Company have been the least valued of the material concerning America written in this period. In his five-volume documentary history of American discovery and colonisation, the eminent historian David Beers Quinn reprints much of the Virginia Company promotional literature with the exception that 'No examples . . . of the sermons preached to potential subscribers are given.' His justification is dismissive: 'they are long-winded and in content only of intermittent interest'.[19] On the whole, first-hand accounts of the business of colonisation are held to be of greater value to the historian than the propaganda of hired pens. This devaluation rests upon an anachronistic understanding of the role of both the sermon and of print in early modern politics. Both were perceived to be inseparable from oratory. When Englishmen sought to establish a colony in America, print, and specifically the sermon, were believed, as forms of oratory, to be

[18] *A declaration of the state of colonie and affaires in Virginia* (London, 1620); *A note of the shipping, men, and provisions, sent and provided for Virginia* (London, 1619); *A note of the shipping, men, and provisions, sent and provided for Virginia* (London, 1620); John Donne, *A sermon . . . preache'd to the honourable Company of the Virginian plantation* (London, 1622); Patrick Copland, *Virginia's God be thanked* (London, 1622); Samuel Purchas, *The kings towre* (London, 1623); Samuel Purchas, *Virginia's verger*, in Samuel Purchas, *Hakluytus posthumus or Purchas his pilgrimes*, 4 vols. (London, 1625), IV.

[19] Quinn, *New American world*, V, p. 233.

crucial to the successful foundation of the new commonwealth. The use of the sermon as the foremost instrument of propaganda reflects the humanistic sensibilities of the Virginia Company's leaders. Indeed, their use of the sermon reveals not only a humanistic belief in the power of oratory but also, as we shall see, a distinctively humanistic vision of the ideology of the new colony for which oratory was understood to be the vehicle.

It is particularly striking that many of the leaders and promoters of the Virginia Company had been educated at St John's College, Cambridge. This common link is, to some degree, reminiscent of the circle of intellectual interest in the New World that had existed previously around the figures of John Dee (also a graduate of St John's) and the Hakluyts. Given, however, the long-standing leadership of St John's College in the *studia humanitatis*, it is more suggestive of the central place of the humanistic imagination in the ambition to establish new commonwealths and of the maturity which that humanistic design reached in the project of the Virginia Company. From this perspective, the position of St John's College is no less noteworthy than the role later played by Emmanuel College in the education of the New England puritans. Henry Wriothesley was the most prominent member of the Company to have attended the college. He was admitted in 1585, graduating in 1589.[20] Alexander Whitaker was educated at Eton and Trinity College, Cambridge, but he had been raised in the Master's Lodge at St John's where his father, William Whitaker, had been one of the most prominent Elizabethan masters from 1587 to 1595.[21] William Crashaw, who not only wrote but also coordinated much of the Company's propaganda, was admitted to St John's in 1588, graduated in 1592, and returned as a fellow from 1594 to 1597.[22] In his preface to Whitaker's *Good newes from Virginia*, he boasts of the author's command of classical languages – the very foundation of the new learning – and of his command of the ornaments of rhetoric, associating these accomplishments with the reputation of Whitaker's father:

I know (and so doe others that know him) hee is able to have written it in Latine or Greeke, and so to have decked it both for phrase and stile, and other ornaments of learning and language, as might shew him no unworthy son of so worthy a father.[23]

[20] *Dictionary of national biography*, eds. Sir Leslie Stephen and Sir Sidney Lee (Oxford, 1917), xxi, pp. 1055–6. In addition to Shakespeare his clients included John Florio; see William Shakespeare, *The Tempest*, ed. Frank Kermode (London, 1958), pp. xxvii–xxviii.

[21] H. C. Porter, *The inconstant savage: England and the North American Indian 1500–1660* (London, 1979), pp. 380–1.

[22] *Ibid.*, pp. 360–1.

[23] Alexander Whitaker, *Good newes from Virginia* (London, 1613), sig. A3v.

Robert Gray, about whom little is otherwise known, is believed to have matriculated from St John's in 1589.[24] Thomas Morton, whose sermon concerned the legality of the colony and who was also a prolific theologian, was admitted to the college in 1584 graduating with a bachelor's degree in 1586 and a master's degree in 1590. He was elected a fellow of the college and remained as a university lecturer in logic until 1598.[25] Gabriel Archer, an officer with Newport's first settlement at Jamestown, was a member of St John's for about two years from 1591.[26] His report on the colony was later published in Samuel Purchas' *Hakluytus posthumus*. Purchas, the most vigorous and prolific promoter of the colony, was again educated at St John's from 1594, gaining his bachelor's degree in 1597 and his master's in 1600.[27]

THE *VITA ACTIVA* AND CORRUPTION

It was within this context of Elizabethan and Jacobean humanism that we must place the political language employed by the Virginia Company. The political landscape of the first years of the Virginia Company's colony has always been clouded. This uncertainty is perhaps surprising, given that Jamestown would become the first permanent English settlement in North America. The problem lies in part with the failure of the records of the first administration of the Company to survive.[28] The absence of those records has contributed to contention among historical accounts of the colony's politics. One patriotic tradition of American history held that the administration of the Company from 1619 by the parliamentary leader Sir Edwin Sandys and, prior to that, the reformed charters of 1609 and 1612, initiated the nation's struggle for liberty.[29] Opposed to this was the argument that the Virginia Company was purely a business enterprise with no political aims.[30] In recent years, this interpretation has

---

[24] See Louis B. Wright, *Religion and empire: The alliance between piety and commerce in English expansion, 1558–1625* (New York, 1965), p. 92; Porter, *Inconstant savage*, pp. 342–3.

[25] *Dictionary of national biography*, xiii, pp. 1057–8.

[26] Porter, *Inconstant savage*, p. 381.   [27] *Ibid.*, pp. 478–9.

[28] On the loss of the Virginia Company's two court books covering the period 28 January 1606 to 28 July 1619, see S. M. Kingsbury, *The records of the Virginia Company of London*, 4 vols. (Washington, 1906–35), I, pp. 25–31.

[29] Alexander Brown, *English politics in early Virginian history* (first published 1901, reissued New York, 1968), pp. 11–13; E. D. Neill, *The English colonisation of America during the seventeenth century* (London, 1871); Gayley, *Shakespeare*.

[30] Kingsbury, *The records of the Virginia Company*, I, pp. 12–15; Craven, *The dissolution of the Virginia Company*, p. 24, 'The true motif of the Company's history is economic rather than political'. The colony, according to this account, was governed along predominantly military lines: Craven, *The dissolution of the Virginia Company*, p. 48; and Herbert L. Osgood, *The American colonies in the seventeenth century*, 3 vols. (first published 1904, reissued New York, 1930), I, pp. 68–71.

prevailed. Surveying the secondary literature, Jack P. Greene observes that 'Virginia's orientation was almost wholly commercial from the beginning.'[31] The context for this understanding of the enterprise has been, as Kenneth Andrews observes, that 'European overseas expansion in this epoch was fundamentally a commercial movement'.[32] Such accounts have emphasised that, in its first years, the colony was ruled by martial law and only gradually adopted some of the legal and political customs of England.[33] From the rudimentary political character of its early years, the colony developed a 'highly individualistic and materialistic' atmosphere in which colonists 'showed little concern for the public weal of the colony and routinely sacrificed the corporate welfare to their own individual ends'.[34]

By contrast with these claims, I shall show that the Virginia Company articulated a political programme in this period. This programme was civic. It was neo-Roman and specifically Classical and Italian republican in its intellectual alignments. Its central precept was that virtue and the active political life of the citizen is necessary to secure the common good. It is true, as patriotic American historians emphasised, that a striking number of Jacobean parliamentarians, who were actively resisting prerogative rule, were also active in the Virginia Company. Such an account cannot explain the participation of many who did not share such sentiments. It is to the *studia humanitatis* that we must turn for a commonly shared language of participation. Humanism provided the aims and the design for the ambition to establish colonies: the design was the foundation of a new commonwealth through virtuous action undertaken for the ends of honour and glory. This language was heuristic; it was employed equally by apologists for absolute rule (including James I himself) and by those who resisted prerogative. It is, however, the *possibility* of resistance offered by humanist discourse within the context of the foundation of a new and remote commonwealth that can account for the great attraction the Virginian venture held for Jacobean parliamentarians.

---

[31] Jack P. Greene, *Pursuits of happiness* (Chapel Hill, 1988), p. 8. See also Edmund S. Morgan, *American slavery, American freedom* (New York, 1975), pp. 44–5, 95, 118.

[32] Kenneth R. Andrews, *Trade, plunder and settlement: Maritime enterprise and the genesis of the British Empire* (Cambridge, 1984), p. 5.

[33] See, for example, Warren M. Billings, 'The transfer of English law to Virginia 1606–1650', in K. R. Andrews, N. Canny and P. E. H. Hair eds., *The westward enterprise* (Liverpool, 1978), pp. 216–18; Nicholas Canny, 'The permissive frontier: the problem of social control in English settlements in Ireland and Virginia', in Andrews *et al.*, *The westward enterprise*, p. 18; David Thomas Konig 'Colonization and the common law in Ireland and Virginia, 1569–1634', in James A. Henretta, Michael Kammen and Stanley N. Katz, eds., *The transformation of early American history* (New York, 1991), pp. 70–92.

[34] Greene, *Pursuits of happiness*, pp. 11, 15.

The civic programme of the Virginia Company was first fully presented in 1609 as the solution to the failures of Elizabethan colonies and to the disasters of the first years of Jamestown. Those historians who have emphasised the role of martial law in the colony have failed to appreciate the Machiavellian undertones of that regime. Moreover, the argument that the Company was purely a business enterprise does not sit easily with the fact that the particular blend of civic thought professed in Company-sponsored pamphlets included that tradition which rejected profit as a corruption of the pursuit of the common good.

In the absence of complete Virginia Company records, this interpretation will rest primarily upon an examination of the Company's promotional tracts. There was, of course, some separation between the image of colonisation which these portrayed and the experience of colonisation. The ideology of the colony itself cannot be reduced to that of the Company. Indeed, I shall argue that in its later period, the Company articulated civic arguments to a large degree in opposition to practices in the colony. The political designs of the Company and the experience of the colony cannot, however, be entirely separated. In their understanding of the ideology of the colonising enterprise, historians have focused upon the colony to the neglect of the Company.

The first reason for not separating the two must be that the ideology of the Company was largely developed in response to the experience of the colony. Moreover, there is evidence that the civic design of the Company could be found outside its promotion, for example in the use of martial law and in the expansion of public participation in the enterprise. It is also true that the civic arguments of the promotional pamphlets were expressed as much by those experienced in the colony, such as Alexander Whitaker and William Strachey, as by hired pens. Certainly the claim to have experience had considerable rhetorical force for Jacobean audiences. Jacobean culture, however, also placed great emphasis upon the power of speech, which included printing. Again, as we shall see in ch. 4, speech was perceived as a form of action and believed to perform fundamental acts in the foundation and conservation of a commonwealth. In this context the Company's promotional tracts are crucial not only to how the adventurers understood their enterprise but also as a central part of that enterprise.

With the arrival of the first colonists in the Chesapeake in 1607, there were signs that the Virginia adventurers had not sufficiently absorbed the lessons of their predecessors. In a letter written in the first months of the colony and returned with Captain Newport, William Brewster remarked that at the head of the river 'ar Rokes and Movntaynes, that prommyseth

Infynyt treasvr'. Strikingly, he added, in the fashion of the Spanish, that the adventurers will 'Conquer this land'.[35] This persistent model of Spanish New World riches is also reflected in Sir Walter Cope, a patentee of the Company, writing to Robert Cecil, Lord Salisbury, James I's Lord Treasurer. 'In stead of mylke', argued Cope, 'we fynde pearle/ & golde Inn steede of honye.'[36] Within twenty-four hours Cope reported that the promise of gold proved false: 'Oure newe dyscovery ys more Lyke to the Lande of Canaan than the Lande of Ophir.'[37] Undeterred, Sir Thomas Smith, treasurer of the Company, reported to Cecil that Newport had promised not to return from his next supply of Jamestown without gold.[38] His promise, however, was overtaken by events.

Having endured a hot and humid first summer, the settlement suffered a bitter winter in 1607–8. The planters failed to establish crops. Hunger, disease, discontent and faction, conflict with the Algonquins and death plagued the colony.[39] George Percy, one of the leaders, summarised the situation:

Our men were destroyed with cruell diseases as Swellings, Flixes, Burning Feuers, and by warres, and some departed suddenly, but for the most part they died of meere famine. There were neuer Englishmen left in a forreigne Countrey in such miserie as wee were in this new discouered Virginia[40]

This news returned to England in 1607 and 1608 through the repeated resupply journeys made by Newport and others.[41] In 1608, John Smith, the most renowned of the colony's leaders, published his *True report*, providing a first hand account without the authorisation of the Company.[42] He conveyed some sense of the problems in spite of the more offensive passages having been edited.[43]

After two years, the state of affairs in Jamestown could hardly have been worse. In late 1608 and 1609, the Company reassessed the project and secured the second charter including, among other changes, the substitution of rule by a president and council with a single governor in the hope of

[35] Undated letter from William Brewster, in Philip L. Barbour, *The Jamestown voyages under the first charter, 1606–1609*, 2 vols. (Cambridge, 1969), I, p. 107.
[36] Sir Walter Cope to Lord Salisbury, 12 August 1607, in Barbour, *Jamestown voyages*, I, p. 108. See also Letters patent, 10 April 1606, in which gold, silver, and copper are named as motives, in Barbour, *Jamestown voyages*, I, p. 24.
[37] Sir Walter Cope to Lord Salisbury, 13 August 1607, in Barbour *Jamestown voyages*, I, p. 111.
[38] Sir Thomas Smith to Lord Salisbury, 17 August 1607, in Barbour, *Jamestown voyages*, I, p. 112.
[39] Barbour, *Jamestown voyages*, I, pp. 127 and 209.
[40] George Percy, *Discourse*, in Barbour, *Jamestown voyages*, I, p. 144.
[41] Barbour, *Jamestown voyages*, I, p. 209.   [42] See Quinn, *New American world*, V, p. 188.
[43] Barbour, *Jamestown voyages*, I, p. 3.

controlling the spirit of faction. At the same time the Company initiated its aggressive promotional campaign. While many of the pamphlets were twenty or thirty pages in length, a number were more substantial volumes. The promotional literature also included numerous letters, verses, and oratory. Indeed, speeches were an important part of the campaign. They were primarily presented as sermons but also as occasional speeches such as addresses to Company meetings. Many were the basis for the pamphlets that followed. Frequently the authors of this diverse literature were not major players in the venture. They served, however, as barometers of the Company's sentiment. The authors possessed close connections within the Company and their publications were either explicitly commissioned or tacitly sanctioned.

This campaign also revealed a major shift in the ideology of the enterprise. Civic values were offered as the solution to the problems of establishing the new commonwealth. A number of the elements that constituted this civic appeal were clearly present in the Elizabethan promotional tracts. What distinguished this Jacobean ideology as civic was not an adherence to any one value recognisably drawn from traditions of civic thought, but rather the proposal of a number of such values related in such a way as to offer a solution to the Company's problems. All these elements were present in the propaganda campaign of 1609–10. To reveal this design, it is necessary at first to approach that literature thematically.

The Virginia Company's promoters consistently defined the colonial enterprise as the foundation of a new commonwealth. When used in a general sense, the term 'commonwealth' referred to a discrete political community embodying the common good of its members. The use of this term by the Company and its promoters to define their ambition is therefore highly significant; their intention was not merely to establish a trading post or a military post, nor merely to conquer foreign lands, nor to expand the existing commonwealth of Britain. The aim was to establish a new civil society. The civic arguments of the company were addressed to that context.

'There is nothing', the colonist Thomas Studley wrote in 1612, reflecting on the previous six years of the Jamestown colony, 'so difficult as to establish a commonwealth.'[44] In 1610, the Virginia Company advertised for 'men of most use and necessity, to the foundation of a Commonwealth'.[45] The promotional authors accordingly structured their discussions

---

[44] T. Abbay and William Symonds, eds., *The proceedings of the English colonie in Virginia* (Oxford, 1612), pp. 10–11.

[45] *A true and sincere declaration of the purpose and ends of the plantation begun in Virginia* (London, 1610), pp. 25–6. See also John Rolfe, *Relation of the state of Virginia*, in *Virginia: Four personal narratives*, Research Library of Colonial Americana (New York, 1972), p. 104.

of the projected plantation in the humanist language of the best form of a commonwealth. Indeed, the tracts promoting the Virginia Company were some of the most vigorous and sustained Jacobean discussions on that theme. A central tension in the discussion was that between the ends of *honestas* and *utilitas*, honour and profit.

The first of the promoters' civic themes was the consistent portrayal of the successful foundation and conservation of the commonwealth as the product of the *vita activa*, or of 'public actions'.[46] This sentiment is reflected in the promotional sermons of William Crashaw and William Symonds. Crashaw, preacher at the Temple church, effectively performed the role of master of ceremonies for the Virginia Company.[47] He was responsible for coordinating much of the promotional material and he drew Symonds, the master of Magdalen School and preacher of St Saviour's, Southwark, into this effort. Crashaw argued, in his sermon before the Company in 1610, that 'The English Christians will not undertake a public action that they will not prosecute to perfection.'[48] Echoing Cicero's dictum that 'All the praise that belongs to virtue lies in action', Symonds represented planting as the ideal field of action in his sermon *Virginia* delivered in April 1609:

Get abroad where vertue is skant, and there, by the advancing of thy wisedom and vertue, thou shalt bee more eminent and famous in a yeare, then at home half of thy ranke shall be all their daies: hidden vertue is neglected, but abroad it is magnified.[49]

In characteristic civic terms, this active life is represented as a duty incumbent upon all. According to Symonds mankind is under a 'duty' to God to 'fill the earth'.[50] Frequently, as in this case, the civic appeal to duty overlapped with religious conceptions of duty, allowing the terms employed in civic thought to be persuasive in religious discourse and vice versa. We will see the same fusion of civic and religious thought in the reform of the sermon through classical rhetoric. Contributing to the same battery of sermons in 1609, Robert Gray, whose identity is otherwise obscure, endorsed the Platonic dictum, popularised by Cicero in *De officiis*, that

---

[46] On *negotium* and the *vita activa* in the civic tradition, see Quentin Skinner, *The foundations of modern political thought* (2 vols., Cambridge, 1978), I, pp. 80, 108, 217–19; Markku Peltonen, *Classical humanism and republicanism in English political thought, 1570–1640* (Cambridge, 1995), pp. 21–34, 63–4, 109.

[47] On Crashaw's position, see Wright, *Religion and empire*, p. 100.

[48] William Crashaw, *A sermon preached before the right honourable the Lord Lawarre* (London, 1610), sig. K3v.

[49] William Symonds, *Virginia* (London, 1609), pp. 31–2. Cicero, *De officiis*, trans. Walter Miller (Cambridge, Mass., 1913), I, 19; see also I, 22 and 58.

[50] Symonds, *Virginia*, pp. 31–2.

'Man is not borne for himself alone'.[51] This sentiment was a premise of the active life. Encouraging those people alarmed by the failures of the colony, Gray exhorted 'We are not borne like beasts for ourselves, and the time present only.'[52]

Crashaw's *Sermon* was the most comprehensive of the promotional tracts in its appeal to the duty to pursue an active life and in its argument that colonisation fulfils the requirements of that life. He attempted a direct translation of Cicero's *De officiis* into the context of establishing the new commonwealth. The sermon opened with a passage from Luke: 'When thou art converted strengthen thy Brethren'. Through Ramist analysis and dichotomous *dispositio*, he drew two arguments from this passage: 'The parts are two: Christ's mercy/ Peter's dutie'. Christ's mercy is the doctrine of the elect. Peter's duty is that if he is one of the elect, he must pursue a virtuous and active life. This duty enjoins 'all others that shall be partakers of this promise' of election, from Peter it is 'derived to the whole Church, and every particular Christian'. Crashaw then applied this lesson to 'the businesse now in hand' with the obvious conclusion that 'it is not voluntary or left indifferently to a mans choice, but (plainly) a necessarie duty'.[53] He then paraphrased Cicero's expansion and qualification of such duties:

But lest any man mistaking or abusing my words, should here cavill and say; Belike then this man holds all damned that are not adventurers to Virginea, and it is a sure signe of a prophane man, if he be not an undertaker in that action, or the like: Take notice that my assertion is qualified with these two limitations: First, that a man must know the true state of this businesse, and true grounds and ends both of his Maiesties gratious grants, and of the undertakers adventure...such therefore wee are farre from condemning, but leave them till they be satisfied of the truth ... Secondly, though a man know it never so well, hee must bee of abilitie to contribute, or else this ties him not: for a man is bound first to maintaine himselfe and his family, and to beare his parte of needful burthens of the Church and State where he lives: then out of that which remaines, such actions as this doe challenge a part. Now whether a man be able or no, hee must be left to his own conscience to give judgement. But herein let a man take heed he flatter not himselfe...the divell delights to make men betray their owne soules.[54]

This passage first corresponds to Cicero's discussion of the priority of duties (I, 57–8). Crashaw's ranking of the duty to assist the Virginian adventure

---

[51] Cicero, *De officiis*, I, 22.
[52] Robert Gray, *A good speed to Virginia* (London, 1609), sig. Dr. On Gray, see Wright, *Religion and empire*, p. 92. This Platonic dictum was popular in contemporary civic thought; see, for example, Henry Crosse, *Vertues common-wealth: or the high-way to honour* (London, 1603), sig. R3r; see also Peltonen, *Classical humanism and republicanism in English political thought*, pp. 149 and 136–9.
[53] Crashaw, *A sermon*, sig. C3r.   [54] *Ibid.*, sigs. Dr–Dv.

behind the duties to family, church and state is comparable to the secondary duty Cicero grants to empire (I, 74–6). His qualification of these duties also corresponds with that made by Cicero (I, 71), as does his warning against false excuses (I, 71). Cicero concluded his caveat to the citizen's public duties with the claim: 'But those who are equipped by nature to administer affairs must abandon any hesitation over winning office and engage in public life' (I, 72). Similarly, Crashaw declared: 'Thus with these two cautions I make my conclusion, that the assistance of this business is a dutie that lies on all men.'[55] This conclusion possessed an unmistakably civic note; all men have a duty to participate in public affairs.

The authors promoting the Virginian colony also agreed with the proposition central to the civic tradition, that virtue is the quality necessary to the successful pursuit of an active life.[56] This belief is seen, for example, in Symonds' representation of the New World as the ideal field for the exercise of virtue. It is also seen in John Smith's use of the related humanist commonplace that 'Vertue be the soule of true Nobilitie' in his dedication of *A map of Virginia* to the earl of Hartford.[57] Following the convention of humanist moral philosophy, the promotional authors portrayed colonisation in terms of a division of the four cardinal virtues: wisdom, justice, courage and temperance. Justice was believed to be fundamental to the success of the colonies. The justice of supplanting the Powhatans and the claims of rival European colonisers were great anxieties. 'We freely confesse', Crashaw acknowledged, 'an action cannot be good, excellent, or honourable, and much lesse can it be necessarie, unlesse it first of all appeare to be lawful: secondly, for the present action, we also confesse and yeeld to this as to a principle of Iustice' (we return to the question of justice in ch. 5).[58] Wisdom, particularly as exemplified in Solomon's Ophirian voyages, was repeatedly demanded of the leaders.[59] The qualities of courage and temperance,

---

[55] *Ibid.*, sig. D2r.

[56] On the place of this proposition in the civic tradition, see Skinner, *Foundations of modern political thought*, I, pp. 88–94.

[57] On the use of this commonplace in early modern English political thought, see Peltonen, *Classical humanism and republicanism in English political thought*, pp. 35–9.

[58] Crashaw, *A sermon*, sig. D3r. On the concern with justifying the Virginian colony in the promotional literature of this period, see Symonds, *Virginia*, p. 10; Gray, *A good speed to Virginia*, sigs. Br–v, B4v, C4v; *A true declaration of the estate of the colonie in Virginia* (London, 1610), pp. 6–12; William Strachey, *The historie of travell into Virginia Britannia* (1609–1612), eds. Louis B. Wright and Virginia Freund (London, 1953), pp. 22–6; Whitaker, *Good newes from Virginia*, p. 19.

[59] See Robert Johnson, *Nova Britannia* (London, 1609), sigs. C2r–v; *A true declaration of the estate of the colonie in Virginia*, pp. 1–2; Richard Crakanthorpe, *A sermon at the inauguration of King James* (London, 1609), sigs. D2r–v; Gray, *A good speed to Virginia*, sigs. A3r–v. On the topic of wisdom in general, see Symonds, *Virginia*, sig. A3r; Crashaw, *A sermon*, sig. K3r; Robert Johnson, *The new life of Virginea* (London, 1612), sigs. A3r–v; Strachey, *The historie of travell into Virginia Britannia*, pp. 8–9; Whitaker, *Good newes from Virginia*, p. 10.

however, were represented as especially vital to the success of the enterprise. They were the conceptual tools believed to be appropriate to redressing the sorry state of the project; the qualities that the audience needed to embrace if they were to be undeterred by the disastrous situation.

Temperance, as we shall see, was prescribed as the solution to the excessive greed that corrupted the enterprise and was particularly required from those who adventured in purse. Courage was said to be necessary if the prospective adventurers, those who adventured in person, were to leave the relative security of England and undertake a dangerous journey to an even more dangerous colony. Potential settlers faced the possibility of loss of property, death by disease, starvation, accident or warfare. In 1612 the Jamestown colony continued to show little improvement or prospect. In this year, Robert Johnson, alderman of London and son-in-law to Company treasurer Sir Thomas Smith, published his second promotional treatise. This tract reveals a dramatic change in emphasis from the Elizabethan arguments used to promote colonies, a marked shift from the promises of El Dorado.[60] Johnson addressed the leaders of the Company and colony:

And first to you the heads and guides of that plantation, it cannot be doubted, but as you are wise and provident men you tooke this worke in hand, for casting wisely that the price thereof might be no lesse then the care of your mindes, the labour of your bodies, and perill of your lives. And seeing you are sure of nothing more then the extremest lots, which either the barren coldnesse of such a naked action in the infancie thereof, or the malice of divellish men can cast upon you, arme your selves therefore against all impediments, to effect those honorable ends that were first intended to be put upon our King, upon our nation, and Christian religion, by that plantation. If the work be more hard and difficult then you took it for, and that you must like Hannibal (piercing the stony Alpes) make cleare way to your desired ends with fire and vinegar; will not your honour be the greater, and your service more acceptable in the performance of it? Nay, if losse of life befall you by this service (which God forbid) yet in this case too, wee doubt not but you are resolved with constant courage, like that noble King Henry the fift, before his triumphant victorie in the fields of Agincourt, where seeing the fewnesse of his own, and multitude of enemies, like a valiant Champion to stir up his little Armie against that great conflict; 'Be cheered my hearts (said he) and let us fight like English men, all England prayeth for us: if here we dye, let this be our comfort, our cause is good, and wee have fathers, brothers, friends and countrimen that wil revenge our deaths.'[61]

[60] On this shift see Charles M. Andrews, *The colonial period of American history* (New Haven, 1934), pp. 99–100. It has also been emphasised by recent commentators: see, for example, Anthony Pagden, *Lords of all the world: Ideologies of empire in Spain, Britain and France c.1500–c.1800* (New Haven, 1995), pp. 67–8.

[61] Johnson, *The new life of Virginea*, sigs. D4r–v.

Death replaced gold as the glory of Virginia. Courage was the quality required to achieve such glory. In addition to paraphrasing Shakespeare, Johnson conformed closely to the topic of courage in the pseudo-Ciceronian *Rhetorica ad Herennium* to support the Company's new emphasis: 'When we invoke as motive for a course of action steadfastness in Courage we shall make it clear that...from an honourable act no peril or toil, however great, should divert us, death ought to be preferred before disgrace.'[62]

Johnson's civic theme of courage and martial vigour was first exploited in the tracts of 1609 and 1610. 'Our forefathers...settled their commonwealths', argued Crashaw, not by 'dalliance and pleasures,'

nay they exposed themselves to frost and colde, snow and heate, raine and tempests, hunger and thirst, and cared not what hardnesse, what extremitie, what pinching miseries they endured, so they might achieve the ends they aimed at.[63]

These appeals consistently conformed to the rhetorical commonplace of courage, as for example in Gray's summary: 'If an honourable death were set before a vertuous minde, it would chuse rather to die heroically, then live opprobriously.'[64]

The promotional authors shared the civic conviction that such a sacrifice of life was justified by the pursuit of the common good.[65] The active life and the exercise of virtue were undertaken to achieve that goal. In his preface to Crashaw's *Sermon*, Thomas West, Lord de la Warre, one of the leaders of the Virginia Company, dedicated the text to the Parliament, observing that the foundation of new commonwealths advanced 'their interest in all endeavours for the common good'.[66] In his first promotional tract, published in 1609, Robert Johnson claimed to have been converted to the cause of establishing colonies having been 'moved so effectually, touching the publike utilitie of this noble enterprise'.[67] The colony was perceived not only to advance the common good of England but also, as a new commonwealth, to possess a common good of its own. John Smith's claim to have endangered his life in the course of his adventures was justified as

---

[62] *Rhetorica ad Herennium*, trans. and ed. H. Caplan (London, 1954), III, 5.

[63] Crashaw, *A sermon*, sig. F4r.

[64] Gray, *A good speed to Virginia*, sig. B4v. For further examples of this argument see Symonds, *Virginia*, pp. 13–14; Johnson, *The new life of Virginea*, sigs. A3r–v; *A true and sincere declaration of the purpose and ends of the plantation begun in Virginia*, pp. 15–16; Crashaw, *A sermon*, sig. H4v; and John Smith, *The generall history of Virginia, New England, and the Summer Isles* (London, 1624), sig. q.

[65] On the common good as the end of civic action, see Skinner, *Foundations of modern political thought*, I, pp. 44–8, 175–80.

[66] Crashaw, *A sermon*, sigs. Ar–A2v.   [67] Johnson, *Nova Britannia*, sig. A4r.

having been undertaken 'as wel for his own discharge as for the publike good'.[68] Members of the Virginia Company routinely justified their actions in these terms. Henry Wriothesley, earl of Southampton, a principal investor and leader of the Company, advised the planting of silk worms for the 'common good' of the colony. A gentleman of the colony, Ralph Hamor, argued that John Rolfe married the 'barbarous' Pocahontas 'merely for the good and honour of the Plantation'.[69]

The Elizabethan promoters of colonies had argued in classical humanist terms that the reward for establishing colonies would both be *honestas* and *utilitas*, honour and profit. The Jacobean promoters signal a marked shift from these ends. The exercise of virtue and the pursuit of the common good were to be rewarded by honour and glory above all.[70] Profit, as we shall see, was portrayed either as secondary or as corrupting. The emphasis upon honour was again found from 1609. *Sauls prohibition staide* by Daniel Price was one of the many sermons both delivered and then published later that year addressing problems of Virginia. Price was chaplain to Prince Henry, soon to be invested prince of Wales, in whom many of the hopes for the future of American colonisation were placed before his death in 1612. He advertised the Virginia colony as fulfilling the ends of 'The glory of God, the honour of our Land, ioy of our Nation'.[71] Similarly, Richard Crakanthorpe, an Essex parson and chaplain to the bishop of London, asked 'what glory shall heereby redound unto God?' from the foundation of the colony: 'What honour to our Soveraigne? What comfort to those his subjects?'[72]

The same shift in emphasis – namely, placing a priority upon honour – was found in the Company's official response to the disastrous loss of the leading vessels in George Sommers' and Thomas Gates' supply fleet of 1609. It was intended that this fleet should bring the new regime of the 1609 charter to the colony. The response to the loss was published with the aim of publicly establishing the ends of the project and was accordingly entitled *A true and sincere declaration of the purpose and ends of the plantation begun in Virginia*. While the anonymous author still maintained that both

[68] John Smith, *A true relation* (London, 1608), sig. B3v.
[69] Purchas, *Hakluytus posthumus*, pp. 1787–8; Ralph Hamor, *A true discourse of the present estate of Virginia* (London, 1615), p. 24.
[70] On honour and glory as the reward for civic action, see Skinner, *Foundations of modern political thought*, I, pp. 100–1, 178–80; Peltonen, *Classical humanism and republicanism in English political thought*, pp. 34–5.
[71] Daniel Price, *Sauls prohibition staide* (London, 1609), sig. F2r.
[72] Crakanthorpe, *A sermon at the inauguration of King James*, sigs. D2r–v. See also Crashaw, *A sermon*, sig. B3v; Abbay and Symonds, *The proceedings of the English colonie in Virginia*, p. 109.

honour and profit were the ends of the plantation, profit had slipped to a secondary position:

The *Principal* and *Maine Ends* (out of which are easily derived to any meane understanding infinit and lesse, and yet great ones) weare first to preach, & baptize into Christian Religion... a number of poore and miserable soules... Secondly, to provide and build up for the publike *Honour* and *safety* of our gratious King and Estates... Lastly, the appearance and assurance of Private commodity to the particular undertakers.[73]

The glory of God and honour had become principal among the stated ends of the enterprise.

The promotional authors concurred not only upon the virtues required to establish the commonwealth, promote the common good and achieve honour and glory. They also agreed upon which vices would corrupt the pursuit of those ends. Indeed, corruption remained a central concern for Jacobean colonisation, as it had been for the Tudors. Roman anxieties about colonisation as a possible source of corruption continued to find voice with both the critics of the enterprise and from promoters. The promoters of the Chesapeake colony constantly complained about 'slanders', 'abuses' and 'discouragements', particularly from 'stage poets', 'players and such like'.[74] Johnson fumes that that 'there is neither common speech nor publike name of anything this day... which is more wildly depraved, traduced and derided by such unhallowed lips, then the name of Virginea'.[75]

There was, of course, much poetry devoted to the promotion of the colony, rather than only deriding it, as Johnson claims. Michael Drayton's ode 'To the Virginian Voyage' was probably first published in 1606 as the newly established council for Virginia prepared their first voyage.[76] The poem presents the voyage according to the familiar ends of honour and glory: 'You brave Heroique Minds... That Honour still pursue'.[77] Similarly in Samuel Daniel's *Musophilus* of 1599, reprinted in 1607 and 1611, Daniel had expressed great optimism in the power of 'heavenly Eloquence' to command men's 'affections' above the power of the sword and over 'all

[73] *A true and sincere declaration of the purpose and ends of the plantation begun in Virginia*, pp. 2–3.
[74] Crashaw, *A sermon*, sigs. H3v, H4v, G2r and K3r; Whitaker, *Good newes from Virginia*, sig. A2r; Johnson, *The new life of Virginea*, sigs. A3r–v; Thomas Dale, *Letter*, in Purchas, *Hakluytus posthumus*, p. 1768; Price, *Sauls prohibition staide*, sig. F2r; Abbay and Symonds, *The proceedings of the English colonie in Virginia*, sig. A2r; Strachey, *The historie of travell into Virginia Britannia*, p. 7; Richard Whitbourne, *A discovery and discourse of Newfoundland* (London, 1622), p. 63.
[75] Johnson, *The new life of Virginea*, sigs. A3v–r.
[76] On dating the poem, see H. R. Woudhuysen, ed., *The Penguin book of Renaissance verse*, selected and introduced by David Norbrook (London, 1992), p. 807.
[77] Drayton 'To the Virginian voyage', in *The Penguin book of Renaissance verse*, p. 431.

the powres of princes can effect'. The sentiment is precisely that great belief in the centrality of eloquence in the conduct of the commonwealth that we have seen to be fundamental to the understanding of the foundation of the colonies. In a much quoted passage, Daniel turns precisely to the possibility that 'The treasure of our tongue...shal be sent/ T'inrich unknowing Nations'.[78]

His optimism finds a response in John Taylor's less frequently cited 'Epitaph in the Barmooda tongue, which must be pronounced with the accent of the grunting of a hogge'. Taylor was a Thames waterman and resident of Southwark, and was placed therefore not only to make acquaintants in the playhouse district on the south bank of the Thames but also to learn gossip from the departing and returning American voyages. The 'Epitaph' was first published in 1613 at the very moment the Virginia Company was turning its attention to the Bermudas. The poem pours ridicule upon the hope of enriching unknowing nations with the English tongue, opening: 'Hough gruntough wough Thomough Coriatough, / Odcough robunquogh', and continuing in the same vein.[79] Here Taylor also succeeds in ridiculing the Algonquin vocabularies produced by Thomas Hariot and John Smith.

Satiric ridicule of hopes for America was also a source of humour in *Eastward ho*, a very successful collaboration by George Chapman, Ben Jonson and John Marston. The play was first produced in 1605 when, after the Treaty of London, colonial interests began to plan the new Virginian venture.[80] In a parody of Ralegh's discovery of Guiana 'Guiana hath yet her maydenhead', the character Seagull declares: 'Come, boys, Virginia longs till we share the rest of her maidenhead.'[81] According to Seagull, 'gold is more plentiful there than copper is with us...Why, man, all their dripping pans and their chamber pots are pure gold.'[82] The authors satirise Ralegh's hunger for gold that was to be sustained through to the instructions to Captain Newport in the first year of the Chesapeake colony. The satire recalls More's virtuous Utopia located in the new world in which the inhabitants disdain material possessions to the extent that they use gold merely for chamber pots. Seagull is unmoved by such moral fortitude and, like Ralegh, thinks merely of the opportunities for plunder.

---

[78] Daniel, *Musophilus*, in *The Penguin book of Renaissance verse*, pp. 716–17.
[79] Taylor, 'Epitaph in the Barmooda tongue', in Noel Malcolm, ed., *The origins of English nonsense* (London, 1998), p. 140.
[80] For the date of the play, see George Chapman, Ben Jonson and John Marston, *Eastward ho*, ed. R. W. Van Fossen (Manchester, 1979), p. 4.
[81] *Ibid.*, III, iii, 15–16. [82] *Ibid.*, 26–30.

Again in 1605, Joseph Hall published *Mundus alter et idem*, a burlesque of accounts of New World voyages. The work was republished in English translation in 1609, at the height of Virginia Company's first promotional drive, under the title *The discovery of a new world*. The work opens with a dialogue between 'The Cambridge pilgrim', Beroaldus, a Frenchman, and Drogius, a Dutchman. Beroaldus is presented as a knowledgeable and well-travelled man. 'I see not', he declares, 'any profit or worth in the world, contained in travell.'[83] Showing no respect for claims for the discovery of New World wonders, he continues: 'Forreine parts are so like ours, that you cannot thinke them strange to yee, though you never saw them before'.[84] For Beroaldus, as for satirists from Barclay onwards, scholarship and self-knowledge are of far greater value than travelling to new worlds. Moreover, as Hall would later elaborate in *Quo vadis? A just censure of travell* (published in 1617), vices are easily adopted in foreign places, just as virtues are easily lost: 'I have (not without indignation) seene too many lose their hopes, and themselves in the way; returning as empty of grace, and other vertues, as full of words, vanitie, mis-dispositions.'[85]

Despite such reservations, 'the Cambridge pilgrim', Beroaldus, and Drogius are inspired by the glory of new discoveries to voyage to a new world: 'It is as great a glory (thinke I) to be called The new worlds dis-coverer, as her conquerer.'[86] The tension of the dialogue is precisely the central tension within humanism which is augmented by anxieties about the New World. It is the tension between corruption and glory. In Hall's work, however, corruption prevails. Just as many New World voyages never left, or were rumoured never to have left, the shores of England, Beroaldus and Drogius abandon the pilgrim before they have even left France (the Virginian voyage planned in *Eastward ho* is similarly wrecked upon the banks of the Thames). The pilgrim continues alone but the new continent he discovers confers no glory; it is a land of vice and luxury, inhabited by gluttony, lechery and women. The principal regions are Tenter-belly, inhabited by gluttons, Letcherania, inhabited by lechers, Fooliana, inhab-ited by idiots, and Shee-landt, inhabited by women. Each of these regions represents precisely those vices of luxury and effeminacy which, Roman history showed, were the product of foreign conquests and which would corrupt civic virtue. The satire, moreover, is tied directly to the Virginian

---

[83] Joseph Hall, *The discovery of a new world: Mundus alter et idem* (London, 1609), p. 9. On Hall's satire, see: Richard McCabe, *Joseph Hall: A study in satire and meditation* (Oxford, 1982).
[84] Hall, *The discovery of a new world*, p. 10.
[85] Joseph Hall, *Quo vadis? A just censure of travell* (London, 1617), sig. A5r.
[86] Hall, *The discovery of a new world*, p. 14.

ventures. The narrator explains that 'Shee-landt', for example, is often mistaken for a part of Virginia: 'The new discovered *Womandecoia*, (which some mistaking both name and nation) call *Wingandecoia*, & make it a part of Virginia) otherwise called *Shee-landt*.'[87] 'Wingandecoia' was derived from an Algonquin word that the English would sometimes use to refer to Virginia. Like John Taylor, Hall ridicules the English attempt to employ Algonquin words. Ralegh's warlike Amazons are parodied as gossiping women (the principal city of Shee-landt is Gossipingoa), obsessed with ornaments, domineering and yet 'generally of meeke and unmanly spririts'.[88] For Sallust, the femininity of Roman soldiers returning from the east was one of the principal causes in the decline of virtue. For Hall, the luxury of foreign lands threatens to soften and make feminine the martial virtues of the English. The habitation of those lands by women who indulge all their feminine vices serves to underline this threat.

These satires were motivated by serious anxieties. Juvenal's satirical accounts of Roman corruption were a model for humanist satire. A central purpose of satire was to reveal the corruption of civic virtue. It is for this reason that much of the humanist opposition to New World voyages, from Alexander Barclay through to Hall, finds its voice in satire.

One of the strongest Jacobean cases against colonisation, while in verse, was not, however, a satire. Ten years after *Musophilus*, Samuel Daniel returned to the theme of colonisation in his 'Epistle. To Prince Henry', 1609–10. This was at the height of the Virginia Company's promotion of the Chesapeake colony and the Company pinned many hopes upon Henry's patronage. Daniel advises Henry against colonisation, seemingly reversing his position in *Musophilus*, or perhaps, in characteristically humanist fashion, seeking to argue *in utramque partem*, to argue, that is, both sides of the question. He draws his arguments directly from Roman history. Great princes will tell you, he warns Henry, 'How glorious theis discoveries and remote/ Plantations are', how blessed they are 'having gott/ Possessions of a world, that never was/ Knowne to our fathers… Besides the inrichment, and the benefitt/ That new detected world, hath brought with it'. 'But yet weigh you', he urges, 'whither this be so.' Are we 'bettred in our state' by the 'excessive vayne/ Of gould?' Had we not 'more/ Of men that time, when wee had less of gould?' It is not simply gold but wealth that is the threat. Wealth erodes civic virtue: 'Examin whither every any state/ Hath not miscarried, when dilisiousnes/ The child of wealth was borne.' He is thinking specifically of Rome. Consider, he continues, 'If Indea [i.e. America] may

---

[87] *Ibid.*, p. 64.   [88] *Ibid.*, pp. 66–8.

not unto Christendome/ As Fatall be, as Asia was to Rome'. Tacitus and Sallust inform these thoughts. Tacitus' *Agricola* is revealed when Daniel turns to the question of civilising the barbarians. 'But some may say', he acknowledges, 'this worke yet glorious was/ For that it did the christien faith extend/ To infidels.' It is true that with time 'those rude lands' will approve 'Th'European arts and Customes'. We shall see in ch. 5 that Tacitus claimed the Romans conquered the Britons less with the sword and more by the corruptions of luxury. As Tacitus put it, the Britons gave the name civilisation to their slavery. Similarly the native Americans, according to Daniel, will be conquered not so much through the sword but through their seduction into luxury: 'they shall curious grow, and delicate/ (Which we call Civill) and enjoy their part/ Of our vaine glories'. Sallust's account of the corruption of Rome through its Asiatic conquests, and Rome's subsequent adoption of 'Asiatic' 'deliciousness', was evident in Daniel's question whether 'Indea' will be as fatal to the English as 'Asia was to Rome'. He then expands upon Sallust's account of the corruption of Rome, both through the wealth conquered in Asia and through the contamination of Romans with 'Asiatic' tastes for luxury:

> we perhaps, arriv'd unto a more
> Then Asiatic weaknes, by the trade
> Of superfluities bred by their store
> And our ymmoderate humors, may be made
> A prey unto some Gothicq barbarous hand.[89]

It would be difficult to imagine a more emphatic rejection of the dangers of profit and possession arising from American colonisation. The 'Asiatic' threat lying within Virginia deepens the perspective of humanists already accustomed to balancing glory and corruption within the civic community: they must consider the possibilities of contamination, they must take the integrity of the commonwealth into the balance.

The promoters of the Chesapeake colony proved to be sensitive to these attacks and anxious to show that the fears were being taken into account. Indeed, the promoters should not be seen to be ideologically opposed to the critics of colonisation, as the apparent hostility of the two sides would suggest. It should hardly be surprising that, having also been educated in

---

[89] Samuel Daniel, 'Epistle. To Prince Henry', in *The Penguin book of Renaissance verse*, pp. 433–6. While Rome conquers both Britain and Asia, culturally the impact of Rome upon the Britons, in the account of Tacitus, is very similar to Sallust's account of the impact of Asia upon the Romans. In the latter case, on Sallust's account, we must ask who conquered whom. There was certainly no concept of historical progress in operation. The motivating issue in each case, as for humanists confronting America, is how a culture that possesses civic virtue can maintain its integrity.

the *studia humanitatis*, the promoters shared the same anxieties and differed only in the sense that they thought it was possible to proceed with caution rather than abandon colonisation. The promoters' consensus upon the corrupting vices was also informed by Roman and Italian civic traditions. According to those traditions, idleness was one of the main threats to the performance of civic duties and the pursuit of an active life.[90] It was idleness that was prescribed as the greatest impediment to the success of the Virginia colony. According to the Company's *True and sincere declaration*, 'Idleness and bestial slouth' was the main cause of the colony's problems and its consequence was that 'every thing [is] returning from civill Propryety, to Naturall, and Primary Community'.[91] Crashaw similarly condemned luxury and extolled martial vigour as the quality necessary for establishing commonwealths:

Stately houses, costly apparell, rich furniture, soft beds, daintie fare, dalliance and pleasures, huntings and horse-races, sports and pastimes, feasts and banquets are not the meanes whereby our forefathers conquered kingdomes, subdued their enemies, converted heathen, civilized the Barbarians, and settled their commonwealths.[92]

In such appeals to martial vigour, by Johnson and Gray on the topic of courage and Crashaw here, we find that the colony's regime of martial law did not substitute for political life but rather complemented the theme of martial discipline in the civic tradition. Crashaw's sentiments were expressed with as much strength by those who lived in the colony as by the Company's hired pens. In his *Map of Virginia* published in 1612, John Smith expanded upon Crashaw's observations from his own experience. Jamestown, he claimed, was overburdened with men who never

did any thing but devoure the fruits of other mens labours. Being for the most part of such tender educations and small experience in martiall accidents, because they found not English cities, nor such faire houses, nor at their owne wishes any of their accustomed dainties, with feather beds and downe pillowes, Tavernes and alehouses in every breathing place, neither such gold and silver and dissolute liberty as they expected.[93]

He argued that this endemic idleness was, more than any other cause, responsible for the disastrous state of the colony:

---

[90] Skinner, *Foundations of modern political thought*, I, pp. 99, 162–6.

[91] *A true and sincere declaration of the purpose and ends of the plantation begun in Virginia*, pp. 10–11.

[92] Crashaw, *A sermon*, sig. F4v.

[93] John Smith, *A map of Virginia* (Oxford, 1612), pp. 37–9. On the opposition between 'dissolute liberty', or licence, and liberty enjoyed with responsibility, see Conal Condren, 'Liberty of office and its defence in seventeenth-century political argument', *History of Political Thought*, 3 (1997), p. 462.

There were many in Virginia meerely projecting, verbal and idle contemplatours, and those so devoted to pure idleness, that though they had lived two or three yeares in Virginia, lordly, necessitie it selfe could not compell them to passe the Peninsula, or Pallisadoes of James Towne... Thus from the clamors and the igno-rance of false informers, are sprung those disasters that sprung in Virginia, and our ingenious verbalists were no lesse plague to us in Virginia, then the Locusts to the Egyptians.[94]

Historians have provided some insight into the apparent apathy of the colonists – an apathy so profound it was held largely to be responsible for the high mortality rate. One problem was that the presence of such a large proportion of soldiers and gentlemen was inappropriate to a project that needed to be essentially agricultural if it was to be self-sustaining (although their presence would have made more sense to the Company, with its civic ambitions, than it does with the hindsight of economic history).[95] Moreover, simple environmental factors such as the salinity of Jamestown's water supply could account for much of the weakness of the settlers.[96] These explanations of the colony's problems do not provide an alternative to the civic diagnosis of the Company. Rather, the civic language of colonists such as Smith and the colony's promoters were the terms through which such threats to the commonwealth as the effects of water salinity were understood.

The problem of faction was also identified as a threat to the continu-ing existence of the commonwealth. The concern with faction reflected both the Jacobean and early modern concern with establishing political consensus and was consistent with the received doctrines of Marsiglio and Bartolus.[97] It should be noted that this concern with consensus was rapidly subordinated if necessary. As we will see in ch. 4, the political rhetoric of the promoters was as much deliberative, and therefore oppositional, as it was a rhetoric of display or demonstration. The political priority of the

---

[94] Smith, *Map of Virginia*, pp. 37–9. On the diagnosis of idleness as a problem in this period of the colony, see also Abbay and Symonds, *The proceedings of the English colonie in Virginia*, sig. A2r; and *A true declaration of the estate of the colonie in Virginia*, pp. 34–5, 'our mutinous loiterers would not sow with providence, and therefore they reaped the fruites of too deare-bought repentance. An incredible example of their idlenes, is the report of Sir Thomas Gates, who affirmeth . . . he hath seene some of them eat their fish raw, rather than they would go a stones cast to fetch wood and dresse it'.

[95] Morgan, *American slavery, American freedom*, pp. 83–4; Karen Kupperman, *Settling with the Indians* (London, 1980), p. 17.

[96] Carville V. Earle, 'Environment, disease, and mortality in early Virginia', in Thad W. Tate and David L. Ammerman, eds., *The Chesapeake in the seventeenth century* (Chapel Hill, 1979), pp. 96–125.

[97] On consensus in early Stuart politics, see Mark Kishlansky, *Parliamentary selection: Social and political choice in early modern England* (Cambridge, 1986). On faction and civic thought, see Skinner, *Foundations of modern political thought*, I, pp. 55–64.

promoters, as we have seen, was participation. Nevertheless faction was a concern. One report remarked with surprise that the plantation had survived its first three years with 'al their factions, mutenies, and miseries'.[98] The new charter of 1609 was designed in part to redress this situation. The Company's tract published shortly after conceded that from returning ships 'ariseth a rumor of the necessity and distresse our people were found in, for want of victual: of which . . . we doe confesse a great part of it'. The author argued, however, that it is possible to

lay aside the cause and fault from the designe, truely and home upon the misgovernment of the Commanders, by dissention and ambition among themselves, and upon Idleness and bestial slouth, of the common sort, who were active in nothing but adhering to factions and parts.[99]

The emphasis upon idleness and faction among the participants in the colony revealed the characteristic civic prescription that the successful foundation and conservation of a commonwealth lay in the character and spirit of its members.[100]

The most dramatic change in the ideology of colonisation under the Virginia Company concerned the propagandists' attitude toward profit. Again this change was first apparent in 1609. Following the series of Elizabethan colonial failures and then the disasters of the early Jamestown colony, the promoters turned from promising profit and riches to denouncing those who pursued profit. They portrayed the desire for profit as one of the vices corrupting the commonwealth. This shift was not confined to the Company's propaganda. On 25 November 1612, the Virginia Company issued a bill of complaint against 'Sir Thomas Mildmaye, James Bryarley, Mathewe De Quester, and Others' for a failure to fulfil promises to invest in the venture.[101] Mildmaye responded that his promise was made when the Company had offered great returns, but now he had 'byn lately told that he this Defendant must expect noe profit of his adventure by the space of Twenty yeares'.[102]

---

[98] Abbay and Symonds, *Proceedings of the English colonie in Virginia*, p. 78.

[99] *A true and sincere declaration of the purpose and ends of the plantation begun in Virginia*, p. 10. On the theme of faction, see also Rolfe, *Relation of the state of Virginia*, p. 104.

[100] On the civic emphasis upon the character and spirit of the citizens, see Skinner, *Foundations of modern political thought*, I, pp. 44–5.

[101] 'Virginia Company vs. Sir Thomas Mildmaye, James Bryarley, Mathewe De Quester, and Others. The bill of complaint, November 25, 1612', in Kingsbury, *Records of the Virginia Company*, III, pp. 34–9.

[102] 'Virginia Company vs. Sir Thomas Mildmaye and Others. The Answer of Sir Thomas Mildmaye to the Bill of Complaint. December 11, 1612', in Kingsbury, *Records of the Virginia Company*, III, p. 40.

The promotional authors drew upon the civic argument that profit corrupts civic virtue.[103] To pursue individual profit while engaged in a public
action, according to this argument, is to place personal interests before
those of the common good. This is not to say republican thought was hostile to private pursuits; one of the principal aims of civic government was to
create the conditions in which citizens could enjoy private lives unthreat-
ened by the invasive claims of arbitrary rule.[104] In such a regime, profit
was a legitimate aim in so far as it was secondary to the common good.
Temperance was represented as the virtue necessary to establishing this
balance.

Some republican sources were sceptical even of the pursuit of collective
wealth, as this was associated with 'Asiatic' luxury and the corruption of
martial values which were believed to have contributed to the downfall of
the Roman republic. 'As soon as riches came to be held in honour', Sallust
recalls of the late republic, 'when glory, dominion, and power followed in
their train, virtue began to lose its lustre.'[105] The authors of the promotional
pamphlets were particularly strong in their attack upon the pursuit of
private profit, but there were also reservations and warnings that there
should be no hopes whatsoever for profit from the enterprise: the aim was
to establish a commonwealth not a business.

Crashaw directly confronted the crisis of profit when dismissing objections against the colony. In doing so, he revealed the sensitivity of his own
arguments to the situation of the Company:

The next discouragement is, the uncertaintie of profit, and the long time that it
must be expected, it be certaine. But I will not wrong you nor myselfe, in seeking
to say much to so base an objection. If there be any that came in only or principally
for profit, or any that would so come in, I wish the latter may never bee in, and
the former out again.[106]

---

[103] On wealth as the corruption of civic virtue, a theme stressed by Roman moralists such as Sallust and
Juvenal, endorsed by Latini, and revived by Machiavelli and Guicciardini, see Skinner, *Foundations
of modern political thought*, I, pp. 42–3, 162–3. On the revival of this theme in Elizabethan and
Jacobean civic thought, see Peltonen, *Classical humanism and republicanism in English political
thought*, p. 79.

[104] See Quentin Skinner, 'The republican ideal of political liberty', in Gisela Bock, Quentin Skinner
and Maurizio Viroli, eds., *Machiavelli and republicanism* (Cambridge, 1990); and Quentin Skinner,
Liberty before liberalism (Cambridge, 1998).

[105] *Sallust*, trans. J. C. Rolfe (London, 1921), xii, 1; see also x–xii. For the revival of this theme in early
modern Britain, see Skinner, *Liberty before liberalism*, pp. 64–5.

[106] Crashaw, *A sermon*, sigs. G2r–v. Crashaw harps on this point: 'But if it be urged further: Why is
there not then present profit, at least after so many voyages and supplies sent? In answere, that *profit
is not the principall end of this action*' (my emphasis), sig. G3v.

Without completely rejecting the ambition for profit, Crashaw adopted the civic line that it must be subordinated to the higher aims of the enterprise. Gray likewise argued that the desire for money was in conflict with virtue and must at best be secondary, praising the Virginia Company for having:

undertaken so honourable a project, as all posterities shal blesse you and uphold your names and memories so long as the Sunne and Moone endureth: whereas they which preferre their money before vertue, their pleasure before honour, and their sensual security before heroical adventures, shall perish with their money, die with their pleasures, and be buried in everlasting forgetfulnes.[107]

MORAL PHILOSOPHY AFTER TOBACCO

While these civic solutions were first addressed to the problems of establishing an American commonwealth in 1609, neither the problems nor the prescription would be fast to fade. Following the great propaganda push of 1609 and 1610, the colony continued to suffer disease, a high mortality rate and disasters such as the wreck upon the Bermudas. When Gates and Sommers eventually reached Jamestown, they found such a dire state of affairs that a decision was taken to abandon the colony. As the few survivors left Chesapeake Bay, it was only their chance meeting with de la Warre's supply fleet that forced a change of heart and the continued survival of the plantation. Against this background, the Company continued to sponsor promotional tracts.

Alexander Whitaker, son of the master of St John's College, Cambridge, was one of those members of Gates' voyage wrecked upon the Bermudas who subsequently arrived in Jamestown at perhaps its most desperate ebb. He opened his *Good newes from Virginia* (published in 1613 shortly before his own death by drowning in the Chesapeake) with an extended passage upon what is now a familiar civic theme of the propaganda:

Be bould my Hearers to contemne riches, and frame your selves to walke worthie of God; for none other be worthie of God, but those that lightly esteeme of riches. Nakednesse is the riches of nature; vertue is the only thing that makes us rich and honourable in the eyes of wise men. Povertie is a thing which most men feare, and covetous men cannot endure to behold: yet povertie with a contented mind

---

[107] Gray, *A good speed to Virginia*, sigs. A3r–v. In the same year, Robert Johnson asks 'are we to looke for no gaine in the lieu of all our adventures?' replying that there is such a hope 'but looke it be not chiefe in your thoughts': Johnson, *Nova Britannia* (London, 1609) sig. Cr.

is great riches: hee truely is the onely poore man, not that hath little, but which continually desireth more.[108]

The Elizabethan desire for New World wealth was again dramatically reversed in this plea 'to contemne riches'. Whitaker emphasised the corrupting power of profit and the necessity for temperance, for curbing the continual desire for more. Wealth is not even granted a secondary position. He esteemed honour as the appropriate reward for action, and portrayed virtue as the means to achieving that end; much of his treatise was an exhortation to the virtues required for the audience to adventure successfully. 'The worke', of establishing the new commonwealth he argued, 'is honourable, and now more than ever sustained by most honourable men.'[109]

In 1615, although the colony was still far from returning a profit to the investors, a couple of years of relative stability encouraged Ralph Hamor, previously secretary to the colony, to publish a treatise in which he expressed greater hope and potential for profit.[110] Hamor devoted part of the tract to persuading merchants to invest. Merchants, he argued, want some 'present returne' of 'commodities'. He promised this return and yet he was still obliged to advise patience and temperance: 'If I may persuade them to be constant in proceedings, some small time longer, the benefit will be the greater and the more welcome when it commeth.'[111] For the remainder of his audience, however, Hamor still held with the argument that civic virtue was the quality required for the foundation of the colony:

I would gladly now by worthy motives, allure the heavie undertakers to persist with alacritie and cheerefulnesse, both for their owne reputations, and the honour of God, and their King, and Countrey. The worthier sort, I meane those Nobles and others of that honourable counsell interested therein, neede no spurre, their owne innate vertues drives them apace.[112]

Again, honour remained the reward of virtuous public action, particularly for those whose birth made them more fit for public actions.

John Rolfe, later famous for having introduced tobacco into the colony, published his *Relation of the state of Virginia* the following year. Rolfe

---

[108] Whitaker, *Good newes from Virginia*, p. 1. He returns to this theme repeatedly through the tract: 'you wealthy men of this world, whose bellies God hath filled with his hidden Treasure: trust not in uncertaine riches, neither cast your eyes upon them; for riches taketh her to her wings as an Eagle, and flieth into Heaven. But bee rich in good works', pp. 26–7, see also p. 32.

[109] *Ibid.*, p. 32.

[110] On the improvement in conditions, see Hamor, *A true discourse of the present estate of Virginia*, p. 16.

[111] *Ibid.*, p. 25.   [112] *Ibid.*, p. 25.

addressed the common objection that if Virginia was such a fruitful country, how was it that men there 'pined with famine'.[113] His answer was a civic diagnosis of the ills of idleness and faction, each of which he claimed was being remedied. In his prescription, we again see the civic emphasis upon the character and spirit of the participants as the key to the colony's success. 'The greatest want of all', he argued, 'is least thought on, and that is good and sufficient men.' With such men, they 'might come with ease to establish a firme and perfect commonweale'.[114]

By the 1620s, with some success in planting tobacco, the promoters of Virginia were ready once more to promise profit. The air of crisis, however, which permeated the colony's early history was not distant and the civic themes of that period proved to be salient. It would be a mistake to attribute that salience wholly to the reputed 'republican sympathies' of Edwin Sandys and Henry Wriothesley, the earl of Southampton, the Company's new administrators.[115] Certainly, Sandys was accused of attempting to establish a 'Brownist republic' in Virginia.[116] The slander would seem to have been directed specifically at Sandys' lengthy negotiations, starting in 1617, with the English 'Pilgrim Fathers', who were at that time resident in Leyden, and were seeking permission from the Company to establish a colony in Virginia.[117] Sandys granted permission but the Pilgrims established the colony at Plymouth, outside the Company's jurisdiction. The accusation of republicanism must, however, be understood within the generally civic character of the Company's activities. Here Sandys is clearly not alone. We have seen that, from the inception of the Company, there was a broad consensus (including gentry figures such as Sandys and merchants such as Robert Johnson) that the colonial project should be understood in terms of a quasi-republican language.

The disputes between the Sandys and Smith factions, leading to the eventual dissolution of the Company in 1625, added to the sense of crisis. The Company was still deeply in debt.[118] Moreover, the interests of the Company and the colonists had steadily diverged over the previous ten years. Property owners 'showed little concern for the public weal of the colony', sacrificing 'corporate welfare' to their 'own individual ends'.[119] Company officials in the

[113] Rolfe, *Relation of the state of Virginia*, p. 102.   [114] *Ibid.*, pp. 103–4.
[115] On the republican sympathies of Southampton and Sandys, see S. L. Adams, 'Foreign policy and the parliaments of 1621 and 1624', in Kevin Sharpe, *Faction and parliament: Essays on early Stuart history* (Oxford, 1978), pp. 144–5. See also Malcolm, 'Hobbes, Sandys and the Virginia Company', pp. 300–1.
[116] *Ibid.*   [117] On the negotiations, see Rabb, *Jacobean gentleman*, pp. 330–1.
[118] Craven, *Dissolution of the Virginia Company*, pp. 33–5.
[119] Greene, *Pursuits of happiness*, p. 11.

colony 'led the way' through their expropriation of Company resources.[120] In this climate, civic argument could be employed as a critique of political corruption as much as a foundational programme. It was in this vein, when writing of the history of the American colonies in 1625, that John Smith returned to the civic theme that the consideration of private gain corrupts the pursuit of the common good: 'the desire of present gaine (in many) is so violent, and the endeavours of many undertakers so negligent, every one so regarding their private gain, that it is hard to effect any publike good, and impossible to bring them into a body, rule, order'.[121] Sandys and Southampton sought to remedy the situation with typically civic solutions: attacking corruption (which was understood as private profit), expanding participation and re-establishing Company plantation, plantation by all and not by individuals.

The reform programme corresponded with a renewed propaganda effort that returned to the Company's earlier civic themes. In 1622 Samuel Purchas composed *Virginias verger*, to be published in 1625 in *Hakluytus posthumus*, his monumental collection of English voyages. Purchas inherited Hakluyt's mantle as the foremost compiler of these accounts in England. In *Virginias verger* he also followed Hakluyt and his successors in presenting glory, and in particular the glory of God, as the highest aim of the enterprise. 'The beginning and the end' of the 'Virginian argument', according to Purchas, was 'whether the Plantation may bring glory to him.'[122] His marginal reference for this argument of glory was to Cicero.[123] Honour remained the principal reward; he presented five 'Arguments for Virginian plantation, as being honourable'.[124] Profit, consistent both with Sandys' policies and conventional Ciceronian moral philosophy, remained subordinate: 'And if Honour hath prevailed with honourable and higher spirits, we shall come laden with arguments of profit to presse meaner hands and hearts to the service of Virginia.'[125] Some of the tension that had opened up between merchant and gentry interests is suggested here. Purchas' solution to that conflict was close to Sandys' own position.[126] Where the common good is being sacrificed to the private ends of one faction, those with higher spirits, who can be trusted to serve the common good (namely, Sandys and the

[120] *Ibid*. See also Morgan, *American slavery, American freedom*, pp. 117–18.
[121] Smith, *The generall history of Virginia*, p. 242. For the continuing secondary position of profit in promotional arguments at this time, see also Samuel Purchas, *Virginias verger*, in Purchas, *Hakluytus posthumus*, p. 1816.
[122] Purchas, *Virginias verger*, p. 1809.   [123] *Ibid*., p. 1813.   [124] *Ibid*., p. 1816.   [125] *Ibid*.
[126] Introduction to [Nicholas Ferrar], *Sir Thomas Smith's misgovernment of the Virginia Company*, ed. D. R. Ransome (Cambridge, 1990), pp. xvii–xviii.

gentry faction), must be trusted with authority. This was a solution, again, which would have been perfectly acceptable to Cicero.

The year 1622 also saw two further sermons commissioned by the Company. The theme of duty, central to Crashaw's sermon, was revived by Patrick Copland in *Virginia's God be thanked*. Copland reminds his audience that they have a 'duty' to pursue 'Gods glory'. He argues that the Virginian plantation offers this opportunity, and offers the conventional rewards of 'her wealth and honour': that is, the wealth and honour of the commonwealth, not private planters.[127] The other sermon was by John Donne, dean of St Paul's, who had sought to become secretary to the Virginia Company in 1609. Donne emphasises that the context of these efforts is the foundation of a new commonwealth: 'Those amongst you, that are old now, shall passe out of this world with this great comfort, that you contributed to the beginning of that Common Wealth.'[128] He then returned to the theme of the necessity of the *vita activa* to the foundation of new commonwealths. As we will see in ch. 4, more clearly than any other of the Company's propagandists, Donne revealed that the production of promotional tracts was regarded as a part of the active life and therefore as central to the foundation of colonies.[129]

Donne's commitment reveals that the unprecedented propaganda campaign launched by the Virginia Company in 1609 was in itself, as an instrument of the *vita activa*, regarded as a central part of the civic effort thought to be necessary to establish the commonwealth. According to a humanistic understanding, the sermons and histories of Virginia would perform the same civic function as had the orations and histories devoted to the foundation and conservation of the Italian city republics. The promotional tracts were, that is, a crucial part of the civic solution to the Virginia Company's problems. This proposition returns us to the question of how seriously we should take the ideology of the Virginian colony as it is expressed in the Company's propaganda. The central position, according to a

---

[127] Patrick Copland, *Virginia's God be thanked* (London, 1622), pp. 27–8.

[128] John Donne, *A sermon . . . preach'd to the honourable company of the Virginian plantation* (London, 1622), p. 44.

[129] *Ibid.*, sig. A3r. This view is expressed metaphorically by Copland whose sermon *Virginia's God be thanked* was published by the Company six months before Donne's sermon: 'How could I, at so earnest entreatie, refuse to adventure this Mite of mine, among so many worthy adventures?', sig. A3r. In the style of Crashaw, Copland's sermon is also devoted to arguing that there is a duty to adventure to Virginia. The implications of Donne's argument are fully explored in Andrew Fitzmaurice, ' "Every man, that prints, adventures": the rhetoric of the Virginia Company sermons', in Lori Anne Ferrell and Peter McCullough, eds., *The English sermon revised: Religion, literature and history 1500–1750* (Manchester, 2000).

humanist and civic view, of such acts of propaganda in the foundation of the commonwealth leads to one conclusion: that these tracts are central to the politics of the colony and that therefore it is precisely in such propaganda that we should look for deliberative statements of policy.

NEWFOUNDLAND AND NOVA SCOTIA

The early 1620s saw not only the continuing struggles of the Virginia Company but also attempts to establish colonies in Newfoundland, Nova Scotia and New England. In addition to the existing and new English adventurers, Scottish, Welsh and Irish interests supported and initiated these projects.[130] On 2 May 1610, four years after the Virginia Council charter was granted, a second colonial charter established the Newfoundland Company. The charter awarded the whole island to the Company, but its focus would be upon the Avalon peninsula.[131] As with the Virginia Company, the Newfoundland Company was composed of an alliance of gentry interests, London capital and west country merchants. A settlement of forty people was established at Cupid's Cove two months after the grant of the charter. The colony never flourished but the toehold remained in the harsh conditions.

In 1616 and 1617 the Newfoundland Company confronted the problem of its limited resources and consequent inability to aid the struggling colony. Mirroring the Virginia Company's method of raising finances in the same years, the Newfoundland Company began to sell licences for private plantation.[132] At the same time, the Bristol merchants withdrew from the Company and secured a grant to establish a settlement in Harbour Grace called Bristol's Hope.[133] Three further private allotments were granted to Sir William Vaughan of Wales, Sir Henry Cary, Lord Deputy of Ireland and soon to be Viscount Falkland, and Sir George Calvert, Secretary of State and later first baron Baltimore.[134] These three men had been contemporaries in Oxford in the 1590s and were well acquainted with each other.[135] While all had backgrounds in the *studia humanitatis*, Vaughan was deeply involved in humanistic pursuits. Particularly striking was his translation of Trajano

---

[130] On Scottish plans see William Alexander, *An encouragement to colonies* (London, 1624); John Mason, *A brief discourse of the new-found-land* (Edinburgh, 1620) reprinted in Cell, *Newfoundland discovered*, pp. 89–99; Robert Gordon, *Encouragements* (Edinburgh, 1625). On Welsh plans, see William Vaughan, *The golden fleece* (London, 1626), and Cell, *Newfoundland discovered*, pp. 13 and 15–26. On Irish plans designed primarily by Henry Cary, Viscount Falkland and George Calvert, Lord Baltimore, for the resettlement of the Catholic 'Old English', see T. C., *A short discourse of the Newfoundland* (Dublin, 1623), in Cell, *Newfoundland discovered*, pp. 227–36; see also pp. 17 and 207–49.

[131] Cell, *Newfoundland discovered*, p. 5.   [132] *Ibid.*, p. 15.

[133] *Ibid.*, p. 17.   [134] *Ibid.*, p. 15.   [135] *Ibid.*, pp. 16 and 46–7.

Boccalini's *The new found politicke* with two of the leading humanists of his generation, John Florio (whom we saw promoting Gilbert's ventures), and Thomas Scott. Boccalini's work expressed a profound disillusionment with the failure of republican politics and the corruption of the court. For Boccalini, the age of virtue had come to an end.[136] Tacitus and Seneca were employed by such disillusioned humanists to show that the only path for virtuous men was withdrawal into contemplation (or, as we shall see in ch. 6, Tacitus could be used to show that continued political involvement demanded the abandonment of virtue). Vaughan appears to have found a further alternative to the corruption of court life, namely, the pursuit of the active life in the New World. In Newfoundland, according to Vaughan, the Golden Fleece would be found among 'Neptune's sheep', the cod of the north Atlantic fisheries. He established a Welsh settlement at Renews in 1618 but the colony folded in a year.

Cary, a member of the Virginia Council from 1609, established a colony in South Falkland in 1623. His intention, apparently, was to provide an opportunity for the resettlement of the 'Old English' in Ireland. The colony did not endure long beyond 1626.[137] Calvert established a colony at Ferryland. With his return to Catholicism in 1625, now as Lord Baltimore, this colony assumed the character of a Catholic refuge. Baltimore took the dramatic step of settling himself and his family in Ferryland in 1628, but his experience of the winter merely focused his efforts upon establishing a Catholic colony on the Chesapeake.

Sir William Alexander of Stirling, a Scot, was yet another recipient of a land title from the Newfoundland Company. Alexander had already gained a reputation as one of the most prominent Scottish poets of his generation. He was granted a large area of land west of Placentia Bay.[138] But Alexander's ambitions for Scottish colonisation could not be contained by this grant. In 1621, James VI and I instructed the Scottish Privy Council to provide Alexander with a patent for the land between New England and Newfoundland. This land would be known as New Scotland, although it was subject to competing claims by the English, Dutch and, particularly, the French. Alexander was progressively bankrupted by the several attempts

---

[136] Trajano Boccalini, *The new-found politicke* (London, 1626). Skinner, *The foundations of modern political thought*, I, pp. 168 and 188–9. On Boccalini as a theorist of reason of state, cf. Maurizio Viroli, *From politics to reason of state: The acquisition and transformation of the language of politics 1250–1600* (Cambridge, 1992).

[137] Cell, *Newfoundland discovered*, pp. 43–5.

[138] John G. Reid, 'Sir William Alexander and North American colonisation: a reappraisal', a lecture delivered at the university of Edinburgh, published by the Centre for Canadian Studies (Edinburgh, 1990), p. 3.

he made to establish colonies. Yet he remained 'exceedingly inflamed' by colonisation and persisted in the accumulation of debts.[139] Once more, we are confronted by the need to explain such persistently unprofitable behaviour. Following the pattern of Newfoundland and Virginia, Alexander was also granted, in 1624, the power to sell land holdings within his patent.

Although plantation had been attempted in Newfoundland for the same period as in Jamestown, the hostility of fishermen and Trinity House to the occupation of the beaches, used for drying fish, probably accounted for the suppression of promotional material. The settlement of this dispute in 1620 by the Privy Council (upon which both Cary and Calvert sat) opened the promotional floodgates.[140] In the same year, tracts promoting the Newfoundland ventures appeared rivalling those of the Virginia Company in volume. Captain John Mason, who had been governor of the Company's Cupid Cove colony since 1615, published *A brief discourse of the new-found-land*. Richard Whitbourne, who had briefly acted as governor of Vaughan's colony, published a treatise arguing the colonisation of Newfoundland that would run to three editions. Vaughan would himself prove to be an even more enthusiastic promoter of his project, publishing three separate works on the subject. Robert Hayman, the governor of the Bristol adventurers' colony, was yet another leader of colonies turned promoter. Hayman used his time in Bristol's Hope not only to produce one treatise and a substantial amount of verse promoting colonisation, but also producing the first English translation of François Rabelais. His choice of translation is significant. Rabelais had produced one of the most scathing of humanist satires of the decay of civic responsibility. In Hayman's work, we see again how close the concerns of humanist satire could come to those of colonial promotion. Like Vaughan, whom he had known at Exeter College, Oxford, Hayman shows that corruption in the Old World could be a basis for adventuring. The New World offered an opportunity for the exercise of virtue.

Henry Cary's plans for a colony produced some promotional literature, which was published in Dublin.[141] Sir William Alexander also appeared to learn from the success of the Virginia Company's promotional campaign, publishing in support of his enterprise within a short time after gaining the patent.[142] The dedications and verse in commendation to the works of

---

[139] Reid, 'Sir William Alexander', p. 3.   [140] Cell, *Newfoundland discovered*, pp. 26 and 32.
[141] T. C., *A short discourse of the Newfoundland*.
[142] Only Calvert failed directly to sponsor promotional tracts, probably for several reasons. He had sufficient money to finance his colonies. Given that he was providing a refuge for Catholics, he had a ready market of personnel. And, perhaps most importantly, advertising Catholic plans for

Vaughan, Mason, Whitbourne, Hayman and Alexander acknowledge their mutual inspiration and the close association of Welsh, Scottish, Irish and English plans for the colonisation of Newfoundland. Both Hayman and Whitbourne acknowledge Cary, Vaughan and Calvert; Mason acknowledges Alexander and commends Vaughan's work; in Vaughan's *Golden fleece*, Alexander and Mason participate in the dialogue (with Boccalini and Tacitus, among others).

A further common element is that the promoters were generally more successful in publishing than in establishing colonies. This mixed success merely underlines the humanist conviction of the fundamental role of oratory as the founding act. Furthermore, it is striking that many of these publications were produced by men who not only were employing their education in the *studia humanitatis* to perform what was perceived to be such an important oratorical role, but who also were actively engaged in, and central to, the conception and implementation of the projects.

These authors wrote against a background of similar difficulties to the Virginia Company. The sense of crisis was deepened by the fact that the numerous attempts to establish colonies in Newfoundland had generally withered in the face of harsh conditions. It is hardly surprising, therefore, that the Newfoundland interests attempted to emulate the propaganda success of the Virginia Company, and that this propaganda was structurally and thematically derivative of the Virginia Company tracts. Addressing Sir Percival Willoughbie, one of the investors, Robert Hayman acknowledged that the ventures had been disastrous:

> Wise men, wise Sir, doe not the fire abhorre,
> For once being sing'd, more wary grow therefore.
> Shall one disaster breed in you a terror?
> With honest, meet, wise men mend your first error.
> If with such men you would begin againe,
> Honor and profit you would quickly gaine.[143]

Courage and temperance are the qualities necessary to overcome disaster, and honour and profit, the ends of Ciceronian moral philosophy, are the rewards. These commonplaces were repeated throughout the tracts

---

colonies would merely arouse public hostility. Certainly Calvert was subjected to personal abuse and the abuse of his religion when in Ferryland and while visiting Jamestown; see Cell, *Newfoundland discovered*, pp. 54–5.

[143] Hayman, *Quodlibets, lately come over from New Britaniola, Old Newfoundland* (London, 1628), p. 34.

promoting the Newfoundland colonies.[144] They are never more apparent than in the substantial volume promoting Newfoundland colonisation written by Richard Eburne, a little-known Somerset vicar.[145] Eburne addressed the objection that 'the adventures are very dangerous and liable to losses of life and goods'. With characteristic bluntness he replied with the example of the Apostles; God 'doth send them forth as lambs among wolves that they should be hated, persecuted, and put to death for his sake'.[146] Public virtues were again to be exercised for the common good and rewarded with honour and glory. The corrupting vices, particularly idleness, were again held to be responsible for the failures of the colonies: 'We must not greatly marvel if our so long continued rest and peace from wars and warlike employments, our unspeakable idleness and dissolute life, have so corrupted and in manner effeminated our people.'[147] In this appeal to martial values, we hear the republican diagnosis of the decline of the Roman republic.

Attempting to establish settlement upon his own holdings of land, Sir William Alexander struck the now familiar theme of a virtuous active life rewarded by glory: 'Where was ever Ambition baited with greater hopes than here, or where ever had Vertue so large a field to reape the fruits of Glory?'[148] These themes are most clearly stated by the Scot Robert Gordon in his *Encouragements* (1625), dedicated to Sir William Alexander and the 'Undertakers in the plantation of New Scotland'. Gordon, like Alexander, filled the dual roles of colonial land-holder and propagandist. His work is one of the least discussed of the early promotional tracts: a deficiency probably accounted for by the fact that it was consistently derivative of the Virginian literature. He wrote in support of the 1620s' campaign promoting colonies in Newfoundland and Nova Scotia. The derivative character of his tract was reflected in the fact that, frequently, he merely plagiarised previous promoters, reprinting long passages from Virginia Company literature without acknowledgement.[149] Gordon announced that he had obtained a patent to

---

[144] Whitbourne, *A discovery and discourse of Newfoundland*, sig. A3r and p. 14; Mason, *A brief discourse of the new-found-land*, p. 99; T. C., *A short discourse of the Newfoundland*, p. 228.

[145] On the author's obscurity and possible motivations, see Richard Eburne, *A plaine pathway to plantations*, pp. xxvi–xxviiii.

[146] *Ibid.*, pp. 58–9. 'What high and worthy enterprise', he argues, 'is there that ever hath without some difficulty been achieved?' p. 75. For this commonplace of courage, see also Hayman, *Quodlibets*, book 2, p. 34; and Gordon, *Encouragements*, sig. E3r, 'Doe wee dreame of difficulties? Then know; that it is out of the greatest difficulties, that spring the greatest honours.'

[147] Eburne, *A plaine pathway to plantations*, p. 120.

[148] Alexander, *Encouragement to colonies*, p. 42.

[149] For example, Gordon's lengthy passage justifying colonisation (*Encouragements*, sig. B4r) is taken, *verbatim*, from *A true declaration of the estate of the colonie in Virginia*, p. 12; his argument that 'no other moderate or mixt course' (*Encouragements*, sig. B3v) of colonisation can be followed

establish a colony and, in this context, he cited the civic commonplace: 'We are not borne to our selves; but to help each other.'[150] In a further Ciceronian commonplace commending the active life, he argued that knowledge alone of the colonial enterprise 'cannot content mee: but knowing that the chiefe commendation of vertue consisteth in action'.[151] In response to the 'difficulties and impediments' bedeviling the foundation of colonies, he then argued:

> Now let us compare our selves with Citizens now, whose credite wee see doeth surpasse ours, although wee bee above them, both in qualitie and richesse. Whence is this woorth of theirs, but from their industrie, and trueth; which beareth them out both to this credite, and respect, as well at home as abroad. Were it not [then] better in these our dayes for us to imitate the foot-steppes of vertue in the Italians, that thinketh it neither dishonourable, nor disparagement unto their greatest Princes, their Dukes, Marquesses, and Countes, to make themselves great, and get patrimonies inlarged by their hazards at Sea? It is their glorie to bee vertuous; and may condemne our dissolutions, and idlenesse, that may as easilie bee great, by such honest and honourable endeavours.[152]

The qualities that, according to Gordon, characterise citizens are those with which we are already familiar from the earlier promotional tracts. He prescribed industry and an active life. He exhorted virtue as the key to the successful pursuit of that life. He condemned the vice of idleness for corrupting these qualities, and he portrayed honour and glory as the reward of good citizens. He revealed that these values were drawn from Italian republican sources. He was careful, however, to stress that a civic ideology need not conflict with a monarchical and aristocratic culture. The derivative character of Gordon's treatise reveals his sense of the history of the problems of colonisation in the enterprises of the Virginia Company and the Elizabethans. His sense of this history showed him to be one of the last propagandists to propose the civic solution to the now Jacobean (rather than simply English) crisis of colonisation.

NEW ENGLAND

There appears to be evidence for the salience of the civic themes of the Virginia Company in the promotional tracts of the Plymouth colony which initially settled under the Virginia Company's charter, albeit outside their territory. The Plymouth leaders William Bradford and Edward Winslow

---

also repeats *A true declaration*, p. 10; his division of the ends of adventurers according to position (*Encouragements*, sig. C2r) reprints a passage from Smith, *The generall historie of Virginia*, p. 221.
[150] Gordon, *Encouragements*, sig. B2v.   [151] *Ibid*.   [152] *Ibid*., sig. Ev.

were acutely aware in their *Relation of Plymouth* (1622) of the potential for
the pursuit of profit to corrupt the common good: 'let every man represse
in himselfe and the whole bodie in each person, as so many rebels against
the common good, all private respects of mens selves, not sorting with the
general convenience'.[153] Robert Cushman concurred in his *Sermon preached
at Plimmoth* of the same year, devoting the sermon to the theme 'Let
no man seeke his owne, but every man anothers wealth.' He concluded
that 'Sweet sympathy is the only maker and conserver of Churches and
commonwealths': a useful argument for a colony with no legal basis.[154]

The Plymouth colony was, of course, concerned with a problem different
from those facing the Virginia Company: that of religious liberty. The civic
emphasis of their tracts may have arisen as much from that predicament
as the disastrous history of English colonisation. In this respect, they anticipate the Massachusetts Bay colony.[155] The civic thought of the Virginia
Company had more in common with the Providence Island Company
of the 1630s in its stress upon virtuous public service.[156] But again, although drawing upon a similar tradition of civic thought, the Providence
Island Company was motivated by religious repression whereas the Virginia
Company was responding to thirty years of commercial disaster. In this respect, the civic themes of English colonisation in the 1630s did not signify
continuity with the Virginia Company but rather marked the end of their
particular crisis and its own distinctive solution.

If the civic ideology used to promote Virginia was discontinuous with
the different models of liberty employed in New England and Providence
Island, what place does the early Virginian model hold in the larger history
of English colonisation? The first context within which this question may
be answered is in a comparison of the character of the Virginia colony with
those in New England. Whereas Virginia is commonly held to be the nurs-
ery of materialistic, individualistic, commercial and proto-capitalist values,
it is frequently contrasted with the communal and religious character of the
New England colonies. These were corporate communities, established by
covenant, which sought to 'subordinate individual interests to the common

[153] William Bradford and Edward Winslow, *A relation of Plymouth* (London, 1624), sig. B3v (see also
     pp. 2–3).
[154] Robert Cushman, *A sermon preached at Plimmoth* (London, 1622), pp. 1, 2 and 13. The western branch
     of the original Virginia Council, which became the New England Council under the leadership of
     Sir Ferdinando Gorges, was at the time threatening 'to give the law along those coasts'; see *A brief
     relation of the discovery and plantation of New England* (London, 1622), in *Sir Ferdinando Gorges
     and his province of Maine*, ed. J. P. Baxter (New York, 1967), p. 225.
[155] On the concern with liberty in Massachusetts Bay, see Karen Ordahl Kupperman, 'Definitions of
     liberty on the eve of civil war: Lord Saye and Sele, Lord Brooke, and the American puritan colonies',
     The Historical Journal, 32 (1989), pp. 17–33.
[156] On the comparison between the Massachusetts Bay and Providence Island colonies, see *ibid.*

good'.[157] The civic designs of the Virginia Company were more remote from the common portrayal of Virginia than from this New England ideal. In fact, in the fundamental premises of their politics, the Virginia Company and the New England colonies were twins. They were separated more by motivations than values.

What, however, were the motivations of the Virginian and Newfoundland adventurers? Since the 1930s, they have been believed to be apolitical and commercial. And yet this understanding must be revised in light of the moral philosophy employed by the adventurers, a moral philosophy that was particularly hostile to commerce. Could, as such early historians as Charles M. Andrews, Charles Mills Gayley and Alexander Brown argued, the issue of parliamentary resistance to the rule of James I have had a role, particularly given that the language in which the colonies were promoted was civic? The difficulty with this argument would be that the language of the *studia humanitatis* was both substantive and heuristic: that is, the *studia humanitatis* were employed both by restless parliamentarians in their promotion of the Virginia colony and by apologists for absolute rule (including James I and VI) in commending the same enterprise. It was, however, the fact that the *studia humanitatis* could be employed as a language of political participation that attracted so many of those who were discontented with James' claims to absolute power. The extraordinary level of gentry participation in the Virginia Company cannot be accounted for by an emerging commercial consciousness among the English gentry because the Company was not understood in commercial terms. The fact that so many members were parliamentarians and that they chose as their leader Edwin Sandys, the leader of parliamentary resistance to James' claims to absolute power, suggests these men were motivated by a desire for political participation.

This suggestion takes greater weight when we find that the *studia humanitatis* are employed by the Company to support an idea of citizenship: the very heuristic character of the *studia humanitatis* provides the answer. With their humanist education, the promoters could have promoted the colony in terms that were not civic. The foundation of the new colony was not portrayed as a Senecan retreat for contemplation, nor was it portrayed in terms of Virgilian pastoral; as a place of withdrawal from the corrupt world.[158] It was not, therefore, presented in terms of those values that

---

[157] Greene, *Pursuits of happiness*, p. 23. Stephen Foster, *Their solitary way: The puritan social ethic in the first century of settlement in New England* (New Haven, 1971); Allen Cardin, 'The communal ideal in puritan New England, 1630–1700', *Fides et historia*, 17 (1984), pp. 25–38.

[158] Cf. Leo Marx, *The machine in the garden: Technology and the pastoral ideal in America* (London, 1964).

reconciled the *studia humanitatis* with absolute rule and the corruption of the court. For Roman writers, the retreat from public life is an end to citizenship and an end to civic life. These themes were vigorously explored in the court cultures of the northern European Renaissance. As we shall see in ch. 6, the alternative to virtuous participation, on the one hand, and withdrawal and contemplation, on the other, was for the subject to enter into the culture of the court, to reject virtue and pursue survival. By contrast, the promoters of the Virginia Company consistently portray colonisation as a theatre of action. The success of the enterprise was held to be dependent upon political participation and the exercise of civic virtues, to be dependent, that is, upon the fundamental elements of citizenship. The foundation of the Virginia and Newfoundland colonies attracted many of those Jacobeans most in sympathy with these Ciceronian ideals. This does not mean that every promoter of colonies was seeking to oppose James' claims to absolute power (Sir William Alexander, for example, would not fit such an explanation). But in a climate in which those claims were made, the pursuit of an active life in the foundation of new commonwealths would have been less likely to bring the subject into conflict with the monarch. Colonising, therefore, offered a field for the exercise of virtue, as so many promoters emphasised, at the very moment when its exercise was limited at home. When had virtue ever, as Alexander pointed out, so large a field.

There is a further context in which the values of the Virginia Company must be questioned. It is now a historical commonplace that the Elizabethan idea of the conquest of the New World was abandoned for a colonisation of commerce.[159] The civic thought employed by the Virginia Company reveals that the shift from the Elizabethan model of conquest was initiated in response to the crisis of 1609. The colonisation of settlement and trade is said to have established the premises of the future commercially based empires of England and France. This interpretation would appear to be consistent with those historians who argue that the Virginia Company was fundamentally a business enterprise. The language of humanism was increasingly employed in the definition of the nature and ends of business in the sixteenth century and in the early seventeenth century. Humanism and civic thought, however, were far from wholly reconciled with commerce. Moreover, foremost among the various strands of the civic tradition employed by the Virginia Company was that which was particularly hostile to commerce; that which rejected the acquisition of wealth as

---

[159] Pagden, *Lords of all the world*, ch. 3. The idea of conquest was not entirely abandoned, as we shall see in ch. 5.

corrupting the common good.[160] The shift from Elizabethan ideas of empire, and the civic ideology of what would become England's first permanent American colony, did not anticipate an individualistic America or a British commercial empire. Rather, as Robert Gordon revealed, the Virginia Company and its immediate successors walked in the footsteps of the Italian republics.

[160] Cf. Peter S. Onuf, 'Reflections on the founding: constitutional historiography in bicentennial perspective', *William and Mary Quarterly*, 46 (1989) pp. 351–3; Richard Vetterli and Gary Bryner, *In search of the Republic: Public virtue and the roots of American government* (Totowa, 1987); J. G. A. Pocock, *Virtue, commerce and history: Essays on political thought and history, chiefly in the eighteenth century* (Cambridge, 1985), p. 272.

CHAPTER 4

Rhetoric – 'not the Words, but the Acts'

THE FOUNDATION OF COMMONWEALTHS

One of the clearest indications of the humanist education of those authors concerned with the New World was that their treatises promoting the colonial designs were composed according to the conventions of classical rhetoric. They were, that is, instances of classical oratory. Of the five disciplines in the humanist curriculum, rhetoric held a central position. The art of rhetoric was defined variously by classical and humanist authorities but always as an act of persuasion. Humanist culture, sometimes referred to as rhetorical culture, placed great emphasis upon the contingency of knowledge. In such an environment, in which knowledge was a matter of plausibility rather than certainty, the ability to persuade was crucial to social and political action. In the *studia humanitatis* the active life of the citizen was represented as vital to the health of the political community. Speech, in particular, was believed in its various forms, including writing and printing, to be one of the most important means through which to pursue action.

Classical rhetoricians and their Renaissance imitators distinguished three *genera*, or kinds, of rhetoric; the forensic, epideictic and deliberative. Each *genus* was distinguished by a context, a function and an end. The context of forensic rhetoric was the law court; its function was accusation and defence and its end, justice. Epideictic, or occasional, oratory, had its genesis in the funeral oration; its functions were praise and blame, and its ends fortune and virtue. The appropriate context for deliberative oratory was the political assembly; its function was 'either hortatory or dissuasive; for... those who speak in the assembly invariably either exhort or dissuade'.[1] Its ends were *honestas* and *utilitas*, or 'honour' and 'advantage'. 'The deliberative', Cicero states, 'is at home in a political debate.'[2]

---

[1] Aristotle, *'Art' of rhetoric*, trans. J. H. Freese (London, 1926), I, iii.3.
[2] Cicero, *De inventione*, trans. H. M. Hubbell (London, 1949), I, v.7.

It was this political *genus* of oratory that was favoured by authors writ-ing to promote the foundation of colonies in the New World. They fre-quently described their attempts at persuasion in terms of exhortation. Lewis Hughes' treatise on the Bermuda islands was, according to the title page, 'written by way of exhortation'.[3] Similarly, Alexander Whitaker opened his tract on Virginia by declaring 'I was greatly emboldened to write these few lines of exhortation, to encourage the noble spirits of so many worthy men'.[4]

Although overwhelmingly deliberative in character the tracts promoting colonies were not devoid of the characteristics of other rhetorical *genera*, particularly the epideictic. As Aristotle observed, exhortation in deliberative rhetoric and praise in epideictic are merely two sides of a coin:

> Praise and counsels have a common aspect; for what you might suggest in coun-selling becomes encomium by a change in the phrase. Accordingly, when we know what we ought to do and the qualities we ought to possess, we ought to make a change in the phrase and turn it, employing this knowledge as suggestion ... if you desire to praise, look what you would suggest; if you desire to suggest, look what you would praise.[5]

John Donne expanded upon this observation in the peroration to his ser-mon before the Virginia Company. Following an overtly deliberative sermon, he concluded:

> To end all, as the Orators which declaimed in the presence of the Roman Emperors, in their Panegyriques, tooke that way to make those Emperors see, what they were bound to doe, to say in those publique Orations, that those Emperors had done so, (for that increased the love of the subject to the Prince, to bee so tolde, that hee had done those great things, and then it convayed a Counsell into the Prince to doe them after.) As their way was to procure things to bee done, by saying they were done, so beloved I have taken a contrary way: for when I, by way of exhortation, all this while have seem'd to tell you what should be done by you, I have, indeed, but told the Congregation, what hath beene done already: neither do I speak to move a wheele that stood still, but to keepe the wheele in due motion; nor perswade you to begin, but to continue a good work, nor propose forreigne, but your own Examples, to do still, as you have done hitherto.[6]

Donne portrays himself as an orator. He acknowledges the two-sided nature of epideictic. He conceded, however, that in fact his own speech had been

[3] Lewis Hughes, *A plaine and true relation of the goodness of God towards the Summer Iles* (London, 1621).

[4] Alexander Whitaker, *Good newes from Virginia* (London, 1613), sig. D2v. See also William Crashaw, *A sermon preached before the right honourable the Lord Lawarre* (London, 1610), sig. K3r; John Donne, *A sermon ... preach'd to the honourable company of the Virginian plantation* (London, 1622), pp. 44–5.

[5] Aristotle, *'Art' of rhetoric*, I, i.36.   [6] Donne, *A sermon*, pp. 44–5.

deliberative, and yet claimed that only praise was necessary. Through this inversion he tempered what had been an overtly political speech, having suggested there could be tensions in such an act.[7] Generally, however, the promoters of colonies did not share Donne's caution.

Having revealed the purpose of their tracts to be exhortation, the promoters next turned to the ends of deliberative oratory. While defined as *honestas* and *utilitas* by Latin authors, these ends were more commonly translated into the vernacular as honour and glory, and profit, wealth and advantage. 'An Oration deliberative', Thomas Wilson declared in his 1553 Ciceronian *Arte of rhetorique*, 'is a meane whereby we do persuade, or disswade... exhorte or dehorte.' 'The reasons which are commonly used to enlarge such matters', he continues, are foremost 'that the thyng is honest' or 'Profitable'.[8] Profit was broadly understood in the classical sense of *utilitas* as any form of advantage, social or political, as well as economic. In the context of discussions of the New World it frequently appeared to refer to the narrow hope of emulating Spanish success in acquiring riches, particularly silver and gold, but this ambition was also understood to be linked to military and political strength.[9]

Upon the failure of Humphrey Gilbert's 1582–3 voyage, Sir George Peckham's son was moved to compose a tract exhorting the settlement of Newfoundland. This tract was composed with the explicit rhetorical aim of 'persuasion': 'I have taken it upon me to write this simple short treatise, hoping that it will be able to persuade such as have bene, and yet doe continue detractors and hinderers of this journey.'[10] Peckham then turned explicitly to 'deliberation' and promoted the 'action' in terms of the deliberative *loci*:

I drew myself into a more deepe consideration, of this late undertaken voyage, whether it were as well pleasing to almightie God, as profitable to men: as lawful as it seem honourable: as well grateful to the Savages, as gainful to the Christians. And upon mature deliberation, I found the action to be honest and profitable.[11]

---

[7] On Donne's equivocal politics, see Annabel Patterson, 'John Donne, kingsman?', in Linda Levy Peck, ed., *The mental world of the Jacobean court* (Cambridge, 1991), pp. 251–72.

[8] Thomas Wilson, *The arte of rhetorique*, ed. Thomas J. Derrick (New York, 1982), p. 34.

[9] On the importance of wealth to political advantage, see Walter Ralegh, *The discoverie of the large, rich and bewtiful empyre of Guiana* [London, 1596], ed. Neil L. Whitehead (Manchester, 1997), pp. 127–8.

[10] George Peckham, *A true report of the late discoveries... by Sir Humphrey Gilbert*, reprinted in Richard Hakluyt, *The principal navigations, voiages and discoveries of the English nation* (London, 1589), p. 704.

[11] *Ibid.*, pp. 703–4.

Sir William Alexander similarly claimed that his Nova Scotia plantation would enable colonisers 'to deserve of their countrey, by bringing unto it both Honour and Profit'.[12] In promoting the Newfoundland colonies, Captain Richard Whitbourne promised 'What the reasons, motives, and inducements are, either of honour, profit, or advantage, which may justly invite your Majesty, and all your good subjects to take some speedy and reall course for planting there, I will endeavour hereafter to shew.'[13] These deliberative *loci* were employed in all the Tudor and early Stuart tracts promoting the various projects for the colonisation of the New World.

This use of deliberative rhetoric is surprising given that it has commonly been argued that there were few if any opportunities for explicitly political oratory under early modern European monarchies. It is claimed that by the sixteenth century 'the oration itself had already become a literary genre rather than a means of political persuasion'.[14] The tensions created by the use of explicitly political oratory (employing models such as the republican Cicero and the democrat Demosthenes) in the courtly culture of early modern England are clearly the cause of Donne's anxiety and equivocation over his use of deliberative rhetoric. Renaissance rhetoricians persisted, however, in discussions of deliberative rhetoric and made great claims for the political achievements of oratory. This power was emphasised by Thomas Wilson in the dedication of his *Arte of rhetorique*, in which he demonstrated the superiority of oratory over arms:

When Pyrrhus, king of the Epirotes, made battle against the Romans, and could neither by force of arms nor yet by any policy win certain strongholds, he used commonly to send one Cineas (a noble orator and sometimes scholar to Demosthenes) to persuade with the captains and people that were in them that they should yield up the said hold or towns without a fight or resistance. And so it came to pass through the pithy eloquence of this noble orator divers strong castles and fortresses were peaceably given up into the hands of Pyrrhus, which he should have found very hard and tedious to win by the sword.

What greater way, asked Wilson, could there be to win countries and to achieve conquest? Yet these claims are said to be anachronistic.[15] From Jacob

---

[12] William Alexander, *An encouragement to colonies* (London, 1624), p. 42.

[13] Richard Whitbourne, *A discovery and discourse of Newfoundland* (London, 1622), sig. A3r.

[14] Christine Roaf cited in Brian Vickers, 'Some reflections on the rhetorical textbook', in Peter Mack, ed., *Renaissance rhetoric* (London, 1994), pp. 83–4. See also Marc Fumaroli, 'Rhetoric, politics, and society: from Italian Ciceronianism to French classicism', in James J. Murphy, ed., *Renaissance eloquence* (Berkeley, 1983), p. 258.

[15] Vickers, 'Some reflections on the rhetorical textbook', pp. 83–4.

Burckhardt in the nineteenth century to Paul Oskar Kristeller in the twentieth it has been argued that 'unlike ancient rhetoric, Renaissance rhetoric was not primarily concerned with the political and even less with the judiciary speech'.[16] In this way the history of rhetoric has been brought in to line with the history of early modern European culture as fundamentally princely, courtly and hierarchical. The history of rhetoric needs to be revised in light of recent research revealing sixteenth- and seventeenth-century perceptions of the English constitution as a mixed form of government.[17] The diminution of the explicitly political role of oratory ignores the multitude of deliberative assemblies below the level of Parliament, foremost of which was the parish council.[18] Moreover, even if the conventions of classical deliberative oratory were not employed in Parliament (and the oratorical conventions of Parliament have not been explored), like each of the rhetorical *genera*, the deliberative *genus* was not bound by its formal contextual associations. It was infinitely flexible in application. Wilson emphasises this point by giving a plea for marriage as his example of deliberative rhetoric. Yet this example has been taken to indicate the impotence of the *genus* rather than its flexibility.

An important instance of the malleability of rhetorical *genera* was the sixteenth-century reform of the sermon. In their contribution to church reform Erasmus and Melanchthon had sought to explain and teach the 'mysteries of scripture' to all audiences. Their desire was that preaching should never be 'frigidly abstract' and would be 'persuasive of a godly life'.[19] Classical rhetoric, which was explicitly designed with the aim of making communication clear, moving and instructive, was harnessed by the religious reformers to their aims.[20] In a move that proved to be particularly popular with reformers, Erasmus and Melanchthon dictated that the sermon should be composed according to the conventions of classical

---

[16] See Paul Oskar Kristeller, *Renaissance thought and its sources*, ed. Michael Mooney (New York, 1979), p. 242. See also Jacob Burckhardt, *The civilisation of the Renaissance in Italy*, 2 vols. (New York, 1958), I, p. 239: 'Bartolomeo Facio complained that the orators of his time were at a disadvantage compared with those of antiquity; of three kinds of oratory which were open to the later only one was left to the former.'

[17] Markku Peltonen, *Classical humanism and republicanism in English political thought, 1570–1640* (Cambridge, 1995); Patrick Collinson, 'The monarchical republic of Elizabeth I', *Bulletin of the John Rylands University Library of Manchester*, 69 (1987), pp. 394–424.

[18] Mark Goldie, 'The unacknowledged republic: officeholding in early modern England', in Tim Harris, ed., *The politics of the excluded, c.1500–1850* (London, 2001).

[19] John W. O'Malley, 'Content and rhetorical forms in sixteenth century preaching', in Murphy, *Renaissance eloquence*, pp. 242–4.

[20] See, for example, Quintilian, *Institutio oratoria*, trans. H. E. Butler, 4 vols. (London, 1920–22), VIII, i.1–ii.1 and XII, x.58–9.

deliberative rhetoric.[21] Given the great role humanists attributed to oratory in political life, one of the consequences of this reform would be to amplify the political power of the sermon. If in the courtly societies of northern Europe there were limited opportunities for the practice of oratory in the formal classical categories (the political assembly, the forensic court, and the occasional speech), the reform of the sermon provided a context in which the humanist vision of the political power of rhetoric could be implemented.

It is striking in this context that the leaders of colonial projects turned so frequently to the clergy and in particular to the sermon as the instruments of promotion. The Reverend Richard Hakluyt, for example, was the foremost Elizabethan promoter of colonies. This relationship was augmented under the Virginia Company. Of the eight orations delivered in 1609 to address the Company's crisis, seven were sermons.[22] Rhetoric was employed because its function was persuasion. All those who wrote to promote the New World colonies were attempting to persuade their audience to 'adventure', as they said, 'in purse and person'.

But the use of rhetoric was also linked to the nature of those enterprises. The promoters repeatedly stated that their ambition was to establish new commonwealths. It is true that the tracts promoting colonisation of the New World have frequently been categorised as travel literature.[23] This categorisation is mistaken. The formal rhetorical texture of the New World literature contrasts with the sparse use of classical rhetorical conventions in contemporary works of travel.[24] The contrast is even clearer with authors who wrote both travel accounts and to promote the New World. John Smith's accounts of his adventures in Turkey and Europe, for example, contain none of the deliberative conventions found in his Virginian writings. The New World tracts are distinguished by the desire to establish new commonwealths and by what, according to classical

---

[21] O'Malley, 'Content and rhetorical forms in sixteenth century preaching', pp. 242–4. On the reform of preaching in England through rhetoric see also Debora Shuger, *Sacred rhetoric: The Christian grand style in the English Renaissance* (Princeton, 1988), pp. 55–117; Quentin Skinner, *Reason and rhetoric in the philosophy of Hobbes* (Cambridge, 1996), pp. 66–7.

[22] See Andrew Fitzmaurice, ' "Every man, that prints, adventures": the rhetoric of the Virginia Company sermons', in Lori Anne Ferrell and Peter McCullough, eds., *The English sermon revised: Religion, literature and history 1500–1750* (Manchester, 2000), p. 26.

[23] See, for example, *The Cambridge bibliography of English literature*, ed. F. W. Bateson (Cambridge, 1969), I, pp. 786–9; and more recently Andrew Hadfield, *Literature, travel, and colonial writing in the English Renaissance 1545–1625* (Oxford, 1998).

[24] Compare, for example, Anthony Sherley, *Sir Antony Sherley his relation of his travels into Persia* (London, 1613); Thomas Coryat, *Thomas Coriat traveller for the English wits* (London, 1616); or Richard Jobson's *The golden trade: or, a discovery of the River Gambra, and the golden trade of the Aethiopians* (London, 1623).

rhetoric, were the linguistic demands of such an enterprise. No such ambition is found in contemporary travel literature. When George Peckham employed deliberative oratory to promote Humphrey Gilbert's planned colony, he placed that oratory in the context of an Athenian debate over what course was best for the 'common wealth'.[25] 'There is nothing', the colonist Thomas Studley wrote in 1612 reflecting on the previous six years of the Jamestown colony, 'so difficult as to establish a commonwealth.'[26] Studley's claim points to the centrality of the commonwealth in the humanists' political imagination. A commonwealth was understood to be a discrete political society.[27] The promoters of colonies aimed for no less – not trading posts, nor simply military posts, nor did they aim merely to expand the commonwealth of England. The private licences which first Elizabeth I and then James I granted to colonisers served to encourage this pursuit of the foundation of new political communities with a separate and semi-autonomous existence from England but under the *imperium* of the crown.

In classical and humanist rhetorical textbooks oratory was represented as the central act in the foundation and conservation of a commonwealth. We have seen that humanist textbooks granted rhetoric a strong political function, particularly through the deliberative *genus*. This idea was famously articulated by Cicero in the opening to *De inventione*. He invited his audience to 'consider the origin of this thing we call eloquence'.[28] 'There was a time', he argued, 'when men wandered at large in the fields like animals... they did nothing by the guidance of reason... there was as yet no ordered system of religious worship nor of social duties; no one had seen legitimate marriage... nor had they learned the advantages of an equitable code of law.' 'At this juncture', he continues

a man – great and wise I am sure – became aware of the power latent in man and the wide field offered by his mind... Men were scattered in the fields... when he assembled and gathered them in accordance with a plan; he introduced them to every useful and honourable occupation, though they cried out against it at

---

[25] Peckham, *A true report of the late discoveries*, sig. B3r.

[26] T. Abbay and William Symonds, eds., *The proceedings of the English colonie in Virginia* (Oxford, 1612), pp. 10–11. For the ambition to establish commonwealths, see also *A true and sincere declaration of the purpose and ends of the plantation begun in Virginia* (London, 1610), pp. 25–6; Robert Tynley, *Two learned sermons* (London, 1609), pp. 67–8; Whitaker, *Good newes from Virginia*, p. 19; William Strachey, *The historie of travell into Virginia Britannia* [1609–1612], eds. Louis B. Wright and Virginia Freund (London, 1953), p. 4; and John Rolfe, *Relation of the state of Virginia* in *Virginia: Four personal narratives*, Research Library of Colonial Americana (New York, 1972), p. 104.

[27] See the discussion of commonwealths in the opening of Sir Thomas Smith, *The commonwealth of England [De republica Anglorum]* [London, 1583], ed. L. Alston (Cambridge, 1906).

[28] Cicero, *De inventione*, I, 2.

first because of its novelty, and then when through reason and eloquence they had listened with greater attention, he transformed them from wild savages into a kind and gentle folk. To me at least it does not seem possible that a mute and voiceless wisdom would have turned men suddenly from their habits and introduced them to different patterns of life.

How, he asked, 'could men believe not only that they must work for the common good but even sacrifice life itself, unless men had been able by eloquence to persuade their fellows of the truth of what they had discovered by reason?'[29] Cicero would repeat this story of the orator's role in the foundation of the commonwealth in his later works. The myth took root in the later classical authors, including Quintilian and Tacitus.[30] This concept of the central role for oratory in the civilising process was fully endorsed by English humanists. Cicero's orator in the wilderness became a commonplace of Renaissance literature. Thomas Wilson, for example, opened his *Arte of rhetorique* with an amplified version of the myth, adding that the role was performed by 'these appoynted of God'.[31]

Richard Eden was one of the earliest of the English humanists to represent his work as an act fundamental to the foundation of new commonwealths. As we have seen in ch. 2, he argued that virtuous acts would be recognised with monuments and that such recognition would spur other men to emulate those acts.[32] In his dedication of *A treatise of the newe India* to the duke of Northumberland, Eden claimed that his translations were precisely such monuments. He recalled that Alexander, upon beholding the tomb of Achilles, lamented that he had not 'suche a trompe [trumpet]' as Homer for his own deeds. Alexander's accomplishments would therefore have no greater name with posterity even though Achilles' exploits 'he thoughte to be much inferiour unto his'.[33] Eden then observed that a book recently came into his hands 'entytled of the newe founde landes' and yet, its treatment was so inadequate to the subject the author may be compared to a man who 'woulde professe to wryte of Englande, and entreated onelye

[29] *Ibid.*, I, 2–3.
[30] Cicero, *De oratore* trans. E. W. Sutton and H. Rackham, 2 vols. (London, 1942), I, 33; cf. Stephen J. Greenblatt, 'Learning to curse: aspects of linguistic colonialism in the sixteenth century', in Fredi Chiappelli, ed., *First images of America*, 2 vols. (Berkeley, 1976), II, p. 565.
[31] Wilson, *Arte of rhetorique*, pp. 17–18. While this understanding of the relation between oratory and the commonwealth was relatively absent from the travel literature of the period it is evident in other contemporary writing where there is a stated concern with the health of the commonwealth. Commerce was frequently defined in such terms and accordingly we find classical rhetoric employed by economic theorists such as John Dee and Gerard de Malynes.
[32] Richard Eden, *The decades of the newe worlde or west India* (London, 1555) reprinted in Edward Arber, ed., *The first three English books on America* (Birmingham, 1885), p. 59.
[33] Arber, *The first three English books on America*, p. 5.

of Trumpington a vyllage wythin a myle of Cambridge'.[34] Eden claimed that his own work would fill this void. He would be to adventures to the New World as Homer to Achilles. His translations would act as the monument to spur English men to employ their virtue in establishing colonies in the New World. In an echo of Cicero's conception of the centrality of oratory to political action, Eden presented himself as participating in the *vita activa* that he was promoting.[35] He was himself participating in, and indeed playing a central role, in the New World enterprise. Without this central role of the orator, he stressed, 'noble enterprises' would be robbed of their 'dignitie'.[36] The consequence would be to confound the 'order of things': a world in which bestiality rather than virtue would be honoured, as when we 'clothe an ape in purple, and a king in sackcloth'.[37] The role of the orator was thus not only in spurring to noble deeds but, at a more fundamental level, in defining the moral philosophy of public life. According to Eden, then, it was to those who perform this role that we had to look for the moral philosophy of New World voyages. His argument that New World colonisation needed a 'tromp' such as Achilles had found in Homer is reprised by subsequent colonial promoters. Philip Sidney, for example, commented that Richard Hakluyt was a 'very good trumpet' for Humphrey Gilbert's ventures.[38]

Similarly, and in typically humanist fashion, Richard Hakluyt maintained that rescue from the 'vasty maw of oblivion' demanded that the acts of Walter Ralegh should be praised and recorded. It is this rhetorical role that he believed to be the principal source of honour in the colonial enterprise. Indeed, according to Hakluyt, the honour of the promoter was as great as that of the coloniser:

I hold those worthy of the highest praise, illustrious and noble knight, who by their labours and by the hazard of their lives have made known to our peoples such an infinite number of the Antipodes, hitherto lying hid. And those, who, of their excellent genius, have recorded the noble deeds of such men, on the imperishable monuments of letters, I consider must be held, if not in greater, certainly in no less honour, and must be no less esteemed.[39]

The basis of this equality of honour was again the conviction that speech, or oratory, is a central political act. In Martyr the Spanish had found

---

[34] *Ibid.*

[35] It is not only in shaping the actions of others that oratory, according to this Ciceronian conception, is perceived as a political act. Even if the orator fails to persuade, he has still acted.

[36] Arber, *The first three English books on America*, p. 5.   [37] *Ibid.*

[38] Humphrey Gilbert, *The voyages and colonising enterprises of Sir Humphrey Gilbert*, ed. David B. Quinn, 2 vols. (Cambridge, 1940), I, p. 93.

[39] Richard Hakluyt, *Epistle dedicatory*, in *The original writings and correspondence of the two Richard Hakluyts*, ed. E. G. R. Taylor, 2 vols. (London, 1935), II, p. 362.

a man whose ability in natural history was no less than that of Aristotle, Theophrastus, Columella or 'even Pliny himself'. And in the consideration 'of mankind and our own species' what, Hakluyt asked, had Cicero, Sallust, Caesar or Tacitus 'written with greater fidelity?'[40] To remind Ralegh that he required a trumpet for his honour, as the Spanish had found in Martyr, Hakluyt borrowed Eden's illustration of the power of oratory: 'Wherefore I can truly say, what once Alexander of Macedon is reported to have said of invincible Achilles: O happy man, who hast found a Homer to the herald of thy praises.'[41] Hakluyt then left open the possibility for filling this role himself: 'Do this [adventure], and you will find at length, if not a Homer, yet some Martyr.'[42]

This Ciceronian notion that the tracts promoting colonies were crucial acts in the foundation of a new commonwealth was stated nowhere more eloquently than in John Donne's sermon to the Virginia Company. Donne selected his text for the sermon from the *Acts of the Apostles*. In the opening of the sermon he echoed Cicero and Quintilian: 'There are reckoned in this booke, 22 sermons of the Apostles; and yet the booke is not called the Preaching, but the Practice, not the Words, but the Acts of the Apostles'.[43] The observation is an axiom of classical rhetoric; that words are acts. If words are acts, then, according to Donne, his own sermon, like those of the Apostles, is an act. He extended this argument to the whole body of literature promoting the colony: 'By your favours, I had some place amongst you, before; but now I am an Adventurer; if not to Virginia, yet for Virginia; for, every man, that Prints, Adventures.'[44] Donne believed that the promotional tracts were themselves acts in the foundation of the new commonwealths because to print was to adventure.

LINGUISTIC POSSESSION

In recent years language has been elevated to central importance in the understanding of colonisation. Historians, particularly literary historians and post-colonial theorists, have increasingly become concerned with the mechanisms of linguistic colonialism, the linguistic means through which the non-European world was possessed by Europeans.[45] Common to these accounts is an emphasis that Europeans encountered a world that was radically different from their own and for which they did not possess the

[40] *Ibid.*, p. 363.　[41] *Ibid.*, p. 364.　[42] *Ibid.*, p. 369.
[43] Donne, *A sermon*, p. 1.　[44] *Ibid.*, sig. A3r.
[45] See, for example Edward Said, *Orientalism: Western conceptions of the orient* (London, 1978); Tzvetan Todorov, *The conquest of America: The question of the Other* trans. Richard Howard (New York, 1984); Stephen Greenblatt, *Marvellous possessions* (Oxford, 1988).

concepts to provide a true account. The only descriptive tools were the categories of European experience. Thus the new was assimilated to the old. This process of linguistic appropriation has been seen as an inevitable epistemic problem whereby the alien can only be understood through the categories of the familiar.[46] It has also been presented, inevitable or not, as an articulation of the emerging capitalist mentality of Europe.[47]

This interpretation of European encounters with non-Europeans is increasingly being challenged. We can now see the possibility that common languages and understandings could be developed in colonial contexts.[48] There is no dispute, however, that in such encounters there was some degree of translation from the alien to the familiar. Certainly in the encounter of early modern English culture with the New World and its inhabitants it is clear that such practices of translation were employed. I will argue that this process of conversion was neither a reflex response to radical otherness nor a possessive proto-capitalism. The process of conversion to Old World values arises from the psychology of persuasion found in classical and humanist rhetoric that was used to compose the English narratives on the New World. We have seen that these tracts were promotional; their mode was persuasion. This aim was often explicitly acknowledged. 'It is an hard matter', observed Richard Whitbourne, 'to persuade people to adventure into strange countries.'[49] There was a consensus among the classical and humanist arts of rhetoric about how such persuasion could be achieved. According to these textbooks, persuasion consists of convincing an audience to accept something they do not already hold to be true. The means of achieving this task is to accommodate the unfamiliar or unpopular proposition to the values of the audience. The historiography that has portrayed the assimilation of alien to familiar has had an unintended and ironic consequence. According to this linguistic account of the violence of the conquests, which is intrinsic to the general account of the violence, the ignorance of the 'other' was an epistemic reflex. If the alien can only

---

[46] This emphasis is shared in a variety of accounts; see J. H. Elliott, *The Old World and the New* (Cambridge, 1970), pp. 16–21; Greenblatt, *Marvellous possessions*, pp. 14 and 23; Antonello Gerbi, *Nature in the New World*, trans. Jeremy Moyle (Pittsburgh, 1985), p. 6; Anthony Pagden, *The fall of natural man: The American Indian and the origins of comparative ethnology* (Cambridge, 1986), p. 4; Wayne Franklin, *Discoverers, explorers, settlers: The diligent writers of early America* (Chicago, 1979), pp. 3–4.

[47] See, for example, Louis Montrose, 'The work of gender in the discourse of discovery', in Stephen Greenblatt, ed., *New World encounters* (Berkeley, 1993), p. 178.

[48] James Clifford, *The predicament of culture* (Cambridge, Mass., 1988); Richard White, *The middle ground: Indians, empires and republics in the Great Lakes region 1650–1815* (Cambridge, 1991); Nicholas Thomas, *Entangled objects* (Cambridge, Mass., 1991).

[49] Whitbourne, *A discovery and discourse of Newfoundland*, sig. C3r.

be understood through the categories of the familiar the actors involved had little choice. The moral responsibility of those concerned is absolved. When seen as rhetorical, the collapse of new into familiar is a deliberate act that carries a moral responsibility.

Quintilian reasoned that to persuade is to prove 'what is not certain by means of what is certain. Indeed this is the nature of all arguments, for what is certain cannot be proved by what is uncertain.'[50] He continues:

> since an argument is a process of reasoning which provides proof and enables one thing to be inferred from another and confirms facts which are uncertain by reference to facts which are certain, there must needs be something in every case which requires no proof. Otherwise there will be nothing by which we can prove anything; there must be something which either is or is believed to be true, by means of which doubtful things may be rendered credible.[51]

For Quintilian, the only way to overcome the audience's uncertainty is to cast the unknown in terms of the known. The act of speaking persuasively consists in moving or turning from the unfamiliar to what is certain or 'held to be certain'. Cicero states that, in this respect, rhetoric is different from all other arts because in the other arts novelty is valued:

> the subjects of the other arts are derived as a rule from hidden and remote sources, while the whole art of oratory lies open to the view, and is concerned in some measure with the common practice, custom, and speech of mankind, so that, whereas in all other arts that is most excellent which is farthest from the understanding and mental capacity of the untrained, in oratory the very cardinal sin is to depart from the language of everyday life, and the usage approved by the sense of the community.[52]

There is some basis in reason to Quintilian's observations on the necessity of appealing to the familiar. For rhetoricians, however, the familiar is regarded as persuasive above all because it is to the familiar that the audience will be emotionally attached. Appeals to the familiar persuade the audience by rousing their emotions. According to Roman rhetoricians, people will

---

[50] Quintilian, *Institutio oratoria*, V, x.8.

[51] *Ibid.*, V, x.11–12. Quintilian is paraphrasing a parallel passage in Cicero, *De inventione*, I, 44–8.

[52] Cicero, *De oratore*, I, 12. Cicero's account of the mode of rhetoric contrasts with Greenblatt's positioning of 'the experience of wonder'. According to Greenblatt, wonder is 'the feature that most decisively links' the early discourse of the New World 'to both philosophical and aesthetic discourse'. He continues: 'For wonder plays a decisive role in the period's philosophy and art . . . that is philosophy (as Socrates had already formulated it) begins in wonder, while the purpose of poetry (as innumerable poets said) was to produce the marvellous' (*Marvellous possessions*, p. 19). Rhetoric, as Cicero points out, is concerned with precisely the opposite and is, in this sense, unique amongst the arts.

frequently not be moved by reason but may be moved by appeals to their emotions. In the opening of *De inventione*, Cicero argues that although through reason men may have discovered a virtuous path, they could only be persuaded to submit to it through eloquence.[53] Through such means they could be persuaded to part with their lives.

It is this rousing of the emotions which rhetoricians claim distinguishes rhetoric from philosophy and from the sciences that are based upon reason. They readily add that this does not mean that oratory does not employ reason. Wisdom, according to the commonplace, would be mute without eloquence; and correspondingly, without reason eloquence cannot aspire to wisdom or virtue.[54] Reason, however, appeals to the intellect alone. An audience may know that a particular course is just or necessary in reason, but they may not wish to submit to it.[55] Those in the assembly may not, for example, wish to risk their lives by waging war even if they know that war may be best for the common good. Once the correct course is laid before an audience, it is only appeals to their emotions and passions that will move them. Logical demonstration of the virtue of a particular action may be beyond their apprehension, whereas appeals to their emotions and character will be most likely to succeed.

This separation of intellect and emotion – intellect for philosophy, emotion for eloquence – is taken to its extreme by the figure of Antonius in Cicero's *De oratore*. Antonius participates in a lengthy discussion of the relation between philosophy and rhetoric in which the speakers emphasise the power of eloquence to attain goals beyond the reach of philosophy. He then relates an anecdote about a man who consulted Publius Crassus upon a marriage. Crassus' advice was 'more correct than comfortable' to his client's interest. Servius Galba challenged Crassus who then resorted to his 'profound knowledge'. Through copious illustrations and analogies, Galba overwhelmed Crassus so that he 'after all admitted that Galba's argument seemed to him persuasive, and very near the truth'.[56] In his portrayal of the power of emotion over reason, Antonius barely stops short of endorsing rhetoric as a means of making the worse appear the better cause – the focus of Socrates' condemnation.

This theory of persuasion is embodied in numerous conventions that comprise the *techne* of rhetoric. The function of the topics, for example, is heuristic. Their role is to find those premises with which the audience

---

[53] Cicero, *De inventione*, I, 3.   [54] *Ibid.*, I, 3–5.   [55] *Ibid.*, I, 3.
[56] Cicero, *De oratore* I, 239–40.

will agree.[57] *Loci communes* are, according to Aristotle, of great assistance to speakers because

the hearers are pleased to hear stated in general terms the opinion which they have already specially formed... Wherefore the speaker should endeavour to guess how his hearers formed their preconceived opinions and what they are, and then express himself in general terms in regard to them.[58]

The necessary condition of the rhetorical syllogism is that it draws its premises from the audience. In this sense it is regarded as 'self-persuasive'.[59] Similarly, Aristotle stresses in his discussion of metaphor that, whereas in poetry figures may be valued for their novelty, in rhetoric 'Metaphors must not be far-fetched, but we must give names to things that have none by deriving the metaphor from what is akin and of the same kind so that, as soon as it is uttered it is clearly seen to be akin.'[60] This rule is applied by Roman and humanist rhetoricians to their discussions of all rhetorical style. The virtues of style are that speech must be clear, appropriate (*accommodata*) and vivid. Both clarity and propriety are directed to what the audience find familiar: to accommodate (*accommodare*) means to fit or adapt one thing to another, to bring the subject within the values of the audience. To be vivid, the subject must be displayed 'in its living truth before the eyes of the mind'.[61] Quintilian states that 'we shall secure the vividness we seek if only our descriptions give the impression of truth, nay, we may even add fictitious incidents of the type that commonly occur'.[62] This vividness appeals to what is believed to be true: 'The mind is always readiest to accept

---

[57] On the heuristic character of the topics see Eleonore Stump, 'Dialectic and Aristotle's *Topics*', in *Boethius's de topicis differentiis*, ed. Eleonore Stump (Ithaca, 1978); and Eleonore Stump 'Topics' in *The Cambridge history of later medieval philosophy*, eds. Norman Kretzmann, Anthony Kenny and Jan Pinborg (Cambridge, 1982).

[58] Aristotle, 'Art' of rhetoric, II, xxi.2. On the nature of the *loci communes*, see also Cicero, *De inventione*, II, 47–8.

[59] See Lloyd Bitzer, 'Aristotle's Enthymeme revisited', in Keith V. Erickson, ed., *Aristotle: The classical heritage of rhetoric* (Metuchen, 1974). See also Cicero, *De inventione*, I, 53, on the character of inductive and deductive reasoning: 'In argumentation of this kind I think the first rule to lay down is that the statement which we introduce as a basis for analogy ought to be of such a kind that its truth must be granted. For a statement on the strength of which we expect a doubtful point to be conceded, ought not itself be doubtful.'

[60] Aristotle, 'Art' of rhetoric, III, ii.12. See Quintilian, *Institutio oratoria*, VIII, iii.73, for a paraphrase of Aristotle's position. The twentieth-century 'linguistic turn' bears some semblance to this classical theory of persuasion. Compare, for example, Wittgenstein on the use of public consensus to justify problematic norms; see Ludwig Wittgenstein, *On certainty*, tr. G. E. M. Anscombe and G. H. von Wright (Oxford, 1974).

[61] Quintilian, *Institutio oratoria*, VIII, iii.62.   [62] *Ibid.*, iii.70.

what it recognises to be true to nature.'[63] Once again Quintilian stresses that 'anything that is selected for the purpose of illuminating something else must itself be clearer than that which it is designed to illustrate'.[64] Such vivid displays, exploiting accepted truths, will arouse the emotions of the audience.

Renaissance commentators on rhetoric adopted these principles of persuasion. For Francis Bacon, the psychology of rhetoric was central to the Ciceronian insistence upon the complementary relation between reason and eloquence. Bacon noted that 'affection beholdeth merely the present' whereas 'reason beholdeth the future and sum of time'. It is the case, however, that 'the present filling the imagination more, reason is commonly vanquished'. The solution was that 'the force of eloquence and persuasion hath made things future and remote appear as present, then upon the revolt of the imagination reason prevaileth'.[65] John Donne, one of the Virginia Company's promoters, summarised this humanist understanding of rhetoric: 'Rhetorique will make absent and remote things present to your understanding.'[66]

The promoters of colonies frequently acknowledged this psychological mechanism of persuasion. Samuel Purchas commented upon the role of rhetorical style in this context:

To sensual Man, nothing more sensible and playne, nothing more piercing and powerful, nothing more pleasing and insinuating, nothing more settling and memorable, nothing more accommodate to common use, then heavenly things in borrowed liveries of metaphorical speech.[67]

He stresses the traditional virtues of style – to teach, to please and to move – while emphasising that metaphor should accommodate the foreign to common use. The Reverend Richard Eburne, who wrote promoting Newfoundland colonies, was even more explicit about the need to appeal to the values of his particular audience: 'my whole purpose and intent is...to do some good this way for and with the meaner sort of our people, to whose capacity, therefore, it was fit and, more than fit, necessary that I should fit

---

[63] *Ibid.*, iii.71. Montaigne's injunction that men should only write of what they have experienced has been seen as a form of anti-rhetoric (see Mary Fuller, 'Ralegh's fugitive gold', in *New World encounters*, ed. Stephen Greenblatt (Berkeley, 1993), p. 223). This opposition between rhetoric and experience ignores the rhetorical commonplace that an orator must make the audience see the matter addressed. In discussing *evidentia* and the description of things, Erasmus observes that 'To give a satisfactory account of all these things not only requires skill and imagination, but it is very helpful to have seen with your own eyes what you wish to depict' (Desiderius Erasmus, *De copia*, in *Collected works of Erasmus*, ed. Craig R. Thompson, (Toronto, 1978–), XXIV, p. 582).
[64] Quintilian, *Institutio oratoria*, VIII, iii.73.   [65] Bacon, cited in Shuger, *Sacred rhetoric*, p. 195.
[66] Donne, cited in *ibid.*   [67] Samuel Purchas, *The kings towre* (London, 1623), pp. 25–6.

and frame my speech'.[68] Similarly, we have already seen Donne, in his sermon to the Virginia Company, claim that 'by way of exhortation' he did not 'propose forreigne, but your own Examples'. Thomas Churchyard dedicated his exhortation to the English nation to colonise, written as an encomium on the voyages of Martin Frobisher, to Thomas Wilson, Privy Councillor and author of the Ciceronian *Arte of rhetorique*. As a rhetorician Wilson would have appreciated Churchyard's stipulation that 'I have chosen familiar things to write upon ... presenting to the people that whiche they are beste acquainted withal.'[69] Again, here we must return to the question of whether an audience that included what Eburne called 'the meaner sort' would have been exposed to the *studia humanitatis*. It is clear that rhetoricians were directly concerned with the means of successfully addressing such audiences.

As Eburne's comment suggests, above all the orator must be a student of the character of man. He must study the different kinds of emotions. While not necessarily making a science of this study, he must possess a shrewd ability to exploit the emotions of the audience before him:

> Who indeed does not know that the orator's virtue is pre-eminently manifested either in rousing men's hearts to anger, hatred, or indignation or in recalling them from these same passions to mildness and mercy? Wherefore the speaker will not be able to achieve what he wants by his words, unless he has gained profound insight into the characters of men, and the whole range of human nature, and those motives whereby our souls are spurred on or turned back.[70]

There was no claim in this theory of persuasion that an emotional attachment to the familiar arises from a failure to comprehend what is unfamiliar. The appeal to the familiar was based not upon a failure of the author's comprehension, nor upon the author anticipating the audience's failure of comprehension, but upon the author's judgement of what would move the emotions of the audience. The audience may readily apprehend that they should invest in or travel to Virginia, they may regard this as a rational choice (having had both the profit and virtue of the enterprise demonstrated to them), but they still may not act because of the attachments of their affections, or because they are afraid. They must therefore

---

[68] Richard Eburne, *A plaine pathway to plantations* [1624], ed. Louis B. Wright (Ithaca, 1962), pp. 7–8.

[69] Thomas Churchyard, *A prayse and reporte of Maister Martyne Forboishers voyage to meta incognita* (London, 1578), sigs. Aiii.v–Aiiii.r.

[70] Cicero, *De oratore*, I, 53. See also *De oratore*, I, 223: 'He ought to feel the pulses of every class, time of life, and degree, and to taste the thoughts and feelings of those before whom he is pleading.' On the heuristic character of rhetoric and the separate claims of philosophy and rhetoric, see also Nancy S. Struever, *The language of history in the Renaissance* (Princeton, 1970), pp. 5–39.

be moved by means of their emotions, and it is that which is familiar to them that will move their emotions.

Even if the audience could understand the alien environment they would not be likely to be moved by, or moved to act upon, that understanding. Here, then, we find a clear separation between epistemic and rhetorical shifts. If the promotional writers could discover a truth different from that held by their audience, they would continue to be constrained by the emotional appeal of what the audience held to be true. William Strachey makes this point in enquiring, in terms of a rhetorical *rogatio*, into what will move his audience to adventure to the New World: 'O our dull Ignorance, depraved wills, or Imperfection of Reason, or all three, how doe yee transport us?'[71]

While the orator must appeal to the familiar in order to persuade, this does not mean that he does not also seek a change in the audience's conception of the subject. The desire for such a change is a necessary condition for persuasion. The act of attempting to persuade initiates two impulses. On the one hand, the orator is attempting to stretch the minds of the audience to encompass something they had not previously held to be true. The other impulse is clearly introspective; the thing that is new is presented in terms of what is familiar. The audiences of Elizabethan and Jacobean authors promoting New World colonies either regarded that world as alien or were indifferent to it. The change sought in the minds of the audience by those authors is to bring them to the belief that the New World embraces the qualities that they value most in the Old. In *A plaine pathway to plantations*, Richard Eburne acknowledges that that process is fundamental to his aims: 'going into a strange place, men cannot but, as it were, naturally desire both to go and to be there with such as they know before and are formerly acquainted with'. 'This matter', he adds, 'is of that moment that it is the first thing and the greatest that troubles the mind of any when speech is made to them of departing hence into any new country, of dwelling in a foreign land.'[72]

---

[71] Strachey, *The historie of travel into Virginia Britannia*, p. 23. While the orator is psychologically motivated and concerned with the emotions, the ethnographer or natural historian, according to the classical distinction, addresses the intellect. Orators may well, however, draw upon both ethnography and natural history in demonstrating the advantages of their argument and in making their subject vivid. In his *Garden of eloquence* (London, 1577) Henry Peacham, for example, includes the figure of *topographia* 'an evident and true description of a place' and suggests Pliny as a source of examples (sig. P, 1r). In *De copia*, Erasmus similarly cites *topographia* under the 'Description of Places' and he also suggests Pliny. Erasmus also discusses amplification through the 'Description of Persons'. For Erasmus, these figures are analysed as means of *evidentia*, or making the material vivid: the term 'figure' is in itself a metaphor for this process of thrusting a matter before the eyes of the audience (p. 587).

[72] Eburne, *A plaine pathway to plantations*, pp. 88–89.

We have seen that it is the heuristic role of rhetorical *loci* to find the values of a particular audience. We have also seen that the *loci* of deliberative rhetoric were extensively employed in the tracts promoting colonies. It is through the manipulation of those ends that the promotional authors were able to accommodate their proposition to the values of their audience. The ends of honour and profit do not equally suit all audiences, all circumstances, or all within a particular audience. Classical and Renaissance rhetoricians acknowledge that the ends of honour and profit will frequently conflict. Cicero observes that 'differences of opinion arise either on the question of which of two alternatives is more expedient, or even supposing there is agreement about this, it is disputed whether the chief consideration should be integrity or expediency'.[73] Quintilian concurs that 'Often we shall again urge that honour must come before expediency' and that 'At other times on the other hand we prefer expediency to honour, as when we advise the arming of slaves in the Punic War.'[74] The principal factors the orator needed to consider in deciding how to deal with such conflicts were the opinions and character of the audience:

But we have still more often to consider personality with reference to what is becoming, and we must consider our own as well as that of those before whom the question is laid . . . For the minds of those who deliberate on any subject differ from one another . . . For when advice is asked by a number of persons it makes a considerable difference whether they are the senate or the people, the citizens of Rome or Fidenae, Greeks or barbarians, and in the case of single individuals whether we are urging Cato or Gaius Marius to stand for office, whether it is the elder Scipio or Fabius who is deliberating on his plan of campaign.[75]

Whereas honour will be appropriate to some of these audiences, profit will motivate others:

Further sex, rank, and age must be taken into account, though it is character that will make the chief difference. It is an easy task to recommend an honourable course to honourable men, but if we are attempting to keep men of bad character to the paths of virtue, we must take care not to seem to upbraid a way of life unlike

---

[73] Cicero, *De oratore*, II, 335. On the conflict of *honestas* and *utilitas*, see Cicero, *De inventione*, II, 174; *Rhetorica ad Herennium*, trans. and ed. Henry Caplan (Loeb Classical Library, London, 1954), III, iv.8–v.9; Cicero, *De officiis*, trans. Walter Miller (Loeb Classical Library, London, 1913), book 3; Wilson, *The arte of rhetorique*, pp. 89–90. This rhetorical conflict may be compared with the arguments of Stephen Greenblatt and Louis Montrose that the conflict between 'piety' and 'greed' in Ralegh's *Discoverie* is a struggle between 'mutually contradictory positions . . . whose incompatibility threatens fatally to undermine the manifest rhetorical intention of the work' (Greenblatt, *New World encounters*, p. xiv; and Montrose, 'The work of gender in the discourse of discovery'). Rather, however, than these tensions undermining rhetoric, rhetoricians argue that it is precisely the role of rhetoric to address and exploit such questions.

[74] Quintilian, *Institutio oratoria*, III, viii.30.   [75] *Ibid.*, III, viii.35–7.

our own. The minds of such an audience are not to be moved by discoursing on the nature of virtue, but by ... demonstration of the advantage that will accrue from such a policy.[76]

Honour is persuasive to honourable men, profit is persuasive to those whose concern is profit.

When urging the deliberative ends of honour and profit, the authors promoting colonies can be seen to heed Cicero and Quintilian's advice upon keeping decorum with the character of the audience. John Smith, for example, attaches particular interests to specific audiences: 'Religion above all things should move us, especially the Clergie, if we are religious, to shew our faith by our works ... Honor might move the Gentry, the valiant, and industrious, and the hope and assurance of wealth, all.'[77] Purchas bluntly pronounces that 'if Honour hath prevailed with honourable and higher spirits, we shall come laden with arguments of profit to presse meaner hands and hearts to the service of Virginia'.[78] Ralph Hamor devoted the first part of his advertisement 'to incourage personal Adventures'. He has attempted 'by worthy motives' to 'allure the heavie undertakers' 'for their owne reputations, the honour of God, and their King, and Countrey'. 'The worthier sort', he adds, 'I meane those nobles and others of that honourable counsell interested therein, need no spurre, their owne innate vertues drive them a pace.' Through this *paralipsis*, Hamor reminds those who would be noble that honour is their end. He then turns to an audience of different character whom he wishes to address in the remainder of the tract:

The merchant onely wants some feeling and present return of those commodities which he is persuaded the countrey affordeth: to them therefore I will address my speech, and if I may persuade them to be constant in their proceedings, some small time longer, the benefit will be the greater.[79]

The ends of honour and profit are also seen to conflict. Crashaw, for example, considers the problem of 'the uncertaintie of profit', answering 'I will not wrong you nor myselfe, in seeking to say much to so base an objection.' 'If there be any', he protests, 'that came in only or principally for profit, or any that would so come in, I wish the latter may never bee in, and the former out again.' He then bases this objection to profit, and the

---

[76] *Ibid.*, III, viii.38–9.
[77] John Smith, *The generall history of Virginia, New England, and the Summer Isles* (London, 1624), p. 221.
[78] Samuel Purchas, *Virginias Verger*, in Samuel Purchas, *Hakluytus posthumus or Purchas his pilgrimes*, 4 vols. (London, 1625), IV, p. 1816.
[79] Ralph Hamor, *A true discourse of the present estate of Virginia* (London, 1615), p. 25.

implicit conflict between profit and honour, in the perception that such a
motive is inappropriate to his audience: 'profit is not the principal end of
this action; if it were, what should so many of the Nobilitie, of the Gentry,
and especially of the Clergy have their hands in it? It is not fit for them to
be Merchants.'[80] Conversely, before an audience of merchants, John Smith
urges profit above all else. Smith leaves no doubt as to his intended audience,
nor his methods of targeting them. Of the publication of a former work, he
observes: 'I caused two or three thousand to be printed, one thousand . . . I
presented to each of the chief Companies in London at their Halls.'[81] Also
conscious of the possible conflict between profit and honour, Sir William
Alexander argues with a sensitivity, as Quintilian puts it, not to upbraid
the audience's way of life:

> howsoever the hope of Honour may flatter a generous spirit, there is no great
> appearance by this means to provide for a family, or for a Posteritie. And if we
> rightly consider the benefit that may arise by this enterprise abroad, it is not onely
> able to afford a sufficient meanes for their maintenance, who cannot conveniently
> live at home, by disburdening the Countrey of them, but it is able to enable them
> to deserve of their Countrey, by bringing unto it both Honour and Profit.[82]

Here Alexander employs the topic recommended by Cicero for reconciling
expediency with honour: 'in a case of this sort, too, when we seem to consult
our security, we shall be able to say with truth that we are concerned about
honour, since without security we can never attain to honour'.[83] In each
of these instances the authors were conscious of writing for a spectrum
of audiences which included the 'meaner sort'. They adjust the aims of
the enterprise to accommodate each of the projected audiences. They do
not, however, when appealing to the 'meaner sort' elevate expedience above
honour. They expect, as Alexander reveals, the lower orders to be moved
by a combination of honour and profit.

 The conflict between the ends of honour and profit was also shaped by
the experience of colonisation. Elizabethan authors, such as Ralegh, are
not afraid to promise huge profits arising from the emulation of Spanish
colonies. The repeated failure to establish such colonies, or to discover such
wealth, is reflected in a reluctance to test the credulity of the audience in the
Jacobean promotional literature. The emphasis upon profit is substituted
by even stronger appeals to civic virtue.[84] Crashaw, as we have seen, curses

---

[80] Crashaw, *A sermon*, sigs. G2r–v and G3v.   [81] Smith, *The generall history*, pp. 230 and 219.

[82] Alexander, *An encouragement to colonies*, p. 42.   [83] Cicero, *De inventione*, II, 174.

[84] On the opposition between civic virtue and wealth, see Skinner, *The foundations of modern political
thought*, 2 vols. (Cambridge, 1978), I, pp. 99, 149–50 and 162–5.

the pursuit of profit as 'base', and wishes those motivated by that pursuit to take no part. Similarly, Robert Gray praises the Virginia Council for having

undertaken so honourable a project, as all posterities shal blesse you and uphold your names and memories so long as the Sunne and Moone endureth: whereas they which preferre their money before vertue, their pleasure before honour, and their sensual security before heroical adventures, shall perish with their money, die with their pleasures, and be buried in everlasting forgetfulnes.[85]

Here Gray follows the commonplace of 'One who prefers the considerations of honour before expediency' recommended in the discussion of deliberative oratory in the *Rhetorica ad Herennium*: 'not he who is safe in the present, but he who lives honourably, lives safely – whereas he who lives shamefully cannot be secure forever'.[86]

We have seen that rhetoric provided the heuristic means to appeal to the values of a specific audience. The necessity for this act of persuasion arose from an uncertainty in the minds of the audience. There was certainly a deep awareness in the English promotion of New World colonies that the strangeness of that world represented the greatest obstacle to the proposed 'adventures'. Whitbourne acknowledged that the necessity for persuasion arose from the difficulty of inducing people to adventure into strange countries.[87] Sir William Alexander lamented of his *Nova Scotia* lease:

But the most wonderful thing of all is this, though now it be clearly discovered, that so few are willing to make use thereof; this doth chiefly proceed from want of knowledge, few being willing to adventure upon that where-with they are not acquainted by their owne experience.[88]

While rhetoric, however, began with the problem of what was uncertain for the audience, expressions of wonder also served a rhetorical purpose. The orator was expected not only to identify the interests of different audiences (those, for example, who pursue honour and those who pursue profit), but was expected to exploit what was antithetical to those interests. The orator would not only appeal, that is, to what was familiar, but would also exploit what was strange. A number of historians have seized upon expressions

---

[85] Robert Gray, *A good speed to Virginia* (London, 1609), sigs. A3r–v.

[86] *Rhetorica ad Herennium*, III, v.9. For further examples of this argument, and the commonplaces of courage to urge the pursuit of honour over profit, see Robert Johnson, *The new life of Virginea* (London, 1612), sigs. D4r–v; 'Nay, if losse of life befall you by this service . . . yet in this case too wee doubt not but you are resolved with constant courage'; Crashaw, *A sermon*, sig. F4r; and Gray, *A good speed to Virginia*, sig. B4v. On courage as a topic of the deliberative end of honour, see Cicero, *De inventione*, I, 159; *Rhetorica ad Herennium*, III, ii.3; and Wilson, *The arte of rhetorique*, pp. 87–8.

[87] Whitbourne, *A discovery and discourse of Newfoundland*, sig. Cr.

[88] Alexander, *An encouragement to colonies*, p. 41. See also Gray, *A good speed to Virginia*, sig. B2r.

of wonder in the New World literature as evidence of the difficulty of translating the experience of alien cultures and environments into familiar terms. The figure of wonder is taken as proof that authors writing about the New World used the familiar to translate the alien because they had reached their epistemic boundaries. According to Stephen Greenblatt, the expression of wonder 'depends upon a suspension or failure of categories and is a kind of paralysis, a stilling of the normal associative restlessness of the mind'.[89] For Greenblatt wonder is rhetorical, but it is a rhetoric of translation forced upon the author by the limits of his language. In rhetorical theory, however, wonder performs a role that derives from the psychology of the audience.

Perhaps the most dramatic of the accounts of wonder in the English accounts of the New World are given in the reports of the wreck of two ships from Gates' and Sommers' fleet for the resupply of Jamestown in 1609 upon the Bermudas, which shortly after were exploited by Shakespeare in *The Tempest*. All these accounts first 'remind' their audience that the Bermudas have always been reputed to be inhabited by devils and spirits and for this reason have always been shunned by sailors:

It may be some are afraid to come hither, because of the strange reports that have gone of these Islands; as that they are the Ilands of divels, and that heere are strange apparitions of divels, and fearefull thundering and lightening, as though Heaven and earth did meet together.[90]

The reports recount the terrifying wreck of Sommers and Gates upon the islands. These expressions of shock and wonder fulfil two textual purposes. The first, as Thomas Wilson had required, is to engage the attention of the audience. 'To make hearers attentive', according to Wilson, 'we maie promise them straunge newes.'[91] In doing so the orator will both express and provoke wonder: 'some straunge wounders maye call up their spirits' and 'if the tyme wil not serve for pleasaunt tales, it were good to tell some straunge thyng, some terrible wonder that they all may quake at the onely hearyng of the same'.[92] 'Boredom', advises Erasmus, 'can be dispelled or avoided' either by telling the audience that there is a threat to their security or with declarations such as 'And now you will hear something you have never heard before'.[93] 'The more unfamiliar the things are', he argues, 'the more pleasure the description will give and the longer one may dwell on it.'[94] Having thus given shape to the fears of the audience, the second role of

---

[89] Greenblatt, *Marvellous possessions*, pp. 19–20.
[90] Lewis Hughes, *A letter, sent into England from the Summer Ilands* (London, 1615), sig. A3v.
[91] Wilson, *The arte of rhetorique*, p. 212. Wilson is paraphrasing *Rhetorica ad Herennium*, I, 7–10.
[92] Wilson, *The arte of rhetorique*, pp. 219–20.   [93] Erasmus, *De copia*, p. 649.
[94] *Ibid.*, p. 588.

wonder is amplification of that image. As Wilson observes 'Thynges notable or straunge, helpe forward amplification.'[95] By inventing the unfamiliar the orator brings the audience into the same moral landscape as that proposition which he is persuading the audience to accept. The unfamiliar, as we shall see, is more easily translated into the familiar than indifference or boredom.

Closely associated with expressions of wonder in accounts of the New World are expressions of a failure of speech. These declarations are again taken by historians to be a sign of encounters with an incommensurable other. Speechlessness is implicit in the idea of the adventurers having reached their linguistic boundaries. The translation of unfamiliar to familiar is seen to be a necessary consequence of such failures.[96] A typical example is seen in Strachey's exclamation that: 'It is impossible for me, had I the voice of a Stentor, and expression of as many tongues, as his throate of voyces, to expresse the outcries and miseries' of those on board.[97] The expression of a failure of language is, however, yet another rhetorical trope. The trope is named *paralipsis* in the *Ad Herennium* and is described by Peacham in terms of a number of figures, and in particular by *aporia*, which he defines as 'when we shewe that wee doubt . . . what to say, or doe, in some straunge and doubtfull matter'.[98] These figures alert the audience to the extraordinary nature of the subject and enable us to 'say that we are passing by, or do not know, or refuse to say that which precisely now we are saying'.[99] Strachey, of course, also finds the voice for expressing, and for amplifying, the wonders he just claimed he cannot tell. The storm 'at length did beate all light from heaven; which like an hell of darknesse turned blacke upon us', 'fury added to fury', 'one storm urging a second more outrageous than the former', 'six and sometimes eight men were not enough to hold the whipstaffe in the steerage', 'the sea swelled above the clouds and gave battell unto Heaven. It could not be said to raine, the waters like whole Rivers did flood in ayre', 'Saint Elmo's fire' hovered about the masts.[100]

There are a number of figurative tools at the orator's disposal for the amplification of the wonderful or unfamiliar. We have seen that, for oratory to achieve its full effect and greatest height, for it to move the audience,

[95] Wilson, *The arte of rhetorique*, p. 247.
[96] The idea is reflected, for example, in Franklin's term 'inexpressibility' (Franklin, *Discoverers, explorers, settlers*, pp. 3–4). See also Greenblatt, *Marvellous possessions*, pp. 19–22; Lorraine Daston and Katherine Park, *Wonders and the order of nature, 1150–1750* (New York, 1998).
[97] Strachey, *A true repertory of the wracke and redemption of Sir Thomas Gates*, in Purchas, *Hakluytus posthumus*, IV, p. 1735.
[98] Peacham, *The garden of eloquence*, sigs. M1v–M2r. For *paralipsis* or *occultatio*, see *Rhetorica ad Herennium*, IV, 37; and Quintilian, *Institutio oratoria*, IX, iii.98.
[99] *Rhetorica ad Herennium*, IV, 37.
[100] Strachey, *A true repertory of the wracke and redemption of Sir Thomas Gates*, pp. 1735–7.

the matter should not merely be narrated but thrust before the eyes of the audience. Renaissance rhetoricians, including Erasmus and Peacham, follow Quintilian in recommending that in oratory, as Erasmus states, 'we fill in the colours and set it up like a picture to look at, so that we seem to have painted the scene rather than described it, and the reader seems to have seen rather than read'.[101] Strachey portrays the tempest and wreck through the figures of *evidentia* or 'vividness' that, as Quintilian observes, display the facts 'in their living truth to the eyes of the mind'.[102] In a passage quoted by Erasmus and Peacham, Quintilian expands his point explaining that if we wish to move and captivate the audience we do not merely state that a town was 'stormed', rather:

we expand all that the one word 'stormed' includes, we shall see the flames pouring from the house and temple, and hear the crash of falling roofs and one confused clamour blent of many cries: we shall behold some in doubt whither to fly, others clinging to their nearest and dearest in one last embrace, while the wailing of women and children and the laments of old men that the cruelty of fate should have spared them to see that day will strike upon our ears.[103]

Strachey follows this principle of augmentation in recounting the wonders of the tempest. Strikingly, when Peacham recounts Quintilian's example of *evidentia*, which he calls the figure *pragmatographia*, he concludes: 'To this figure belong the descriptions of warres, tempests, shipwrackes... and of all such like.'[104]

The rhetorical exercise in making the subject vivid accounts for the formulaic repetition of the marvels of the wreck upon the Bermudas, such that some authors appear even to lift their descriptions from rhetoricians' examples of *evidentia*. Lewis Hughes recounts the story of how Gates and Sommers

had their ship so shaken and torn with a cruel tempest, as she received so much water as covered to tire [two tiers] of Hogsheads, above the ballast, so as men stood up to the middles with buckets and kettles to baile out water, & continually pumped for three daies and three nights together.[105]

---

[101] See Erasmus, *De copia*, pp. 577–8; and Peacham, *The garden of eloquence*, sig. A3r, and sigs. O4v–P1r where he refers to this function as the figure '*Pragmatographia*, a description of thinges, whereby we do as plainly describe any thing by gathering togeather all the circumstaunces belonging unto it, as if it were moste lively paynted out in colloures, and set forth to be seene.'

[102] Quintilian, *Institutio oratoria*, VIII, iii.61–2.   [103] *Ibid.*, VIII, iii.68–9.

[104] Peacham, *The garden of eloquence*, sig. P1r. See also sig. A3r: 'By figures he [the orator] may make his speech as cleare as the noone day: or contrarywise... he may stirre up stormes, & troublesome tempestes.'

[105] Hughes, *A letter... from the Summer Ilands*, sigs. [A,4]r–v.

Exhausted, the men resign themselves to death and take their leave of each other: 'them that had comfortable waters fetcht them out, and dranke one to another, taking their last leave one of another'. We may compare this last embrace with Peacham's translation of Quintilian 'others hang on their friendes, to bid them farewell for ever'.[106] Jourdain's account of the tempest recites the same commonplace of the final exchange of farewells.[107] Yet another report portrays the scene at length, again borrowing from Quintilian's instance of how to represent such a disaster, for example in the wailing of women: 'an Egyptian night of three daies perpetual horror; the women lamented; the hearts of the passengers failed'.[108]

Having vividly portrayed the wreck upon the Bermudas, having brought to life the audience's nightmare of what might be entailed by the Virginian voyage, these writers then transport their audience to the discovery that the Bermudas in fact embody all that they most value. The adventurers discover:

the hidden and long concealed truth, touching the state of the Barmuda Ilands ... the Barmuda Islands are not only accessible and habitable, but also fertile, fruitfull, plentifull, and a safe, secure, temperate, rich, sweet and healthfull habitation for Man, and especially for English bodies.[109]

From islands of devils the Bermudas are revealed to be ideal not only for the habitation of all men but in particular for Englishmen or the audience itself.

The shift from the strange to the familiar is not, however, entirely linear in this promotional literature. In rhetoric the orator also learns to attack the opposition case. It is necessary, that is, for the orator to attempt the redescription not only of the strange into the familiar, but also to attempt the redescription of the familiar, in so far as it obstructs the proposition, into the strange or base. We shall, according to the discussion of deliberative rhetoric in *Rhetorica ad Herennium*:

show that what our opponent calls justice is cowardice, and sloth, and perverse generosity; what he has called wisdom we shall term impertinent, babbling, and offensive cleverness; what he declares to be temperance we shall declare to be inaction and lax indifference; what he has named courage we shall term the reckless temerity of the gladiator.[110]

---

[106] Peacham, *The garden of eloquence*, sig. O4v.
[107] Sylvester Jourdain, *A discovery of the Bermudas* (London, 1610), pp. 4–7.
[108] *A true declaration of the estate of the colonie in Virginia* (London, 1610), pp. 21–6.
[109] William Crashaw, ed., *A plaine description of the Bermudas, now called the Sommer Ilands* (London, 1613), p. 3.
[110] *Rhetorica ad Herennium*, III, iii.6.

It is necessary not only to prove that the proposition which concerns some uncertainty in the audience's mind is in fact consistent with their beliefs, but also to prove that what your opponent – or the audience, in their resistance – holds up as certain is in fact undesirable, foreign or uncertain. For Robert Gray, such attachments are the chief obstacle to the settlement of Virginia: 'neither is it necessary for anie man to beleeve reports, though probable, nor to follow strange projects be they never so likely, so long as he hath home inbred hopes to relie upon, and assured certainties to satisfie his future expectation'.[111] There are, again, a number of tools at the orator's disposal to perform the task of unsettling the familiar. These include the figure of *meiosis*, but foremost among such devices in Renaissance thought, as Quentin Skinner has stressed, is the figure of *paradiastole*.[112]

Eburne's attack upon the certainties of home is blunt:

> Be not too much in love with that country wherein you were born, that country which bearing you, yet cannot breed you, but seemeth and is indeed weary of you. She accounts you a burden to her and encumbrance of her. You keep her down, you hurt her and make her poor and bare; and, together with your own, you work and cause, by tarrying within her, her misery and decay, her ruin and undoing...

The audience discover that what was familiar and certain only appeared to be so. Having eroded the emotional ties that hold the audience from adventuring, Eburne then transports the familiar from the concrete to the abstract: 'And if you will needs live in England, imagine all that to be England where Englishmen, where English people, you with them, and they with you, do dwell.'[113]

In a similar fashion, William Symonds undermines his audience's sense of security in their families, their occupations and any faith they may have in the benevolence of their country, because he sees each of these 'certainties' as a barrier to 'adventuring'. He argues:

> I am not ignorant, that many are not willing to goe abroad and spread the gospel, in this most honourable and christian voyage of the Plantation of Virginia their reasons are diverse according to their wits. One saith England is a sweete country. True indeede... but nothing so fruitfull, as Virginia... O but, saith another, my kindred would not be forsaken. Kindred? What kindred?... Atheists and

---

[111] Gray, *A good speed to Virginia*, sig. B2r.
[112] For the figures *meiosis* and *paradiastole*, see Peacham, *The garden of eloquence*, sig. N4v. For a discussion of these figures, see Quentin Skinner, 'Thomas Hobbes: rhetoric and the construction of morality', in *Proceedings of the British Academy*, 76 (1991); and Skinner, *Reason and rhetoric in the philosophy of Hobbes*.
[113] Eburne, *A plaine pathway to plantations*, pp. 11–12.

Papists...have sowed such cockell among our wheat, that in many places a man is in no such perill to be cheated and cosened, if not murthered and poisoned, as among his own kindred that are affected that way...

Having continued in this vein to find arguments that arouse his various possible audiences, Symonds then uses the figure of *evidentia* to amplify the misery of England. The shopkeeper 'grinds the face' of the 'honest poore labourer'. The 'metal man' cannot keep his family from the almes box. And the poore woman, with children at her knee, works day and night with her needle 'deluding the bitterness of her life with sweet songs'. She sings: 'Helpe Lorde, for good and godly men doe perish and decay...And when the week is ended, she can hardly earne salt for her water gruel to feede upon the Sunday. Many such sweets are in England.'[114] The vivid portrayal of corruption undermines the audience's emotional attachment to home.

Like Eburne, Symonds repeatedly balances the decay of England with the seeming 'strangeness' of the New World, where he finds the lost prosperity and virtue of old England can be revived:

And so here is an answere to a third objection, which some doe make: What should a man do abroad? A man would willingly keepe the poore reputation and respect he hath. If I go out of my Country, I shall be but swallowed up among strangers... The Lord answereth this objection thus. Feare not 'Abram, I will bee thine exceeding great rewarde', I will by thee doe so great things in a strange place, that thy name shall be remembered, as my name, which I will put upon thee. Sure it is very true, that manie a man, while he staieth at home, liveth in obscuritie, as in the darkest night, though his vertues and worth deserve better respect...Get abroad where vertue is skant, and there, by the advancing thy wisdome and vertue, thou shalt bee more eminent and famous in a yeare, then at home half of thy ranke shall bee all their daies: hidden vertue is neglected, but abroade it is magnified.[115]

Symonds inverts the location of the audience's fear of the unknown. The certainties of home are shown to be illusions, and the unknown state of this 'strange land' is found to be the blank space where these certainties can be revived.

There is a common figurative shift in the move from uncertainty to certainty and, in the case of opposition, in the move from certainty to uncertainty. In both cases the audience is transported from the physical

---

[114] William Symonds, *Virginia* (London, 1609), pp. 16–22. See also Robert Copland, *Virginia's God be thanked* (London, 1622), p. 34, who appears to paraphrase Symonds in establishing the same argument. Gray, as we have seen, is conscious that it is not 'necessarie for anie man...to follow strange projects...so long as he hath home inbred hopes to relie upon' He then argues that these 'assured certainties' existed only in the past. Now 'there is neither preferment nor employment in our countrey' (*A good speed to Virginia*, sigs. B2r–B3r).

[115] Symonds, *Virginia*, pp. 31–2.

and temporal to the moral and spiritual. The familiar is located in the abstract. The audience are detached from their material moorings. Above all, the shift from physical to moral enables the author to locate certainty in a sphere which is itself not affected by or is, rather, enhanced by physical transportation.[116]

The arguments that seek to unsettle the certainties that hold the audience from adventuring appear to be addressed to those who might adventure in person, in particular, rather than to potential investors. Many members of that audience would not, however, have possessed the grammar-school or university education that informed the authors' arguments. We must question, therefore, whether these arguments or the rhetorical frame of honour and profit, drawn from Academic moral philosophy, could be appreciated by that audience. It is important to note that many yeomen possessed a grammar-school or equivalent education. Moreover, it is striking that a notoriously disproportionate number of the members of early colonising ventures were gentlemen. Karen Kupperman observes that: 'Gentlemen... were six times as numerous proportionally in Virginia as in England.'[117] While taking both these facts into consideration, however, it is clear that an increasing proportion of those who adventured in person were of the 'common sort'. To understand the effectiveness of humanist rhetorical promotion it is also important to remember the close relation we have discussed between humanism and reformed religion. Through the introduction of deliberative rhetoric into the sermon, the vocabulary and values of classical rhetoric had become familiar to a broad audience. Classical rhetoric was particularly attractive to reformers because they believed it had the power to move not just the educated but all audiences. The authors promoting colonies employed the tools of the *studia humanitatis* to reach all these audiences including the 'common sort'. Humanism, that is, was not a barrier between the author and a 'popular' audience but was precisely the basis upon which authors were able to reach that audience.

PLAIN STYLE AND 'ASIATIC' CORRUPTION

One of the strongest arguments for finding the beginnings of liberal individualism and capitalism in early modern English writing on the New

---

[116] In this spirit, Donne's advice to the Virginia Company is first to seek a spiritual kingdom and not a temporal kingdom; see Donne, *A sermon... preach'd to the honourable company of the Virginian plantation*, pp. 11–13.

[117] Karen Kupperman, *Settling with the Indians* (London, 1980), p. 17. Many of the early reports complain of the burden of these men upon the colony; see John Smith, *A map of Virginia* (Oxford, 1612), pp. 37–9; T. Abbay and William Symonds, ed., *The proceedings of the English colonie in Virginia* (Oxford, 1612), sig. A2r.

World has been the use of the 'plain style' of writing by the authors of that literature. As Debora Shuger has observed, 'The relation of the plain style to the rise of modern science and modern individualism has frequently been remarked.'[118] The rhetoric of plain style which gathered pace in the sixteenth century is said to have made possible the expression of a 'self-conscious individuality', to have signalled 'the shift from communal to private', to have encouraged the 'diagrammatic and analytic functions of language in print culture' and to have provided the language of capitalist commerce.

Theories of plain style opposed the excessive use of ornament in language, representing it as florid and overdressed. They recommended a plain and simple style of speaking. This movement gathered impetus from the reforms of French rhetorician and logician Peter Ramus who removed invention and judgement from the art of rhetoric, arguing they were properly the province of dialectic. This reform encouraged the analytical separation of thought from language. Thus arguments for plain style demanded that orators should use no more words than things. These arguments were famously articulated by Francis Bacon and later by Thomas Sprat. Bacon criticised the previous generations for rhetorical excess:

For men began to hunt more after words than matter; more after the choiceness of the phrase, and the round and clean composition of the sentence, and the sweet falling of the clauses, and the varying and illustration of their works with tropes and figures, than after the weight of matter, worth of subject, soundness of argument, life of invention or depth of judgement.[119]

Sprat described the scientific style of the Royal Society in the same terms, praising its fellows for having returned 'to the primitive purity, and short-ness, when men deliver'd so many things, almost in an equal number of words'.[120]

Historians have argued that these principles of style were employed by sixteenth- and seventeenth-century writers on the New World and have linked that style to the individualism and possessiveness that they argue is found in those authors. Anthony Pagden, for example, notes that Samuel

---

[118] Shuger, *Sacred rhetoric*, p. 8. The classic study of plain style and the 'modern' mind is Morris Croll, *'Attic' and Baroque prose style: Essays by Morris Croll*, ed. Max Patrick and Robert O. Evans (Princeton, 1966). See also G. L. Hendrickson, 'The origin and meaning of the ancient characters of style', *American Journal of Philology*, 26 (1905); Wilbur Samuel Howell, *Logic and rhetoric in England, 1500–1700* (Princeton, 1956); Walter J. Ong, *Ramus, method, and the decay of dialogue* (Cambridge, Mass., 1958). For an exploration of the theme in an early modern colonial context, see Perry Miller, *The New England mind: The seventeenth century* (New York, 1939).

[119] Cited in Skinner, *Reason and rhetoric in the philosophy of Hobbes*, p. 273.   [120] *Ibid.*, pp. 361–2.

Purchas claimed that most of the authors he collected in his *Hakluytus posthumus* of 1625 had written without 'art', 'each Traveler' merely 'relating what is the kind that he hath seene'. According to Pagden 'It was in this way, by detaching the "speculator" from the "observer", that America, and more significantly the Americans, were finally incorporated into something resembling the original Baconian project'.[121] A crucial passage that has led historians in this direction has been Montaigne's claim in *On cannibals* that his simple servant was his principal source of information on the New World. According to Montaigne the simplicity of his servant was the basis of the reliability of his descriptions:

for clever people observe more things and more curiously, but they interpret them... They never show you things as they are, but bend and disguise them according to the way they have seen them... We need a man either very honest, or so simple that he has not the stuff to build up false inventions... Such was my man... So I content myself with his information, without inquiring what the cosmographers say about it.[122]

Reading this passage, Stephen Greenblatt argues that

In the period's travel literature, the texts written by those who claim to have seen the new lands for themselves, it is style that plays the authenticating and legitimating role played by Montaigne's servant. For the most part the style is humble, unimaginative, uninventive, and hence by implication reliable.[123]

In support of this argument Greenblatt also cites Purchas claiming: 'I mention Authors sometimes of meane qualitie... for the meanest have sense to observe that which themselves see, more certainly then the contemplations and Theory of the more learned.'[124] For Pagden this style is seminal to empirical science and commerce; for Greenblatt – who is concerned with the reification of the wondrous in these texts – it is the conduit of possession.

The image which historians appear to accept of writers on the New World as simple men who write in a plain style does not always hold true. Purchas praises William Strachey's report on the wreck upon the Bermudas – which Shakespeare ransacked for *The Tempest* – for his 'copious discourse' and for having written in 'Rhetorics full sea and spring tide'. Purchas was himself generally purple in his prose. But on the whole the evidence for the use of plain style in the New World narratives is overwhelming. In 1609 Richard Rich, a relative of Robert Rich, second earl of Warwick (a leader of the Virginia Company), and a soldier in the Jamestown colony,

---

[121] Anthony Pagden, *European encounters with the New World: From Renaissance to Romanticism* (New Haven, 1993), p. 85.
[122] Cited in Greenblatt, *Marvellous possessions*, p. 146–7.   [123] *Ibid.*, p. 147.   [124] *Ibid.*, p. 146.

published an account in verse of his experience in the colony. Yet despite
his pedigree and his decision to write in verse, Rich appeals to the quality,
attributed by Montaigne to his servant, that he is a simple man: 'I am a
Soldier, blunt and plaine, and so is the phrase of my newes.'[125] John Smith,
a governor of Jamestown in its first years, makes precisely the same claim
in his *General history of Virginia, New England and the Summer Isles*: 'The
style of a soldier', he declares, 'is not eloquent.'[126] Plainness is more fitting
to the martial virtues.

John Mason, a ship's captain, was appointed the second governor of
the Newfoundland Company's Cupid's Cove colony in 1615.[127] In 1620 he
published his *Brief discourse of the new-found-land* which he claimed was
'unpolished and rude bearing the countries badge where it was hatched,
merely clothed with plainesse and trueth'.[128] Sir Walter Ralegh, another
ship's captain, similarly argued that his *Discoverie of . . . Guiana* of 1596 was
written 'without the defence of art . . . I have studied neither phrase, forme,
nor fashion'.[129]

To disguise the presence of rhetoric was, of course, one of the first rec-
ommendations of rhetorical textbooks, but these disavowals of eloquence
were also essential to being seen to be plain – or 'blunt and plaine' as Rich
described himself. The badge of plain style is found throughout this literature. Little is known about the Reverend Richard Eburne, a west country
preacher and author of *A plaine pathway to plantations*, one of the most
exhaustive and elaborate tracts promoting colonisation published in 1624.
But Eburne repeatedly insists upon the text as 'these plaine . . . labours of
mine'.[130] And we have seen that Purchas, one of the most florid of the
promoters, claimed that there was 'nothing more sensible and playne . . .
nothing more accommodate to common use, then heavenly things in borrowed liveries of metaphorical speech'.[131]

It has been well documented that the claim to a plain style was particularly
valued by Puritans and the claim is accordingly found in the title of the
puritan Reverend Lewis Hughes' *Plaine and true relation of the Bermudas* of
1616.[132] The Reverend William Crashaw, who acted as a kind of master of

[125] Richard Rich, *Newes from Virginia* (London, 1610), sigs. A3r–v.
[126] *The General History of Virginia, New England, and the Summer Isles*, sig. Ar.
[127] Cell, *Newfoundland discovered*, pp. 12–13.
[128] John Mason, *A brief discourse of the new-found-land* (London, 1622), reprinted in Cell, *Newfoundland discovered*, p. 89.
[129] Ralegh, *The discoverie . . . of Guiana*, sig. A3v.
[130] Eburne, *A plaine pathway to plantations*, pp. 4 and 7–8.
[131] Purchas, *The kings towre*, pp. 25–6.
[132] On Puritans and plain style, see Miller, *The New England mind*.

ceremonies for the Virginia Company, had mixed in the flourishing puritan circle in Cambridge in the 1590s when he had become a fellow of St John's College under the patronage of the master, Dr William Whitaker. William Whitaker was one of the leaders of the puritan circle. Another leader of that circle was William Perkins, the prominent exponent of the plain style in preaching and author of the one the first arts of sacred rhetoric, *The art of prophesying* of 1592, to be published in England.[133] When Perkins died, Crashaw was appointed as an editor of his collected works that were published in 1603.[134] Apart from publishing his own sermon promoting the Virginian colony in 1610, Crashaw was also the editor of Alexander Whitaker's *Good newes from Virginia*. Whitaker was the son of Crashaw's former patron, the master of St John's College. In his preface to Whitaker's treatise Crashaw acknowledges that Whitaker could 'have adorned it' had he wished 'for I know (and so doe others that know him) hee is able to have written it in Latine or Greeke, and so to have decked it for phrase and stile, and other ornaments of learning and language, as might shew him no unworthy sonne of so worthy a father'. And yet, Crashaw observes, what 'hee hath sent us' is 'this plaine, but pithie and godly exhortation'.[135]

These claims to plain style were not confined to Puritans. George Percy, brother to Henry Percy, the earl of Northumberland, and a soldier in Virginia claimed that in his report he did not 'intend to use any eloquent style'.[136] Stephen Parmenius, a Hungarian Protestant humanist in exile at Oxford was employed as the voyage 'orator' in Sir Humphrey Gilbert's final and disastrous attempt to colonise Newfoundland in 1583. He drowned with Gilbert when the pinnace the *Squirrel* was swamped off the coast of Newfoundland, but not before he had the opportunity to send off a letter from St John's harbour in which he claimed not to have the 'leisure...to vary and multiply words'.[137] This distancing from leisure, as we shall see, was vital to the spirit of the claim to plain style.

It is, of course, well known that theories of plain style found their origins in classical disputes between Attic and Asiatic oratory. I shall argue that

---

[133] Shuger, *Sacred rhetoric*, p. 69.

[134] H. C. Porter, *The inconstant savage: England and the North American Indian 1500–1660* (London, 1979), p. 362.

[135] Whitaker, *Good newes from Virginia*, sigs. A3v and Cr. For the claim to employ few words, see Whitbourne, *A discovery and discourse of Newfoundland*, sig. Bv; Peckham, *A true report*, p. 704; Abbay and Symonds, *Proceedings of the English colonie in Virginia*, sig. A2r; Hamor, *A true discourse of the present estate of Virginia*, p. 1.

[136] George Percy, *A true relacyon of the procedeings and occurrentes of momente which have hapned in Virginia* [c.1625], in *Virginia; Four personal narratives*, p. 261.

[137] Parmenius in Hakluyt, *The principal navigations*, pp. 697–9. See also, Stephen Parmenius, *The new found land of Stephen Parmenius*, ed. David B. Quinn (Toronto, 1972).

the concern of promoters of New World colonies to identify themselves as plain speaking was motivated by those classical disputes and not by Baconian empiricism or proto-liberal individualism. Classical and humanist rhetorical textbooks place the plain style among two or three, or sometimes an indefinite, number of styles of oratory. Most of these textbooks would recommend the use of the style that was in decorum with the circumstances; thus the grand style would be inappropriate in the classroom as much as the plain style would have been inappropriate to Pericles' funeral oration. Nevertheless, controversy attached to the question of which style to employ.

When he was nearing the end of his career, Cicero was attacked by Calvus and Brutus for using what they described as an 'Asiatic' style. He left his record of these disputes in his last two works: the *Brutus*, and the *Orator* written as a reply to the charge. The charge was that his language was too rich in ornament, studied in its rhythms and excessive in emotional appeals. The school of oratory to which Calvus and Brutus belonged demanded a return to what they described as 'Attic' purity. Supposedly basing their principles upon fourth- and fifth-century Greek orators, particularly Lysias, Thucydides and Xenophon, they prescribed a plain and clear style with a minimum of ornament and an emphasis upon instruction rather than stirring the emotions.

What generated this dispute was an anxiety in Greek rhetorical schools that the purity of the Greek language was being corrupted by the introduction of foreign words and diction. One focus of that anxiety was the impact of Alexander's conquering armies in Asia upon Greek culture. Plutarch claimed that Alexander was disturbed by the 'fineness and delicacy' of his armies after their conquest of Persia, that they became accustomed to lying in 'beds soft and delicate'. In the words of Thomas North's 1579 translation of the *Life of Alexander*, Alexander reproaches his men: 'Are you ignorant, that the type of honor in all our victories consisteth, in scorning to doe that which we see them doe, whom we have vanquished and overcome?'[138] And yet, after a further passage of time, Alexander 'beganne to apparel him selfe after the facion of the barbarous people', a sight which 'grieved the Macedonians much'.[139] These anxieties were readily transferred from Greece to Rome. In Cicero's *Brutus* Pomponius argued that:

[138] Plutarch, *The lives of the noble Grecians and Romans*, trans. Thomas North (Oxford, 1928), pp. 220–1.
[139] *Ibid.*, p. 226.

The ground or so to speak the foundation, on which oratory rests is, you see, a faultless and pure Latin diction...But lapse of time has brought about some deterioration in this respect both at Rome and in Greece. For as to Athens, so to our city, there has been an influx of many impure speakers coming from different places.[140]

In Tacitus' *Dialogue on oratory* we find that some of the criticism of Cicero stuck. The figure of Aper comments: 'Cicero himself, as is well known, had his detractors: they thought him turgid and puffy, wanting in conciseness, inordinately exuberant and redundant – in short, anything but Attic.'[141] Calvus thought him 'flabby', and Brutus, according to Tacitus, believed Cicero to possess that most Asiatic of qualities: he was, that is, 'emasculate'.[142]

These concerns were in fact just part of a far greater anxiety, that the conquests of Rome would produce a wealth and an effeminate and 'Asiatic' luxury which would corrupt the martial virtues upon which the very greatness of the Republic had been established in the first place. This was precisely the diagnosis that Roman moralists such as Sallust and Juvenal gave for the fall of the Republic. Sallust describes an unstoppable lust for the spoils of victory and armies taught to covet 'Asiatic' luxury.[143] He presents this decline in the *War with Catiline* in which he also describes Catiline, one of the chief agents of destruction, as a man of great eloquence but little wisdom. The 'Asiatic' corruption of oratory is but a part, albeit a central part, of the corruption through which empire threatens citizenship.

I would argue that it is in this context that the English Renaissance revival of plain style must be placed; within the corresponding English revival of civic thought in which luxury and wealth are represented as dangerous to the pursuit of the common good. Given the role played by empire in both Greece and Rome in the creation of 'Asiatic' luxury, English promoters were particularly alert to the possibility of corruption arising from the acquisition of New World territories. They were careful not to use the language of empire when describing the planned colonies and proposed instead the foundation of new 'commonwealths' that would be separate from the English commonwealth, but under the English crown. Given

---

[140] Cicero, *Brutus*, trans. G. L. Hendrickson (Cambridge, Mass., 1939), 258. See also Cicero, *Orator*, trans. H. M. Hubbell (Cambridge, Mass., 1939).

[141] Tacitus; *A dialogue on oratory* (Cambridge, Mass., 1970), 18.   [142] *Ibid.*

[143] *Sallust*, trans. J. C. Rolfe (London, 1921), xii.1, see also x–xii. See also Quentin Skinner, *Liberty before liberalism* (Cambridge, 1998), p. 64; David Armitage, *The ideological origins of the British empire* (Cambridge, 2000), pp. 126–8.

the role played by empire in the 'Asiatic' corruption of Greek and Roman language, the use of plain style in the business of founding and conserving those new commonwealths was essential to maintaining the integrity of civic virtues. While it has been remarked that the use of plain style by these authors (and, indeed, Renaissance plain style generally) was a step toward individualism, possession and a commercial empire, the authors themselves would have understood Atticism as something completely opposite. The extensive claims to an Attic or plain style were a barometer of the anxiety about the corruption that the new colonies could generate and a rejection of wealth and profit as the motivation, or even as a desirable consequence, of establishing those colonies.

CHAPTER 5

Law and history

From the 1970s historians began to emphasise that the English colonised America not by settlement but conquest. The lands of Amerindians were seized by force of arms, just as the Spanish had conquered Mexico and Peru.[1] More recent studies have emphasised that English colonisers were uncomfortable with the language of conquest and employed natural law arguments that were more appropriate to agricultural settlers than to conquistadors.[2] It is argued that these natural law claims underpinned the development of a commercial ideology of expansion. The use of the argument of *terra nullius*, for example, is said to reveal assumptions about the exploitation of the land that would underpin the expansion of commerce in the seventeenth and eighteenth centuries. Each of these interpretations, whether emphasising conquest or natural law, has drawn material from the early modern English tracts justifying colonisation to support their argument. Both would have that literature to be more coherent than it is. In fact, English promoters of colonies in the first century of colonising plans employed a whole battery of frequently conflicting arguments. These arguments were not only incoherent between authors and across time, but often the same author would resort to a range of mutually contradictory arguments.[3] In this chapter I consider not only the use of ideas associated with the justification of agricultural colonies and conquest but also two arguments concerning the justification of colonies which have been ignored by historians. First,

---

[1] See, for example, Francis Jennings, *The invasion of America: Indians, colonialism, and the cant of conquest* (New York, 1975); and Robert A. Williams, Jr, *The American Indian in western legal thought: The discourses of conquest* (New York, 1990).

[2] See, for example, Anthony Pagden, *Lords of all the world: Ideologies of empire in Spain, Britain and France c.1500–c.1800* (New Haven, 1995); Richard Tuck, *The rights of war and peace: Political thought and the international order from Grotius to Kant* (Oxford, 1999).

[3] Cf. John T. Juricek, 'English claims in North America to 1660: a study in legal and constitutional history' (Ph.D., University of Chicago, 1970); John T. Juricek, 'English territorial claims in North America under Elizabeth and the early Stuarts', *Terræ Incognitæ*, 7 (1975), pp. 7–22; Christopher Tomlins, 'The legal cartography of colonization, the legal polyphony of settlement: English intrusions on the American mainland in the 17th century', *Law and Social Inquiry*, 26, 2 (2001), pp. 315–72.

promoters employed legal humanism equally if not more than natural law and conquest to justify colonies. These justifications rested upon historical record and, while a history of involvement in America has frequently been noted to have been used to justify colonies, the legal humanistic context for understanding those claims has not been appreciated. Significantly, and in contrast to the use of natural law, legal humanism did not directly support a commercial understanding of colonisation. Secondly, and crucially, promoters routinely denied any intention of taking possession of others' lands (even while justifying the possibility of possession); yet these denials have been treated simply as cynical or have been passed over (presumably because they do not fit the picture of a possessive European expansion). The incoherence in the justification of colonies revealed a deep neo-Roman anxiety that expansion was a cause of corruption (it is this anxiety rather than cynicism which underlay the denials of possession). The legal arguments employed by English promoters of colonies were not being used simply to justify possession; they address an anxiety about foreign possessions, an anxiety which is most clearly revealed in their denials that the colonisers have any intention to possess the Amerindians' property.

RELIGIOUS JUSTIFICATIONS

Promoters of the foundation of new colonies were concerned to justify the colonies, or projected colonies, against two claims: first, against the rights of indigenous societies in America; and second against the claims of other European nations. A religious mission was frequently cited first among the justifications of colonisation and was directed in particular against the claims of the indigenous inhabitants. In Hakluyt's *Discourse of western planting*, the first chapter is devoted to a proof 'That this western discoverie will be greately for the inlargemente of the gospell of Christe, whereunto the Princes of the refourmed Relligion are chefely bounde, amongeste whome her Ma.tie ys principal'.[4] Some forty years later, Samuel Purchas expressed substantially the same sentiment:

God is the beginning and the end... The first and last therefore in this Virginian argument considerable, is God; that is whether we have commission from him to plant, and whether the Plantation may bring glory to him: This in regard of us and our scope; that in regard of it and the lawfulnesse thereof'.[5]

---

[4] Richard Hakluyt, *A discourse of western planting*, in *The original writings and correspondence of the two Richard Hakluyts*, ed. E. G. R. Taylor, 2 vols. (London, 1935), II, p. 214.
[5] Samuel Purchas, *Virginias verger*, in Samuel Purchas, *Hakluytus posthumus* (London, 1625), p. 1809.

As Purchas concludes, the propagation of religion was frequently believed to be vital to the justification of the enterprises. It was not, however, always represented as a necessary condition. Some promoters failed to emphasise the Christian mission. The letters patent granted for the foundation of the Council for Virginia in 1606 included among the colony's ends the

the glorie of his divine maiestie in propogating of Christian religion to such people as yet live in darknesse and myserable ignorance of the true knowledge and worshippe of god and may in tyme bring the infidels and salvages lyving in those partes to humane civilitie.[6]

In contrast, however, the letters patent granted to Humphrey Gilbert in 1578 (the first granted to an English colonising venture intended for America) omit any explicit reference to a Christian purpose. Rather, they state, in common with the 1606 letters patent for Virginia, that Gilbert had a licence to discover and occupy 'such remote heathen and barbarous landes... not actually possessed of any Christian prince'.[7] It would appear that the assumption underlying that declaration is the Calvinist belief that the only legitimate society is a godly one, but missionary zeal was absent. Whether or not a religious mission was necessary to justify colonies, it was certainly not regarded by most promoters as sufficient; they would rarely stand on this sole legal leg.

Scepticism of religious justifications was generated in part by the publication of accounts condemning Spanish practices. The author of the *True declaration of the estate of the colonie in Virginia* observed that

to preach the Gospell to a nation conquered, and to set their soules at liberty, when we have brought their bodies to slaverie; It may be a matter sacred in the Preachers, but I know not how iustifiable in the rulers who for their meere ambition, doe set upon it the glosse of religion.[8]

There was, moreover, a consensus among English promoters of colonies that it would be necessary first to make savages civil before they could be receptive to religious doctrine.[9] While in this way religion could help justify the aim of establishing colonies and civil society – rather than merely missions – religion was simultaneously made a more remote objective.

---

[6] Philip L. Barbour, ed., *The Jamestown voyages under the first charter, 1606–1609*, 2 vols. (Cambridge, 1969), I, p. 25.

[7] *Ibid.*, pp. 188 and 24.

[8] *A true declaration of the estate of the colonie in Virginia* (London, 1610), pp. 8–9.

[9] Hakluyt, *A discourse of western planting*, p. 215; William Crashaw, *A sermon preached before the right honourable the Lord Lawarre* (London, 1610), sig. [D4]r.

Among secular justifications of colonisation, the Roman law doctrine of conquest was frequently employed in English colonial plans. Conquest was held to establish *de facto* title and a *de jure* claim when based upon a just war. The right of conquest had been central to the Spaniards' justification of their American colonies and English promoters repeatedly called for the emulation of the Spanish success. For English humanists, justification by conquest could be accommodated to the humanist appetite for glory. The letters patent granted by Henry VII to Sebastian Cabot and those granted by Elizabeth I to Ralegh established rights to 'conquer and possess'.[10] It has often been noted that Ralegh modelled himself upon the conquistador.[11] In his Latin dedication to Sir Walter Ralegh of an edition of the *Decades* of Peter Martyr, Richard Hakluyt portrayed Ralegh in terms of the glory of conquest. Ralegh at the time was engaged in the attempt to colonise Roanoke under the governor John White. According to Hakluyt: 'to posterity no greater glory can be handed down than to conquer [*domare*] the barbarian, to recall the savage and the pagan to civility, to draw the ignorant within the orbit of reason'.[12]

NATURAL LAW: *RES NULLIUS*, TRADE AND FRIENDSHIP

It is frequently commented, however, that northern Europeans abandoned their sixteenth-century attempts to imitate the Spanish conquest of the New World; they failed to discover similar quantities of precious metals.[13] Commerce and agriculture would instead become the economic basis of their plans for colonisation. It was necessary, therefore, to employ legal arguments more appropriate to agricultural colonisation. The doctrine, according to this account, which proved particularly useful was the Roman and natural law argument of *res nullius* (from which *terra nullius* is derived) which understood title to be based upon the exploitation of land.[14] Early modern discussions of *res nullius* were largely derived from sixteenth-century Thomists at the university of Salamanca. The Salamanca Thomists,

---

[10] Pagden, *Lords of all the world*, p. 64.

[11] See, for example, Charles M. Andrews, *The colonial period in American history* (New Haven, 1934), pp. 99–100; Pagden, *Lords of all the world*, p. 67.

[12] *The original writings and correspondence of the two Richard Hakluyts*, p. 368.

[13] Andrews, *The colonial period in American history*, I, pp. 99–100; or more recently Pagden, *Lords of all the world*, pp. 67–8.

[14] See Francisco de Vitoria, *On the American Indians* in Vitoria, *Political writings*, eds. Anthony Pagden and Jeremy Lawrance (Cambridge, 1991), p. 280, 'in the law of nations (*jus gentium*) a thing which does not belong to anyone (*res nullius*) becomes the property of the first taker, according to the law *Ferae bestiae* (*Institutions*, II.i.12), therefore if gold in the ground or pearls in the sea or anything else in the rivers has not been appropriated, they will belong by the law of nations to the first taker'.

from Francisco de Vitoria through to those strongly influenced by the Salamanca school, such as Bartolomé de Las Casas and Jose de Acosta, had been concerned with the legality of Spain's conquest of American civilisations. Salamanca authors had argued that the legitimacy of a society rests in whether it observes the law of nature.[15] The knowledge and use of the laws of the nature was taken to be a fundamentally human and social capacity. These Thomists argued that Spain had conquered civilisations that provided abundant evidence of their observance of the laws of nature, both in their technologies and their political organisation. The only just intervention in these New World societies, according to the Salamanca authors, could have been with a missionary purpose.

English readers were aware of the history of Spanish conquest throughout the sixteenth century, although the first full account to be published in England was Richard Eden's inclusion of Gonzalo Fernández de Oviedo's *History* in his *Decades* in 1555. The publication in England of authors influenced by the Salamanca school had to wait until the rise in interest in colonial ventures at the time of Elizabeth's grant to Sir Humphrey Gilbert of a patent to establish colonies. In 1583 Las Casas' *Brevissima relacion de la destruycion de las Indias* (first published in Seville in 1552) was printed in an English translation in London.[16] The edition included an appendix that recorded the famous dispute between Las Casas and Juan Ginés Sepúlveda over the rights of the American Indians. This translation of Las Casas and the appendix were reprinted in Purchas' *Hakluytus posthumus* in 1625. In 1604 Edward Grimstone also published a translation of José de Acosta's *Naturall and morall historie of the East and West Indies*.[17]

These English translations were clearly not, however, the only available sources for an English audience of the ideas of the Salamanca school. Continental editions of the authors were also available, for example, in the monumental *America* published by Theodore de Bry. The familiarity of these authors to English audiences, and particularly to those planning to establish colonies, is reflected in the frequency with which they were cited in promotional tracts. In 1584, in the *Discourse of western planting*, Hakluyt

---

[15] See Vitoria, *On civil power*, in Vitoria, *Political writings*.

[16] H. C. Porter, *The inconstant savage: England and the North American Indian 1500–1660* (London, 1979), p. 152. This work was a summary of Las Casas' *Historia de las Indias* that remained in manuscript.

[17] Grimstone was a humanist scholar of substantial reputation. He also translated Pierre d'Avitty's *The estates, empires, & principalities of the world* which praised mixed constitutions; see Markku Peltonen, *Classical humanism and republicanism in English political thought, 1570–1640* (Cambridge, 1995), p. 178.

cited the *Historia* of Las Casas the year after its translation in an account of
the Spanish destruction of the Indies.[18] Ralegh invoked the Spanish atroc-
ities, noting that the story was 'written by a Bishop of their own nation
called Bartholomew de las Casas, and translated into English and many
other languages, entitled The Spanish Cruelties'.[19] State papers record the
circulation of Acosta's *History* prior to its first English edition. Shortly after
the publication of the *History* in Seville (in 1590) the work was presented to
the Secretary of State, Robert Cecil, by Richard Wright, one of the directors
of Ralegh's colonial interests in Virginia.[20] Cecil then requested Hakluyt to
make an abstract of the work.[21] This abstract was made ten years before the
English edition of Acosta was published, yet other references to his work
can also be found in England in the 1590s, notably by Thomas Hariot, as
the work became entangled in Ralegh's attempts to prove the existence of
El Dorado.[22]

The histories of the Thomists served two purposes for English promoters.
The first was to provide a condemnation of Spanish colonies from Spanish
mouths and so to undermine the legitimacy of Spanish claims to title over
the New World. The second was the English promoters' reversal of the
implications of the Salamanca school's natural law arguments for native
rights. According to many English promoters (at least at those times when
they were employing natural law arguments), the North American natives
differed from the people encountered by the Spanish in that they were
simple and had not realised the potential to exploit the laws of nature. Their
systems of government and technology were perceived to be rudimentary.
They lived, according to William Symonds, 'but like Deere in heards, and
(no not in this stouping age, of the grey headed world, ful of yeres and
experience) have not as yet attained unto the first modestie that was in
Adam, that knew he was naked'.[23] The implication is that having failed
to observe the law of nature and exercise a right of property in the land,
the native Americans had never established ownership. As Gray observed
'So man may say to himself: the earth was mine, God gave it me . . . and
yet I stay and take it not out of the hands of beasts and brutish savages,
which have no interest in it, because they participate rather of the nature

[18] *The original writings and correspondence of the two Richard Hakluyts*, p. 309. Hakluyt also cited
     Oviedo in the same account.
[19] Cited in Porter, *The inconstant savage*, p. 175.
[20] George Bruner Parks, *Richard Hakluyt and the English voyages* (New York, 1961), pp. 137, 138 and 135.
     The directors of Ralegh's interest included Thomas Smith, later secretary of the Virginia Company
     and East India Company. Wright also later held an East India Company position.
[21] The abstract has been preserved with an incorrect date; see Parks, *Richard Hakluyt*, p. 138.
[22] *Ibid*.   [23] William Symonds, *Virginia* (London, 1609), p. 15.

of beasts then men.'[24] The suggestion is that the English have no case to answer in defending their possession of the land because the natives have no legal claims. We shall see, however, that even with this position Gray stresses that the English will nevertheless 'stay and take it not'.

The natural law implication that the land must be exploited is fully explored in those tracts. 'Who will think', William Strachey argued,

it is an unlawful act, to fortefye, and strengthen our selves (as Nature requires) with the best helpes, and by sitting down with Guards, and forces about us, in the wast and vast, unhabited groundes of their amongst a world of which not one foot of a thousand, do they either use or know how to turne to any benefit, and therefore lyes so great a Circuit vayne and idle before them?

The promoters are frequently careful to stress that these arguments are derived from an understanding of natural law. As John Donne observed in his sermon before the Virginia Company,

In the law of Nature and Nations, a land never inhabited, by any, or utterly derelicted and immemorially abandoned by the former Inhabitants, becomes theirs that will possesse it. So also is it, if the inhabitants doe not in some measure fill the Land, so as the Land may bring forth her increase for the use of men: for as a man does not become proprietary of the Sea, because he hath two or three Boats, fishing on it, so neither does a man become a Lord of a maine Continent, because hee hath two or three Cottages in the Skirts thereof. That rule which passes through all Municipal Lawes in particular States, *Interest rei – publicai ut quis re sua bene utator*, The State must take order, that every man improove that which he hath, for the best advantage of that State, passes also through the Law of Nations, which is to all the world, as the Municipall Law is to a particular State, *Interest mundo*, the whole world, all Mankinde must take care that all places be emproved, as farre as may be, to the best advantage of Mankinde in generall.[25]

As several commentators have noted, Donne's debt here is not only to the Salamanca school but also to Grotius who developed the law of nations, or *jus gentium*, into a theory of international law.[26]

Res nullius was not, however, the only natural law argument employed by the promoters. They also appealed to the natural law rights of trade and friendship. Friendship for both humanists and Thomists was based

---

[24] Robert Gray, *A good speed to Virginia* (London, 1609), sigs. Br–v. See also Gray's argument that there 'is not *meum* or *tuum* amongst them: so that if the whole land be taken away from them, there is not a man that can complaine of any particular wrong done unto him', sig. C4r.

[25] John Donne, *A sermon . . . preach'd to the honourable company of the Virginian plantation* (London, 1622), pp. 25–7.

[26] See David Armitage, 'Making the empire British: Scotland in the Atlantic world 1542–1707', *Past and Present*, 155 (May 1997); Noel Malcolm, 'Hobbes, Sandys, and the Virginia Company', *The Historical Journal*, 24 (1981).

in natural law. It was perceived to be the cement of community, and it was friendship, therefore, which enabled people through communities to maximise their use of the gifts of nature. William Strachey justified colonisation upon the basis of friendship arguing: 'Now, what greater good can we derive unto them then the knowledge of the true and everliving God? And what doth more directly and rarely minister that effect, then Society? and to ioyne with them in friendship?'[27] From the argument of friendship an argument of trade could also be derived from the law of nature because, as Anthony Pagden observes, for the Thomists 'at a deeper level... trade is a part of the communication between men'.[28] Accordingly, Strachey extends his justification of the colony from friendship into an argument from trade and he derives each of these from the 'law of nations' and natural law:

I must ask them [the objectors to the justice of the colony] agayne, in which shall we offer them [the natives] Iniury? for proffering them trade, or the knowledge of Christ?... why, what Iniury can yt be to people of any Nation for Christians to come unto their Fortes, Havens, or Territoryes, when the Law of Nations (which is the lawe of god and man) doth privelege all men to doe so, which admits yt lawfull, to trade with any manner of People... the Salvages themselves may not impugne, or forbid the same in respect of Common fellowship and Community betwixt man and man.[29]

This appeal to trade was enthusiastically adopted as a justification for colonising. The concept of trade in these justifications was extended metonymically to include the trade of spiritual goods. Again echoing Vitoria, the *True declaration of the estate of the colonie in Virginia* states that Christianity must be preached in the New World in

one of these three waies: [1] Either meerly Apostolically, without the helpe of man, (without so much as staffe [2] (or meerly imperiallie, when a Prince hath conquered their bodies, that the Preachers may feede their soules; [3] Or mixtly, by discoverie, and trade of merchants; where all temporall meanes are used for defence, and security, but none for offence, or crueltie.

The author concludes that not only is the third course preferable, but also finds that it is religion which the English offer in exchange: 'The third, belongs to us, who by way of merchandising and trade, doe buy of them pearles of the earth, and sell to them the pearles of heaven.'[30] It is striking, however,

[27] William Strachey, *The historie of travell into Virginia Britannia* [1609–1612], eds. Louis B. Wright and Virginia Freund (London, 1953), pp. 18–19.
[28] Anthony Pagden, *The fall of natural man: The American Indian and the origins of comparative ethnology* (Cambridge, 1982), p. 77.
[29] Strachey, *The historie of travell into Virginia Britannia*, pp. 22–3.
[30] *A true declaration of the estate of the colonie in Virginia*, pp. 6–7.

that the reversal of *res nullius* to justify possession is forgotten for the moment. Natives, who have previously been described as possessing no property rights and no understanding of the laws of nature, are now in a position to trade. The author acknowledges that imperial conquest – and implicitly, the usurpation of natural property rights – cannot be justified by saving souls. The author continues by arguing of this 'third course' that: 'if it be unlawfull it must precede from one of these three grounds, either because we come to them, or tarrie and dwell and possesse part of their country amongst them'. In reply to the objection the author states that the right of trade and friendship is grounded in the law of nations and nature, claiming: 'Is it not against the lawe of nations, to violate a peaceable stranger, or to denie him harbour?'[31]

William Strachey who, as we have seen, also employed the argument of *res nullius* to deny that the 'Indians' possessed the land, is also found tacitly contradicting this argument in his appeal to the natural law right of trade. Strachey is anxious to avoid the comparison of the English with the Spanish who had been described by Las Casas as devouring wolves:

a righteous man according to Solomon ought to regard the life of his beast, so surely Christian men, should not shew themselves like Wolves to devour ... and therefore even every foote of Land which we shall take unto our use, we will bargayne and buy of them for copper, hatchets, and such like commodities.[32]

Previously we saw Strachey arguing that Virginia was a waste and vast uninhabited land which the natives put to no use. Now the natives possess sufficient property rights to be able to sell their land. The same assumption was made by Crashaw. He raised 'the doubt of lawfulness of the action' and conceded 'we ... yeeld to this as to a principle of Justice'. He concluded 'A Christian may take nothing from a heathen against his will, but in faire and lawfull bargain.' 'It is most lawful', he argued,

to exchange with other Nations, for that which they may spare ... we will take nothing from the Savages by power nor pillage, by craft nor violence, neither goods, lands nor libertie, much lesse life ... But what may they spare: first, land and roome for us to plant in ... Again, they may spare us Timber, Masts, Crystal (if not better stones) Wine, Copper, Iron, Pitch, Tar, Sassafras, Sope ashes (for all these and more, we are sure the Countrey yeeldes in great abundance) ... These things they have, these they may spare, these we neede, these we will take of them.

---

[31] For this argument, see Vitoria, *On the American Indians*, pp. 278–81.
[32] Strachey, *The historie of travell into Virginia Britannia*, p. 26.

In return Crashaw offered the spiritual trade:

we will give them more, namely such things as they want and neede, and infinitely more excellent than all we take from them: and that is
{1.Civilitie for their bodies,}
{2. Christianity for their soules}
The first to make them men: the second happy men.[33]

The use of the argument of trade with its implicit recognition of property rights reflects a lack of confidence in employing the argument of *res nullius*. Moreover, it reflects a preparedness to employ whichever argument suits the occasion (an axiom, as we have seen, of humanist rhetoric), with little concern for self-contradiction.

CONQUEST AND JUST WAR

The same crisis of confidence is revealed when we find the promoters, having established a right to colonise peacefully on natural law principles (distancing themselves from the Spanish devouring wolves) then falling back upon the argument that they may employ force and violence. While Jacobean authors did retreat from hopes of gold and silver, contrary to the generally accepted view they did not entirely abandon the argument of conquest.[34] Robert Gray considered the case in which the English were 'unwronged or unprovoked' by the natives. In such circumstances 'By what right or warrant', he ponders, 'we can enter into the land of these Savages, and plant ourselves in their places'. Joshua's advice to his people, he argued, was to 'destroy God's enemies' who were 'Perrizzites, and Giants' but may be any 'abominable Idolators'. He continues:

Moreover, all Politicians doe with one consent, hold and maintain that a Christian King may lawfullie make warre upon barbarous and savage people . . . [if] the war be undertaken to this end, to reclaime and reduce those Savages from their barbarous kinds of life, and from their brutish and ferine manners, to humanitie, pietie, and honestie . . . And Lipsius alledgeth Saint Austustine for proofe hereof whose words are these, *Qui licentia iniquitatis eripitur, utiliter vincitur.* Those people are vanquished to their unspeakable profite and gaine.

Here natural law arguments are overturned in favour of Justus Lipsius' reason of state (we will return to the use of reason of state in the following chapter). When resorting to arguments based upon force and conquest,

---

[33] Crashaw, *A sermon*, sigs. D3v–[D4]v.
[34] See, for example, Andrews, *The colonial period in American history*, I, pp. 99–100; Pagden, *Lords of all the world*, pp. 67–8.

however, most promoters preferred to appeal to the Roman law doctrine of just war. The right to resist force with force – *vim vi repellere licet* – was reserved if the prior natural rights were refused. Strachey echoed Gray when he declared 'All the Injury that we purpose unto them, is but the Amendment of these horrible Heathenishness' but he was more careful when he concluded that the colony could 'barter' with the Indians:

in all love and friendship, until for our good purposes towardes them, we shall fynd them practize vyolence, or treason against us (as they have done at our other colony at Roanok) when I would gladly knowe ... whether we may stand upon our owne Innocency or no, or hold yt a scruple in humanity, or make it any breach of Charity (to prevent our owne throats from the cutting), to draw our swordes, *et vim vi repellere*.[35]

The natural law arguments of friendship and trade are employed to support the arguments for conquest. The author of *A true declaration of the estate of the colonie in Virginia* argued 'they have violated the lawe of nations, and used our Ambassadors as Ammon did the servants of David: If in him it were a just cause to warre against the Ammonites, it is lawfull, in us, to secure our selves, against the infidels.'[36] The author returns to this theme:

If anie man alleadge, that yet wee can possesse no farther limits, than was alloted by composition, and that *fortitudo sine iustitia, est iniquitatis Materia*, fortitude without justice is but the firebrand of iniquitie. Let him know that Plato defineth it, to bee no iniustice, to take a sword out of the hand of a madman; that Austen hath allowed it, for a lawfull offensive warre *quod ulciscitur iniurias* that revengeth bloudie iniuries. So that if iust offences shall arise, it can bee no more iniustice to warre against infidells, that it is when upon iust occasions wee warre against Christians.[37]

In these appeals to war the argument of *res nullius* (and its commercial associations) is pushed further into the margins. The weakness of *res nullius* is revealed once more when we find Donne (who previously argued from *res nullius*) basing an argument for force upon the fact of agricultural cultivation by the natives:

Again if the Land be peopled, and cultivated by the people, and that Land produce in abundance such things for want whereof their neighbours, or others (being not enemies) perish, the Law of Nations may justifie some force, in seeking, permutation of other commodities which they neede, to come to some of theirs.[38]

---

[35] Strachey, *The historie of travell into Virginia Britannia*, pp. 25–6.
[36] *A true declaration of the estate of the colonie in Virginia*, pp. 9–10.
[37] *Ibid.*, p. 12.   [38] Donne, *A sermon*, pp. 25–7.

While appropriating the arguments of the Salamanca school, English promoters had very different purposes from the Thomists. The justice of the Spanish colonies was the central concern of the Salamanca theologians and of Salamanca-influenced histories, together with the philosophical questions that that concern provoked. The Salamanca theologians and historians were deeply concerned with the nature of man, and the problems of the New World served as the occasion for examining this abstract question. The English promoters of colonies were also deeply, but not solely, concerned with the justice of colonising. For humanists, as for Cicero, 'the single virtue' of justice 'is the mistress and queen of virtues'.[39] But for the promotional orator justice was above all a necessary condition of the proof that a cause was both honourable and expedient. The English promotional tracts commonly attend first to the 'lawfulness' of the enterprise and then to the ends of their deliberation. Accordingly, William Crashaw observes: 'we freely confesse an action cannot be good, excellent or honourable, and much lesse can it be necessarie, unlesse it first of all appeare to be lawful: secondly, for the present action, we also confesse and yeeld to this as to a principle of Iustice'.[40] By contrast with the Salamanca authors, the English promoters do not move from the question of justice to more abstract concerns, rather they move directly to their concern with how to establish colonies. When the impediment of justice is removed, the readers can be directed to the honour and advantage of the adventure. The difference is not that the Spanish writers see the colonies as unjust and the English as just (the confidence of the English is too weak for such a simple opposition), but that the Salamanca authors move from justice to abstract issues whereas the turn of the English rhetorical argument is to practical ends.

LEGAL HUMANISM

We have seen natural law arguments employed primarily to counter possible indigenous claims to title over the colonised land. Anxiety over the legality of the colonies, however, had two sources. The priority of English claims was also made against the claims of rival European colonisers. Natural law arguments were frequently implicit when those claims were established. William Strachey, for example, comments that some corrupt people have objected 'how the undertaking [of the Virginian plantation] cannot be lawful. Why? Because the King of Spayne hath a primer Interest into the

---

[39] Cicero, *On duties*, trans. and ed. M. T. Griffin and E. M. Atkins (Cambridge, 1991), 3.28.
[40] Crashaw, *A sermon*, sig. D3r.

Country.' He continues 'No Prynce may lay clayme to any more amongst these new discoveryes... then, what his people, have discovered, tooke actual possession of, and passed over to his right.'[41] The implicit natural law assumption is that title rests upon occupation. Again, this assumption has been seen as seminal to the development of a commercial basis to colonisation. It was certainly an assumption present in most claims to the priority of title in disputes with other European colonisers. This use of natural law is consistent with similar disputes between European countries over the possession of fishing rights and trading privileges.

It has not, however, been appreciated that, in the early period of English colonising projects, natural law arguments played only a secondary role in the rivalry with other European colonisers. Promoters devoted far greater space to historical claims. While it has often been commented that those historical arguments performed a legitimising rhetoric, it has not been recognised that the arguments constituted an entirely separate legal basis for colonising: namely, legal humanism. The links between legal humanism and a commercial basis for expansion are far weaker than those based upon natural law.

At the beginning of the fifteenth century, Roman law held a pre-eminent position in European legal scholarship and practice. Two factors were central to that dominance. The first was the treatment by scholastic jurists of the Code of Justinian as *ratio scripta*, written reason, and therefore as a mirror of natural law. The second factor was that the pope was credited to be the highest authority in Roman law. This position was based upon the claim that the Emperor Constantine granted *dominium* to the western Empire.[42] Through the second half of the fifteenth century and the sixteenth century, the position of Roman law was challenged by humanists. The Italian humanist scholar Lorenzo Valla first proved in the 1440s that the Donation of Constantine was a forgery, thus undermining the temporal authority of the pope. Following Valla, a succession of legal scholars with humanist training insisted that the Code must be understood as a historical document in need of interpretation rather than an 'immediate valid source of law'.[43] When the law schools then conceded this approach they began to question what could be a satisfactory basis to law. The consensus which arose was that each country should fall back upon its indigenous customary laws. This conclusion encouraged more detailed historical investigations into 'the precise character of those customary laws'.

---

[41] Strachey, *The historie of travell into Virginia Britannia*, pp. 9–10.
[42] Quentin Skinner, *The foundations of modern political thought*, 2 vols. (Cambridge, 1978), I, p. 202.
[43] *Ibid.*, p. 205.

As a consequence 'discussions about legal and political principles tended to resolve into discussions about historical precedents'.[44] This comprehensive revision of European legal principles has become known as 'legal humanism', having been inspired by and conducted in terms of the methods of humanist textual analysis as well as by the central position of history in the *studia humanitatis*. The movement found fertile ground in England, where Roman law had never penetrated to the same degree that it had in other European countries, and where there was a correspondingly strong tradition of customary, or common, law.

In 1610 *The true declaration of the estate of colonie in Virginia* compared the Donation of Alexander (whereby the pope donated possession of the New World to the Spanish) with the Donation of Constantine. The author drew the conclusion that Lorenzo Valla's proof that the Donation of Constantine was a fraud must also render that by Alexander a fraud. Given, that is, that the Donation of Constantine was fake then Pope Alexander could not have possessed the temporal power to grant land to a prince.[45] The reference here to Valla's rejection of the Donation of Constantine is an appeal to the foundations of legal humanism. For the author, the Donation of Constantine must first be dismissed in order to substitute the Donation of Alexander (which had been printed by Richard Eden in 1555) with custom and precedent as the legal basis for European occupation of the New World. In presenting the argument from custom the author then provided a detailed history of English colonisation in the New World. This confident assertion of the legal humanist case was made possible only because the promoter had entered what was, by the time of the Virginia Company, a well-established historical project following legal humanist principles to establish the legitimacy of English colonisation in America.

When English colonising activity in America gained great impetus in the 1570s and 1580s, the organisers and promoters had for the first time seriously to address themselves to the legality of their action over the vigorously pursued counterclaims of Spain. John Dee addressed the problem in his *Art of navigation* (1576–8) that had been written for a private audience. For Dee, the obstacle to English title in North America was the apparent priority of the discovery of the New World by Columbus. The customary case for the Spanish also seemed stronger given their continuous occupation of the Americas following the voyage by Columbus. Using medieval Welsh

---

[44] *Ibid.*, p. 208. On the development of legal humanism, see also Julian H. Franklin, *Jean Bodin and the sixteenth-century revolution in the methodology of law and history* (New York, 1963); Donald Kelley, *The foundations of modern historical scholarship* (New York, 1970).

[45] *A true declaration of the estate of the colonie in Virginia*, p. 16.

sources, Dee (himself Welsh) repudiated the Spanish case with the fantastic story of the voyage by the Welsh prince Madoc in 1170. Madoc, Dee argued, crossed the Atlantic and established a colony. He also cited the Cabots as the first to discover the mainland of North America, the area of greatest interest for the English.

Dee's case gained support from English Catholics who stepped in to finance Humphrey Gilbert's floundering plans. The Spanish ambassador, Bernardino de Mendoza, reported that Spain's missionary ambitions in England were threatened by the possibility that an exodus of English Catholics would leave to establish American colonies in order to escape persecution: 'the small remnant of good blood in this sick body would be drained away'.[46] A threat was issued through priests that English Catholics who established colonies in the New World would 'immediately have their throats cut as happened to the French [Protestants] who went with Juan Ribao [Jean Ribault]'.[47] Attempting to reassure his co-religionists, the leader of the Catholic enterprise, Sir George Peckham, consulted Dee on the legality of the plans. Dee recorded in his diary 'A meridie hor 3 1/2 cam Sir George Peckham to me to know the tytle for Norombega in respect of Spayn and Portugall parting the whole worlds discoveryes'.[48] Peckham sufficiently valued Dee's advice to pay him with 5,000 acres of his New World holdings. The following year (with Gilbert now dead), Peckham's son, George Peckham, published his *True report of the new found land* in which the third chapter professed to 'shewe the lawfull title, which the Queen most excellent Maiestie hath unto those countries'.[49] Following Dee, Peckham stated that that title rests almost wholly upon the story of Madoc, now greatly enlarged, and the voyages of the Cabots. Peckham argued that the 'Spanish Chronicles' record an oration by 'Mutezuma that mighty Emperor of Mexico' in which he told his people 'we are not naturally of this Countrey... our forefathers came from a farre Countrey, and their King... returned again to his naturall Countrey, saying, he would send such as should rule and governe us'.[50] Madoc, according to Peckham, is the only possible candidate for Montezuma's myth. His role in establishing American societies is further confirmed by the debt that the Amerindians' languages have to Welsh; a debt revealed, for example, by the common signification of the

[46] *The voyages and colonising enterprises of Humphrey Gilbert*, ed. David B. Quinn 2 vols. (Cambridge, 1939), I, p. 279.
[47] *Ibid.* [48] *Ibid.*, II, p. 280.
[49] Richard Hakluyt, *The principal navigations, voiages and discoveries of the English nation* (London, 1589), p. 709.
[50] *Ibid.*

word 'penguin' in both Wales and the 'sayd countries'. Here the philolog-
ical skills employed in the development of legal humanism would seem
to have degenerated into unintentional burlesque. Accordingly, it is commonly suggested that the Madoc myth was 'weak' and 'far-fetched'.[51] The
promoters were, however, serious in their employment of the myth but
its utility can only be understood when it is placed in a legal humanist
framework.[52]

In his *Discourse on western planting* published the year after Peckham's
True report, Richard Hakluyt also devoted a chapter to establishing 'That
the Queen of England's Title to all the west Indies or at leaste to as moche
as from Florida to the Circle acticke is more lawfull and righte then the
Spaniardes or any other christian Princes'.[53] 'Are wee to answer', he continues, 'the most injurious and unreasonable donation graunted by Pope
Alexander the sixte...of all the west Indies to the kinges of Spaine?' As we
have seen, it was the ambition of legal humanism to address legal claims
upon this allegedly false basis by an appeal to historical precedent. Hakluyt
accordingly responded to the problem of the Donation with further evidence on Madoc:

for the first point wee of England have to shewe very auncient and auctentical
Chronicles written in the welshe or brittishe tongue, wherein wee finde that one
Madock ap Owen Guyneth a Prince of North Wales beinge wearye of the civill
warres and domesticall dissentions in Contrie, made twoo voyadges oute of Wales
and discovered and planted large Countries wch he founde in the mayne Ocean
south westwarde of Ireland, in the yere of our Lorde 1170.[54]

He then supports this argument with the now familiar claims about the
Welsh language agreeing in many aspects with the languages spoken in the
north of the American continent. And he refers the reader to an edition of
Humphrey Lloyd's *History of Cambria* published the same year in which
the Madoc myth is again repeated.

Legal humanism dictated that the stronger the precedent the stronger the
case. Promoters of colonies correspondingly searched further than the myth
of Madoc to build the case for English title. Having made his claims for

---

[51] Pagden, *Lords of all the world*, p. 81.
[52] Williams, *The American Indian in Western legal thought: The discourses of conquest*, pp. 170 and 178,
does not identify the basis in legal humanism for the argument of precedent and accordingly fails to
appreciate this context for the Madoc myth. Anthony Grafton, *New worlds, ancient texts: The power
of tradition and the shock of discovery* (Cambridge, Mass., 1992), p. 147, argues on the basis of the use
of Madoc that the Elizabethans 'went not to ancient but to medieval sources for their justifications
of English empire abroad'. The legal humanistic basis of the use of Madoc reveals this opposition
between medieval and classical sources to be overdrawn.
[53] Hakluyt, *Discourse of western planting*, p. 290.   [54] *Ibid.*

Madoc, Dee had also pointed out that the voyages of the Cabots, licensed by Henry VII and beginning in 1497, had preceded every other European nation in the discovery of the north American continent. This link between the Cabots and the English case for north American title was publicised for the first time in 1580 by John Florio, then tutor in Italian at Oxford and later one of the most skilled of English humanists. Florio's claim was made in a translation of the account of the voyages of Jacques Cartier previously published in the history of Ramusio:

> there is none, that of right may be more bold in ther enterprice than the Englishmen, the land being first found out by John Gabot the Father, and Sebastian Gabot, one of hys three sonnes, in the yeare 1494, in the name and behalfe of King Henry the seaventh, as both by the foresaid Ramusius in his first Volumes, and our owne Chronicles, and Sebastian Gabots letters patents yet extant, and in his Mappe maye be seene: so there is no nation that hath so good a righte or is more fit for this purpose, than they are.[55]

Following the conventions of legal humanism, Florio based his claims upon the increment of histories, chronicles, patents and documents, such as maps. His translation was made at the request of Richard Hakluyt, who was in contact with Dee at the time, and was clearly in part promoting Gilbert's rights under his recently obtained patent. It has been held that Florio's preface was the product of Hakluyt's ventriloquism. 'The translator of Montaigne', we are told by George Bruner Parks, was not likely to be interested in such a subject.[56] His genius was rather, according to E. G. R. Taylor, 'for language and letters'.[57] Clearly, however, when the colonising ventures are understood in the context of the revival of 'language and letters', that is, in the context of the *studia humanitatis*, then Florio's humanist credentials would suggest that the ventures were vital to his interests and that he was perceived to be specially qualified to assist. Indeed, as we have seen, his interest was revealed by his continuing involvement in the promotion of colonies more than twenty years later.

We find the Cabot precedent employed by Hakluyt just two years after Florio's translation, with Hakluyt stating in his preface to the *Divers voyages* that he has

> first put down the title which we have to that part of America which is from Florida to 67 degrees northwarde, by the letters patents granted to John Cabote and his three sonnes, Lewis, Sebastian and Santius, with Sebastians own certificates to

---

[55] *The original writings and correspondence of the two Richard Hakluyts*, I, p. 166.

[56] Parks, *Hakluyt*, p. 64.

[57] *The original writings and correspondence of the two Richard Hakluyts*, I, p. 21.

Baptista Ramusius of his discoverie of America, and the testimonie of Fabian, our own Chronicler.[58]

He then recites the documentary evidence of voyages in the present volume as proof of the same title and within ten lines he reminds the reader that 'the last yere' he sponsored the translation of Cartier. Again here we see the incremental building of the legal humanist case for title, but in this instance the increment of historical precedent is built with the assistance of the humanist gift for advertising and self-reference.[59] This legal humanist snowball gains increasing momentum through 1583 when Peckham, whom we have seen citing Madoc, also cites the Cabots on the question of title. The following year, Hakluyt produced his *Discourse of western planting* in which he not only appealed to the precedent of Madoc when refuting the Donation of Alexander, but also provided a detailed account of the exploits of the Cabots.[60]

The legal humanist case was constructed through the collaboration of leaders of colonial enterprises, such as Peckham and Gilbert, with the humanist promoters of those enterprises such as Florio, Hakluyt and Dee (although, importantly, leaders such as Peckham, Gilbert and Ralegh were also humanists and promoters). Through close consultation, these men developed a consensus on historical myth and events that would constitute the basis of their case. This case was then strengthened through mutual references in print. Such self-reference was highly complementary to the spirit of legal humanist principles. Indeed, so complementary are humanist self-promotion and legal humanism that it would seem that our understanding of the success of legal humanism must take greater account of the practices of self-promotion, and the exploitation of print.[61] It is in this way, through fusing the skills of incremental self-promotion in print with the principles of legal humanism and then applying this practice to the colonial enterprise, that colonisation could become the legitimisation of itself.

With the accumulation of testimony, the legal humanist case began to take the form of a project. That project reached a climax in Hakluyt's monumental *Principal navigations, voiages and discoveries of the English nation*, published in 1589. Hakluyt was not concerned solely with colonisation in

---

[58] *Ibid.*, p. 180.
[59] See Lisa Jardine, *Erasmus, man of letters* (Princeton, 1993), on the humanists' employment of their skills for self-promotion.
[60] *The original writings and correspondence of the two Richard Hakluyts*, II, pp. 290–313.
[61] The standard accounts of legal humanism (such as Franklin, *Jean Bodin*; Kelley, *The foundations of modern historical scholarship* and Skinner, *The foundations of modern political thought*) predate recent work on the ways in which humanists manipulated print for the purposes of self-promotion.

America. His interests also concerned the development of trade to the east and to some degree they were also antiquarian. Those broader interests are reflected in the content of the first two parts of the *Principal navigations*. There is no overt employment of legal humanism in those pages. It is all the more striking, therefore, when we turn to the third and last book concerning voyages to the 'West', to the Americas, that Hakluyt employed the legal humanist case as his frame. To establish the customary right of the English to colonial America, Hakluyt presented a detailed historical account of English interests in that continent. He provided 'letters, Privileges, Discourses, Observations' including letters patent and emphasising first-hand accounts (all too often these first-hand accounts are understood as a nascent empiricism when the emphasis upon them was being driven, at least in part, by the ideological demands of legal humanism).[62] He begins with Madoc and then provides a detailed account of the acceptance by Henry VII of Columbus' offer to voyage to the west under the English crown (he had rehearsed this argument in *Western planting*). He moves from the Cabots to William and John Hawkins and proceeds in this fashion through the following 300 pages to the projects of Gilbert and the exploits of Ralegh, whose patent was still valid at the time of publication. Each account adds yet greater weight to the accumulative nature of the legal humanist case.

Hakluyt's work was merely the first of a series of histories promoting the English colonisation of America that find their inspiration in the argument for title from custom and precedent. He published a second edition of the *Principal navigations* from 1598 to 1600, this time in three volumes with a whole volume devoted to the western voyages. In 1612 William Strachey completed the manuscript (which was not printed) of his *History of travell into Virginia Britannia*. While he confined this work to the foundation of the new Chesapeake colony, Strachey presented the account in the form of a history in order to address the problem of title. The abstract of the 'Praemonition to the reader' declares 'Wherin (as the foundation to all the succeeding busines) is derived downe to our tymes, the antient Right and Clayme, which wee make to this part of America'.[63] The 'foundation' of the business was in an 'antient Right'; that is, upon the history of English enterprise in the New World. His argument for English title accordingly followed Hakluyt in a repetition of English interest based upon Madoc, the

---

[62] For emphasis upon the proto-empiricism of first-hand accounts, see Karen Kupperman, *Settling with the Indians* (London, 1980) and Anthony Padgen, *European encounters with the New World: from Renaissance to Romanticism* (New Haven, 1993).

[63] Strachey, *The historie of travell into Virginia Britannia*, p. 7.

Cabots, Gilbert and Ralegh. Upon this foundation Strachey then provided a detailed account of the land and people based upon the experience of the previous six years. This account further cements the legal humanist claim to title, furnishing a further chapter of involvement.

The last years of the Virginia Company saw the production of two further works in this genre, namely, John Smith's *Generall historie of Virginia, New England, and the Summer Isles* (1624); and Samuel Purchas' *Hakluytus posthumus, or Purchas his pilgrimes* (1625). As Purchas' title indicates, he relied heavily upon both the aims and material of Hakluyt. Like Hakluyt's, his work was not concerned solely with the American plantations but, where it was, he repeated the now standard arguments from precedent. Smith, on the other hand, confined himself solely to the history of English interest in colonial America. As such, the whole work is contained within the logic of the legal humanist enterprise. He presented an account of English colonisation that was entirely historical and began with the 'ancient' records of Madoc, the Cabots, Gilbert and Ralegh.[64] The work provided the history of the Virginia Company's adventure as the conclusion to that account, the final chapter in the historical argument for title.

The legal humanist validation of English title to the New World was not confined to these voluminous histories. As we have seen, promotional tracts such as the *True declaration of the estate of the colonie in Virginia* and Johnson's *Nova Britannia* made detailed examinations of English title by reference to the explicitly legal humanistic concerns with the Donation of Constantine. Indeed, the great body of the legal humanist argument for title is presented in those numerous promotional tracts that characteristically open with an historical account of English colonising projects as the explicit legitimation of the present enterprise. Thus, while the beginnings of the case can be discerned in such early tracts as Peckham's *True report*, Hakluyt's *Western planting* and *Divers voyages*, or in editions of texts such as Florio's *Cartier*, the authors of Jacobean promotional tracts, including Crashaw, Symonds and Gray, present elaborated versions of the same case. Those promotional tracts included the projects the earlier promoters were attempting to legitimise as the legitimation, in turn, for the Virginia Company's claims.

Typical of these is Robert Johnson's *Nova Britannia*. Johnson devotes a large proportion of his narrative to the familiar history of English

---

[64] John Smith, *The generall historie of Virginia, New England, and the Summer Isles* (London, 1624), p. 1.

enterprises, providing a detailed account of Elizabethan attempts and placing this history in the context of the rivalry for possession with Spain.[65]
He repeatedly underlines the self-referential nature of this historical project
in justification. Hakluyt had nimbly supported his case by reference to his
own work and to the work of others whom he had sponsored. He had attempted to provide claims of custom with depth at the same moment they
were being initiated. Johnson, by contrast, confidently refers the reader to
Hakluyt's 'Book of English voyages' as sufficient testimony in itself of the
English right to possess.[66] The legal humanist project had now reached
a maturity whereby it was perceived in itself to be sufficient to establish
English title. As Johnson summarised, there are 'divers monuments already
publisht in Print to the world, manifesting and shewing that the coast
and parts of Virginia' have an ancient English claim and are therefore the
property of King James.[67] To erase any doubt that his historical argument
for title would have its basis in legal humanism, Johnson then compares
the Donation of Alexander with the 'donation of Constantine whereby
the Pope himselfe doth hold and claime the Citie of Rome and all the
Western Empire'. Following legal humanist tradition and, in particular,
Valla's demonstration that the Donation of Constantine was a fraud, he
then dismissed it as a valid basis for papal authority. This first donation, the
Donation of Constantine, was from a 'temporal Prince to the Pope'. The
second, the Donation of Alexander, 'from the Pope to a temporal Prince, I
doe verily guess they be neere of kinne'. The first was 'fabulous', the second
was 'ridiculous'.[68]

NOSTALGIA FOR NATIVE VIRTUES

We have seen that the English promoters' concerns with legal questions
were pre-eminently practical. They were less concerned with philosophical
and abstract matters than were the Salamanca school. They employed arguments of natural law, conquest and legal humanism to practical ends. The
discovery of peoples previously unknown to Europeans did, however, provoke English promoters, like other Europeans, to consider such questions
as the nature of man and the course of human history. Such considerations
were closely tied to the practical question of whether the establishment
of colonies was legitimate. It has been observed that frequently the image
of the native presented by promoters was convenient to the ambition to

[65] Robert Johnson, *Nova Britannia* (London, 1609), sigs. Bv, B2r, B3r.
[66] *Ibid.*, sig. B2r.   [67] *Ibid.*, sig. A4v.   [68] *Ibid.*

establish colonies. It has not been appreciated that that image also frequently reflected the central anxieties of the colonial enterprise.

For their understanding of the native, promoters drew both upon the assumptions of natural law and upon Roman and Greek histories. Natural law assumptions supported the perception that indigenous cultures were relatively simple compared with those of Europeans and that such cultures were therefore at an earlier stage of history. This theory, which shared the same field of assumptions as the argument of *res nullius*, was in itself a quasi-legitimising discourse. The explicit conclusion was that colonial intervention would advance these people to a more desirable place in history, one which was particularly receptive to an understanding of theology and thus to saving their souls. As Crashaw observed,

for the time was when we were savage and uncivill, and worshipped the divell, as now they do, then God sent some to make us civill, others to make us christians. If such had not been sent us we had yet continued wild and uncivill, and worshippers of the divell: for our 'civilitie' wee were beholden to the Romanes, for our 'Religion' to the Apostles and their disciples. Did we receive this blessing by others, and shall we not be sensible of those that are still as we were then?[69]

Roman historians were routinely employed to support this theory. Promoters observed that the Romans had found Britain in much the same state as Britons found America. According to Robert Johnson, 'we had continued brutish, poore, and naked Britaines to this day, if Julius Caesar and his Roman legions (or some other) had not laid the ground to make us tame and civill'.[70] This observation had been made earlier in Theodore De Bry's edition of Hariot's *Brief and true report* in which the comparison of John White's drawings of Ancient Britons and Virginians was noted as having been made 'for to showe how that the Inhabitants of the great Bretannie have bin in times past as Savage as those of Virginia'.[71] These claims were repeated throughout the Elizabethan and Jacobean tracts promoting colonies.[72]

The comparison of Ancient Britons and modern Americans has been shown to reveal an incipient progressive theory of history.[73] In the hands

---

[69] Crashaw, *A sermon*, sig. [C4]v.   [70] Johnson, *Nova Britannia*, sig. C2r.
[71] Thomas Hariot, *A brief and true report of the new found land of Virginia*, ed. Theodore de Bry (Frankfurt, 1590), sig. Er.
[72] See also Alexander Whitaker, *Good newes from Virginia* (London, 1613), pp. 23–7; John Rolfe, *Relation of the state of Virginia* (1616), in *Virginia: Four personal narratives* (New York, 1972), p. 111; Richard Eburne, *A plaine pathway to plantations* [London, 1624], ed. Louis B. Wright (Ithaca, 1962), p. 29 and pp. 55–6; Purchas, *Hakluytus posthumus*, p. 1755.
[73] David Armitage, 'The New World and British historical thought', in Karen Kupperman, ed., *America in European consciousness 1493–1750* (Chapel Hill, 1995).

of Enlightenment philosophers, that progression was perceived to be fundamental to the triumph of the final stages of commercial society. Subsequent generations of historians have enthusiastically endorsed this proto-commercial interpretation of early American history. It is needless to state that the early promoters of American colonisation did not have David Hume or Adam Smith in mind when comparing Picts and American Indians. Moreover, the modernising interpretation of the comparisons overlooks an ambivalence which expresses not one but two models of history. We find these authors simultaneously confident of the virtues of historical progress and also nostalgic for the virtues of a golden age. To understand this ambiguity, we have to turn precisely to those Roman historians with whom the promoters supported the idea of progress.

Tacitus was held to be foremost among Roman historians in late Elizabethan and Jacobean England. He was believed to have provided two accounts of Roman encounters with 'primitive' cultures, the *Germania* and the *Agricola*; the latter was a popular source for the image of the Ancient Britons.[74] It is clear in both these works that the attitude of Tacitus to the primitive tribes was ambivalent. In *Agricola*, he was concerned to celebrate the valour of his father-in-law in the conquest of Britain. But this Roman alone was the subject of praise. He lamented the corruption of previous colonial administrations in Britain. The Romans are represented as luxurious, avaricious and oppressive. He admired the British tribes for their courage and industry. In the mouth of Galgacus, a leader of the Britons, Tacitus says of the Romans 'To plunder, butcher, steal, these things they misname empire'.[75] The tribes were defeated not only through Agricola's martial virtues but more completely through their abandonment of their own virtues in favour of the Roman corruption: 'little by little the Britons went astray into alluring vices: to the promenade, the bath, the well-appointed dinner table. The simple natives gave the name of "culture" to this factor of their slavery.'[76]

In *Germania* the focus was less upon the corruption of the Romans and more upon the tribes' embodiment of the virtues of civic life. The description is not utopian but Tacitus expressed great admiration for the

---

[74] For doubts about Tacitus as the author of the *Germania*, see A. N. Sherwin-White, *Racial prejudice in imperial Rome* (Cambridge, 1967). The text was unquestioningly accepted in the Renaissance, however, as the work of Tacitus.

[75] Tacitus, *Agricola*, trans. M. Ogilvie (Cambridge, Mass., 1970), 30; David Armitage, 'Literature and empire', in Nicholas Canny, ed., *The origins of empire*. vol. I of *The Oxford history of the British empire*, ed. Wm Roger Louis (Oxford, 1998), p. 109.

[76] Tacitus, *Agricola*, 21; see also 11 and 15.

Germans. The tribes were 'uncorrupted' by luxury, possessing no more than they needed and sharing with those who were in want. They possessed a strong sense of duty and were unsurpassed in martial virtues. They also exhibited a mixed form of quasi-republican government.[77]

When put in the context of his larger work, these short accounts take an even greater significance. In the *Annals* and *Histories*, Tacitus described imperial Rome as a society in which virtue had declined. The martial virtues were no longer observed. The period was one in which luxury had corrupted the citizens. In this context, while not ideals, the images of the Britons and Germans were a reproach to the decline in the Romans' civic virtues.

It is, of course, well documented that Tacitus enjoyed great popularity in Europe and in England in the late sixteenth and seventeenth centuries, in the period in which English colonial activity in America commenced in force. The reading of Tacitus in early modern Europe clearly had, at the least, a double aspect. The first was consistent with the rise of Machiavellism. According to this reading, the subject of the prince should adopt dissimulation and dishonesty because these were the only means of survival in a corrupt world. But perhaps the dominant understanding of Tacitus was one of nostalgia for a lost civic virtue. In this sense, Tacitism was an extension of Ciceronian humanism. In this final section of this chapter we explore the Ciceronian readings of Tacitus in a New World context; these were the readings that reflect an anxiety about corruption. In the following chapter we turn to the reading of Tacitus as a critique of the Ciceronian perspective.

Early modern promoters of English colonies made comparisons between Ancient Britons and Native Americans in the context of the second, nostalgic, reading of Tacitus. Those comparisons recalled the anxiety of Tacitus about the relative corruption of the Romans and revealed a similar anxiety on the part of the promoters. Robert Sidney provided a telling example of this reading of Tacitus. Robert Sidney's father, Henry, had initiated the colonisation of Ireland under Elizabeth and his brother Philip had been deeply involved in Humphrey Gilbert's projects to colonise America. Robert, in turn, was a central figure in the Virginia Company.[78] In a marginal note in his copy of Lipsius' edition of Tacitus' *Agricola*, he drew attention to the Britons', as he put it, 'servitu[de] under the Ro[mans]'.[79]

Readers of Tacitus knew that history could be repeated not only through Britons civilising Americans, as Romans had civilised Britons, but through

---

[77] Tacitus, *Germania*, trans. M. Hutton (Cambridge, Mass., 1970), 11–16.
[78] Milicent V. Hay, *The life of Robert Sidney* (Washington, 1984), pp. 225–7.
[79] Armitage, 'Literature and empire', p. 109, n. 50.

Britons corrupting Americans as Romans had corrupted Britons. This anxiety was expressed first in the repeated charges made in tracts promoting colonies that English society was indeed corrupt and that the colonising enterprises were themselves corrupted by greed, faction and idleness: charges, that is, which were in line with the reception of Tacitus in this period. We have seen that William Crashaw used the assumptions of *res nullius* and progress in his justification of the Jamestown colony. Yet we have also seen that Crashaw was deeply concerned with the themes of corruption and we find him as ready to appeal to a golden age of history as a progressive theory of history:

Stately houses, costly apparell, rich furniture, soft beds, daintie fare, dalliance and pleasures, huntings and horse-races, sports and pastimes, feasts and banquets are not the meanes whereby our forefathers…subdued their enemies…and setled their commonwealths: nay they exposed themselves to frost and colde, snow and heate, raine and tempests, hunger and thirst, and cared not what hardnesse, what extremitie, what pinching miseries they endured, so they might atchieve the ends they aimed at.[80]

Contemporary Britons were perceived as soft by comparison. In a passage that was to be echoed repeatedly in subsequent enterprises, Thomas Hariot complained in his 1588 account of the Roanoke colonists:

Some also were of a nice bringing up, only in cities or townes, or such as never (as I may say) had seene the world before. Because there were not to be found any English cities, nor such faire houses, nor at their owne with any of their olde accustomed daintie food, nor any soft beds of downe or fethers: the country was to them miserable, & their reports thereof according.[81]

In his *Map of Virginia*, John Smith supported this impression that it was particularly through their experience of colonising that the English were revealed to be corrupt. Jamestown, he claimed, was overburdened with men who never

did any thing but devour the fruits of other mens labours. Being for the most part of such tender educations and small experience in martiall accidents, because they found not English cities, not such faire houses, nor at their owne wishes any of their accustomed dainties, with feather beds and downe pillows, Tavernes and alehouses in every breathing place.[82]

As a consequence of such 'idleness and bestial slouth', according to the Virginia Company's *True and sincere declaration of the purposes and ends*

---

[80] Crashaw, *A sermon*, sig. [F4]r.   [81] Hariot, *A brief and true report*, sig. A4v.
[82] John Smith, *A map of Virginia* (Oxford, 1612), pp. 37–8.

of the plantation begun in Virginia, 'every thing [is] returning from civill Propryety, to Naturall, and Primary Community'.[83]

At the same time that they lamented their own corruption the promoters did not exclusively represent the Americans to be backward and savage. As Karen Kupperman has shown, promoters frequently praised elements of native cultures and did not necessarily see them as set apart by savagery.[84] Native government, manners, athleticism, oratory and martial valour were all sources of admiration. William Strachey, secretary of the Virginia colony from 1609 to 1611, provided not only one of the most comprehensive accounts of a native society but also one of the most ambivalent. He made the customary observations upon the simplicity of the native culture and upon the obnoxious nature of some of its practices. But he also commented upon the natives' possession of the classical virtues. He described the leader Powhatan as a 'strong and able saluadge, synowie, active, and of a daring spirit, vigilant, ambitious, subtile to enlarge his dominions'.[85] Of the natives generally, he notes that 'the men are very strong of able bodies, and full of agility, accustoming themselves to endure hardnes, to lye in the woodes under a tree, by a smale fire in the worst of winter in Frost and Snow'.[86] By contrast, we have seen that the promoters frequently attributed the problems of the English to their inability to endure such hardships, whereas, according to Crashaw, they had held such virtues in ancient times. Strachey notes that the natives worship the devil out of fear but compares them in this respect with 'the Romaynes [who] did [worship] their hurtful god Veious' from the time of Romulus. The comparison recalls Machiavelli's account of Roman religion, which he praised for instilling civic virtues through the use of fear. It is striking that while the promoters frequently described the Indians as possessing the faculty of eloquence, Strachey also remarked that they possessed the Attic virtue to 'have but few words in their language' with which to describe things.[87] He admired the martial virility of the men

[83] *A true and sincere declaration of the purposes and ends of the plantation begun in Virginia* (London, 1610), pp. 10–11.

[84] Kupperman, *Settling with the Indians*. See also James Tully, 'Placing the *Two Treatises*', in Nicholas Phillipson and Quentin Skinner, eds., *Political discourse in early modern Britain* (Cambridge, 1993), pp. 279–80; Robert Berkhofer, Jr, *The white man's Indian: Images of the American Indian from Columbus to the present* (New York, 1979), pp. 72–80; Axtell, *The invasion within*; and Alden T. Vaughan, 'From white man to red skin: changing Anglo-American perceptions of the American Indian', *American Historical Review* 87 (1982), pp. 917–52, for eighteenth-century anxieties raised by the virtuousness of native cultures when compared with European corruption. These authors point out that the development of a progressive theory of history allowed such anxieties to be dismissed. Sixteenth- and early seventeenth-century Englishmen were more likely to subscribe to a cyclical view of history, however, and could not dismiss their anxieties with the same confidence.

[85] Strachey, *The historie of travell into Virginia Britannia*, p. 57.

[86] *Ibid.*, p. 74.   [87] *Ibid.*, p. 59.

'The men bestowe their without the doores, scorning to be seen in any effemynate labour'.[88] Again, here we find the contempt for 'Asiatic' effeminacy that Roman historians believed had been responsible for the decline of the republic. Moreover, Indian culture was uncorrupted by luxury. It was a culture in which people possessed no more than they needed: 'and (indeed) to saye triuth their victuall is their chief riches'.[89] The observation may be compared with the opening to Whitaker's *Good newes from Virginia*: 'Be bould my Hearers to contemne riches... Nakedness is the riches of nature; vertue is the only thing that makes us rich.'[90]

It has frequently been noted that White's paintings of both Indians and Ancient Britons, which appeared in the de Bry edition of Hariot's report, portrayed both subjects, native American and Briton, in classical poses and embodying the martial virtues.[91] White's representations of warrior women, in particular, recall the frequent references in Tacitus to the women, such as Boadacea, who led the Britons' rebellions against the Romans. It has also been assumed that the caption to White's paintings, which claimed that the Britons were 'in times past' like the inhabitants of Virginia, suggests the expectation that the Americans would one day progress to civility.[92] Given that the promoters of English colonies portrayed contemporary English civil society as corrupt, however, White's paintings and Hariot's caption, like the promoters' frequent comparisons of Ancient Britons and native Americans, can be seen to reflect two anxieties in the colonising projects. First, the comparison which Indians provided with Britons of the past – a past in which Crashaw declared they had been truly virtuous – clarified the corruption of the English in the present. Thus we may read that the English having 'been in times past like the Virginians' meant that in times past the English had been virile, martial and virtuous, like the Virginians of the present. This was certainly the impression of de Bry when he republished Hariot's *Report* with the engravings he made from White's paintings. As de Bry observes in his 'Epistle to the reader', although the native Americans have no 'true knowledge of God...Yet they passe us in many things'.[93] At the top of his list was continence. Perhaps the greatest reproach to the femininity of present day Englishmen were White's images of warrior women. Even women in the past possessed the martial qualities that Englishmen

---

[88] *Ibid.*, p. 81.   [89] *Ibid.*, p. 115.   [90] Whitaker, *Good newes from Virginia*, p. 1.
[91] John White, *The American drawings of John White 1577–1590*, ed. Paul Hulton and David B. Quinn, 2 vols. (London, 1964), I, pp. 9–12.
[92] Armitage, 'The New World and British historical thought'; Peter Burke, 'America and the rewriting of world history', in Kupperman, *America in European consciousness*, pp. 42–4.
[93] Hariot, *A brief and true report*, 'Epistle to the reader'.

lacked. As Hariot's commentary noted 'The women of the pictes above said were not worser for the warres then the men.'[94] The second fear provoked by the comparison of ancient Britons and native Americans was that the natives might one day be like the English: that is, they, also, might one day be 'civilised' through being corrupted. As Tacitus had lamented of the Ancient Britons, the native Americans might also come to give the name 'culture' to their slavery.

THE DENIAL OF DISPOSSESSION

It is clear that the perceived virtues of the Indians posed a threat to the English promoters concerned with civic corruption.[95] Given these perceptions, it is particularly striking that the promoters, often again contradicting themselves, repeatedly stated that there was no intention to violate the integrity of Indian society and no intention to take anything that the Indians possessed. Again these anxieties about foreign possessions had a solid foundation in Roman history. We have seen that in *The war against Catiline*, Sallust argued strongly that the virtue of the Roman republic had been undone by the corrupting influence of Rome's foreign possessions. First Sulla and then Catiline had employed soldiers who had been corrupted by their exposure to the luxury of Asia. These men, he argued, became avaricious, 'which renders the most manly body and soul effeminate'.[96] Rather than bringing glory, foreign *imperium* threatens an 'Asiatic' and effeminate commonwealth.[97] Cicero expresses similar concerns in *De officiis*. The corruption of the Spartans, he argued, was 'inflamed by desire for conquest'. Following this course greatness of spirit descends into 'wilfulness and an excessive desire for pre-eminence'.[98] Cicero expands this problem of conquest into a more general concern about the justice of empire, a concern that exceeds fears for the republic and extends to the treatment of other people. While for Cicero the strongest human ties are the closest, there is also an unlimited fellowship among humanity.[99] There was a time, he argued, when

---

[94] *Ibid.*, sig. E2v.

[95] Tully, 'Placing the *Two Treatises*'; Berkhofer, *The white man's Indian*, pp. 72–80; Axtell, *The invasion within*; and Vaughan, 'From white man to red skin' describe a similar threat to English colonisers in the eighteenth century.

[96] *Sallust*, trans. J. C. Rolfe (London, 1921), X.1–XII.3.

[97] On the limits to the concept of *imperium* in early modern British political thought, see Armitage, 'Literature and empire' and David Armitage, *The ideological origins of the British empire* (Cambridge, 2000).

[98] Cicero, *On duties*, I, 64.   [99] *Ibid.*, 51–3.

the empire of the Roman people was maintained through acts of kind service and not through injustices, wars were waged either on behalf of allies or about imperial rule; wars were ended with mercy and through necessity... In this way we could more truly have been titled a protectorate than an empire of the world.[100]

This practice was eroded and was rejected entirely by Sulla who was followed by Caesar 'a man whose cause was unrighteous and whose victory fouler still; he did not confiscate the property of individual citizens, but embraced entire countries and provinces under a single law of ruin'.[101] Earlier in *De officiis*, Cicero had distinguished between true and false glory. It is not glory, he argued, to steal from one group and give to another. He appeared to have both Sulla and Caesar in mind as having committed this injustice to both Romans and foreign cities. 'It is not', he argued, 'those who inflict injury, but those who prevent it, whom we should consider the men of courage and of great spirit.'[102]

Whereas historians have repeatedly, if not systematically, examined the legal claims to possession by the English promoters of colonies, they have ignored the denials of possession which do not fit the standard account of a possessive European expansion. The Virginia Company was particularly careful to emphasise that its aim was not the possession of the land of others.[103] In his *Virginia*, the company promoter William Symonds raised the anxiety over possession, noting that there had been objections to the enterprise because 'the country, they say, is possessed by owners, that rule and governe it in their owne right: then with what conscience, and equitie can we offer to thrust them, by violence out of their inheritances?'[104] One of the promoters' answers to this charge was that there was no intention whatsoever to forcibly possess the property of another people. William Crashaw also raised the 'doubt of lawfulness of the action'. According to Crashaw: 'A Christian may take nothing from a heathen against his will, but in faire and lawfull bargain.' 'We will take nothing', he continues, 'from the Savages by power nor pillage, by craft nor violence, neither goods, lands nor libertie, much lesse life.'[105]

---

[100] *Ibid.*, II, 26–7.   [101] *Ibid.*, 27.   [102] *Ibid.*, I, 65.

[103] Most accounts of the legal arguments of the Virginia Company promoters focus on their claims to possession, passing over their denials of having any such intention; see Axtell, *The invasion within*, p. 132; L. C. Green and Olive P. Dickason, *The law of nations and the new world* (Edmonton, 1989); Williams, *The American Indian in western legal thought*, pp. 210–11; Pagden, *Lords of all the world*, pp. 93–4; Tuck, *The rights of war and peace*, pp. 122–4; Juricek, 'English claims in North America to 1660: a study in legal and constitutional history'; Juricek, 'English territorial claims in North America under Elizabeth and the early Stuarts'; Tomlins, 'The legal cartography of colonization'.

[104] Symonds, *Virginia*, p. 10.   [105] Crashaw, *A sermon*, sigs. D3v–[D4]v.

English promoters of colonies did, as we have seen, make claims to the right to possess land in the New World, but their accompanying denials of any intention to possession show those claims to have been deeply equivocal and contradictory. Typically, the promoters move from denying an intention to possess the lands of another people to justifying the presence of the Company in the Chesapeake by appeals to the law of nations – that is, to the right to trade – or, as we have seen, by making the partly contradictory claim that the land was *terra nullius*. In *The historie of travell into Virginia Britannia*, William Strachey questioned the right to possess, arguing 'surely Christian men, should not shew themselves like Wolves to devoure...'. He answered with the argument that the land would not be forcibly possessed: 'and therefore even every foote of Land which we shall take unto our use, we will bargayne and buy of them for copper, hatchets, and such like commodities'.[106] The tension is nowhere more evident than in Robert Gray's *A good speed to Virginia*. Gray raised the customary anxiety over possession: 'The first objection is, by what right or warrant we can enter into the land of these Savages, and plant ourselves in their places.' In accordance with Company policy, he disavowed any such intention: 'the answer to the forsaid objection is, that there is no intendment to take away from them by force that *rightful* inheritance they have in that Countrey'.[107] As late as the 1620s Francis Bacon declared, in his essay *On plantations*: 'I like a *Plantation* in a Pure Soile; that is, where People are not *Displanted*, to the end, to *Plant* in Others. For else, it is rather an Extirpation, then a *Plantation*.'[108] There was little stomach to revive the image of the Romans' treatment of the Ancient Britons found in Tacitus or to ignore Cicero's warnings about empire. There was no desire to dramatise the passage in *Agricola* to which Robert Sidney had been drawn. There was no desire, that is, to civilise the native Americans as the Romans had civilised the Britons, to resort to 'robbery, slaughter, plunder' and give it the 'lying name of imperium'.

---

[106] Strachey, *The historie of travell into Virginia Britannia*, p. 26.

[107] Gray, *A good speed to Virginia*, sig. [C4]r, my emphasis.

[108] Francis Bacon, *The essayes or counsels, civill and morall*, ed. Michael Kiernan (Oxford, 1985), p. 106. It comes as little surprise that Bacon should place this desire in the context of the civic ambitions of the company, declaring that the venture should be controlled: 'rather [by] Noblemen, and Gentlemen, then Merchants: For they looke ever to the present Gaine' (p. 107).

CHAPTER 6

The Machiavellian argument for colonial possession

Historians have distinguished two attitudes in early modern Europe to the problem of the possession of the New World. The first, supported primarily by theologians, particularly the school of Salamanca, was cautious and sceptical concerning the scope of European claims to property in the New World. Opposed to the theologians, according to this account, were the humanists. Humanists were closely associated with colonial ventures – unsurprisingly, given their emphasis on the *vita activa*. They are said to have allowed their preoccupation with glory, particularly the glory of conquest, to encourage their unapologetic justifications of the enterprises (Sepulveda was merely one of many such enthusiasts).[1]

This portrayal has neglected a central tension within Renaissance humanism. Humanists, as we have seen, balanced their pursuit of glory with a careful vigilance against corruption. This anxiety was in part based upon the threats of wealth and luxury that were believed to arise from conquest, but it also encompassed the related question of possession. The humanist promoters of English colonial projects were profoundly concerned with justifying the adventures, but this concern was not motivated simply by

---

[1] The most recent representative of this view is Richard Tuck, *The rights of war and peace: Political thought and the international order from Grotius to Kant* (Oxford, 1999). See also Anthony Pagden, *The fall of natural man: The American Indian and the origins of comparative ethnology* (2nd edn, Cambridge, 1986); L. C. Green and Olive P. Dickason, *The law of nations and the New World* (Edmonton, 1989). The dichotomy is sustained by Robert A. Williams, *The American Indian in western legal thought: The discourses of conquest* (Oxford, 1990), who, however, refers to the Thomistic Salamanca theologians as 'Thomistic-Humanist' (p. 93). It is certainly clear from a reading of Vitoria, for example, that he had also been educated in the *studia humanitatis*. Compare the discussion of the fundamental points of opposition between Thomists of the Salamanca school and humanists, in Quentin Skinner, *The foundations of modern political thought*, 2 vols. (Cambridge, 1978), II, p. 141. See also Francisco de Vitoria, *Political writings*, eds. Anthony Pagden and Jeremy Lawrance (Cambridge, 1991), p. xiv: 'it is a mistake to attribute the originallity of Vitoria's work, as many scholars have done, to a happy marriage of Thomism and "Christian Humanism" . . . he came to regard humanist textual scholarship on the Bible as the slippery slope which had led to Protestant heresy'. The similarities between humanist and Thomist attitudes to colonial possession were not grounded upon any humanist influence upon the Salamanca school.

their pursuit of glory. It also reflected a fear that colonial possession would corrupt the commonwealth, or worse, would reveal the corruption of the commonwealth (both the English commonwealth and the new commonwealth which was to be established). Moreover, the promoters articulated a Ciceronian concern with justice for its own sake. They were concerned, that is, with issues of justice as they relate to the human community and not just the commonwealth. Indeed, as we have seen in the previous chapter, these promoters frequently progressed beyond the justification of possession to a denial that the possession of the lands of other peoples was a part of the colonial design.

The failure to discern a strong anxiety within humanism about colonial possession has distorted our understanding of the circumstances in which the first unapologetic claims to possession were made by the promoters of colonies. Those circumstances were shaped by a central dispute within sixteenth- and seventeenth-century humanist moral philosophy: between a conventional Ciceronian insistence on the primacy of honesty and a Machiavellian and Tacitean emphasis upon expedience and necessity. Anxieties over possession flowed from a Ciceronian concern with preserving honesty. From this perspective, not only had wealth to be avoided, but also the cardinal virtue of justice had to be observed; colonies needed to be justified. According to a Machiavellian and Tacitean perspective, justice was the least troubling of the virtues. The introduction of Machiavellian languages into colonisation allowed the concern with the justice of possession to be dismissed. For the first time, possession could be asserted without any such fears.

In this chapter, I will compare two writers, one 'literary' and one directly involved in colonial projects: William Shakespeare and Captain John Smith. Both have been considered crucial to an understanding of early modern colonisation. Both, I shall argue, adopted a Machiavellian critique of the prevailing Ciceronian model of colonisation supported by the Virginia Company. Through their use of this ideology, these writers made it possible to claim possession of others' lands without the limitation of justice. The first confident claims to English colonial possession were made, that is, through the language of reason of state.[2]

---

[2] I take a conventional view of the thought of Machiavelli as fundamental to the post-Machiavellian emergence of reason of state. For this view see, for example, Skinner, *The foundations of modern political thought*. Cf. Maurizio Viroli, *From politics to reason of state: The acquisition and transformation of the language of politics 1250–1600* (Cambridge, 1992) on a separation between Machiavelli and post-Machiavellian reason of state. Whether Machiavellian or not, my interest here is with the rise of the values of expedience and necessity. See footnote 11 on the possibility of a pre-Machiavellian concept of reason of state.

Consistent with the proto-commercial interpretation of early modern colonisation, historians have understood the colonial impulse in terms of a drive for the possession of the New World. We have seen that these claims are misleading. In accordance with its anxieties over wealth and luxury, the Virginia Company repeatedly stressed that it did not desire the dispossession of other peoples.[3] We have seen that William Crashaw raised the 'doubt of lawfulness of the action', declaring: 'A Christian may take nothing from a heathen against his will, but in faire and lawful bargain.' 'We will take nothing', he continued, 'from the Savages by power nor pillage, by craft nor violence, neither goods, lands nor libertie, much lesse life.'[4] In answer to the question 'by what right or warrant we can enter into the land of these Savages, and plant ourselves in their places', Gray observed: 'the answer to the forsaid objection is, that there is no intendment to take away from them by force that righful inheritance they have in that Countrey'.[5] And we have also seen that as late as the 1620s Francis Bacon declared, in his essay *On plantations*: 'I like a *Plantation* in a Pure Soile; that is, where People are not *Displanted*, to the end, to *Plant* in Others. For else, it is rather an Extirpation, then a *Plantation*.'[6]

This civic understanding of colonial legitimation ('civic' because it arises from a concern with corruption) was essentially one of Ciceronian humanism. The guiding concern was that *honestas* must always be placed before *utilitas*. 'We freely confesse', Crashaw acknowledged, 'an action cannot be good, excellent, or honourable, and much lesse can it be necessarie, unlesse it first of all appeare to be lawful: for the present action we confesse and yeeld to this as to a principle of Justice.'[7] Crucially, the promoters argued that there would be no possession of the territory of others or that, if there was, possession would be just. They made no claims which systematically subordinated justice to necessity.[8] This choice was deliberate, not conventional. The Company was not unaware of the fashion for Machiavellian

---

[3] Most accounts of the legal arguments of the Virginia Company promoters focus on their claims to possession, passing over their denials of having any such intention. See James Axtell, *The invasion within: The contest of cultures in colonial North America* (Oxford, 1985), p. 132; Green and Dickason, *The law of nations and the New World*; Williams, *The American Indian in western legal thought*, pp. 210–11; Anthony Pagden, *Lords of all the world: Ideologies of empire in Spain, Britain and France, c.1500–c.1800* (New Haven, 1995), pp. 93–4; Tuck, *The rights of war and peace*, pp. 122–4.

[4] Crashaw, *A sermon preached before the right honourable the Lord Lawarre* (London, 1610), sig. D3v–[D4]v.

[5] Robert Gray, *A good speed to Virginia* (London, 1609), sig. [C4]r.

[6] Francis Bacon, *The essayes or counsels, civill and morall*, ed. Michael Kiernan (Oxford, 1985), p. 106.

[7] Crashaw, *A Sermon*, sig. D3r.

[8] This is not to suggest that arguments of reason of state cannot be incorporated into a conception of what is just, but justice was not a priority for the critics of the Virginia Company.

arguments of necessity, or 'policy', in which expedience was placed before virtue. Crashaw felt obliged to observe on the title page to his sermon
printed in 1610 that 'the lawfulnesse of that Action [establishing the colony]
is maintained . . . not so much out of the grounds of Policie, as of Humanity, Equity, and Christianity'. This rejection of reason of state is not simply
high minded, it is central to a philosophy of government that had only
been strengthened by experience. We have seen that the emphasis upon
expedience and profit was held responsible for previous colonial failures
and was deemed inappropriate to an enterprise in which death, and not
riches, was believed to be the most likely source of glory.[9]

For scepticism of the Ciceronian humanism in which early modern
colonisation was promoted, we must look again to the ideological context
of Jacobean England and early modern Europe. The ideals of Ciceronian
moral philosophy increasingly came under attack in the sixteenth and early
seventeenth centuries. Writing against the background of the wars of religion, humanists such as Lipsius employed the histories of Tacitus to represent the ideals of the Ciceronians as 'lofty yet forlorn'.[10] Tacitism, as it
has come to be known, was an ideology more appropriate to survival in
the court. In the courtly world, according to Tacitus, deceitful men flour-
ish while virtuous men perish. Yet, the reading of Tacitus in early modern
Europe clearly had, at the least, a double aspect. Perhaps the dominant
understanding of Tacitus was one of nostalgia for a lost civic virtue. In this
sense, Tacitism was an extension of Ciceronian humanism (this was the
Tacitism we saw in the previous chapter). There were two possible lessons

---

[9] See, for example, Robert Johnson, the treasurer of the Company, who addressed the leaders of the
    colony in 1612 when it showed little improvement or prospect, arguing: 'Nay, if losse of life befall
    you by this service . . . yet in this case too, wee doubt not but you are resolved with constant courage',
    in Robert Johnson, *The new life of Virginea* (London, 1612), sigs. D4r–v. Johnson's civic theme of
    courage and martial vigour was first exploited in the tracts of 1609/10. Gray summarised succinctly
    in *A good speed to Virginia*, sig. B4v, 'If an honourable death were set before a virtuous mind it would
    choose rather to die heroically than to live opprobriously.' On the *topos* of courage used to support
    the argument of *honestas*, see Fitzmaurice, 'The civic solution to the crisis of English colonisation,
    1609–1625', 42, 1 (1999), pp. 37–8.

[10] Markku Peltonen, *Classical humanism and republicanism in English political thought, 1570–1640*
    (Cambridge, 1995), p. 125. The nature of early modern Tacitism has recently generated debate.
    Richard Tuck, *Philosophy and government 1572–1651* (Cambridge, 1993), has argued that Tacitus was
    read in a way that overturned Ciceronian humanism. Markku Peltonen, *Classical humanism and
    republicanism in English political thought*, has emphasised that most 'Tacitist' authors were nostal-
    gic for Ciceronian virtue. J. H. M. Salmon, 'Seneca and Tacitus in Jacobean England', in Linda
    Levy Peck, ed., *The mental world of the Jacobean court* (Cambridge, 1991), has shown that Tacitus
    could be read to support several humanist positions. See also Blair Worden, 'Ben Jonson among
    the historians', in Kevin Sharpe and Peter Lake, eds., *Culture and politics in early Stuart England*
    (Basingstoke, 1994); Peter Burke, 'Tacitism', in T. A. Dorey, ed., *Tacitus* (London, 1969); and Peter
    Burke, 'Tacitism, scepticism and reason of state', in *The Cambridge history of political thought*, eds.
    J. H. Burns and Mark Goldie (Cambridge, 1991).

from Tacitus for the virtuous subject. The bad fortune of public life could be suffered stoically, or the subject could withdraw from public life, given that participation demanded a descent into flattery and trickery. There was, however, another possible reading of Tacitus which was more consistent with the rise of Machiavellism, and with which we shall be concerned in this chapter.[11] According to this reading, the subject would adopt the behaviour of dissimulation, deceit, flattery and trickery because this was the only means of survival in a corrupt world. It was this, perhaps more pessimistic, version of Tacitus and a corresponding Machiavellism which was employed to critique the civic thought of the Virginia Company.

WILLIAM SHAKESPEARE, *THE TEMPEST*

Most eloquent among these critiques, although not subsequently recognised as such, was Shakespeare's *The Tempest*. For a generation, the play has attracted a great deal of attention, particularly within post-colonial theory, not (as I will argue) as a repudiation of Jacobean colonial ideology, but as an exemplum of 'colonialist discourse'. While post-colonial theory is a field that claims no great degree of coherence, it has been united by two concerns. The first is the cultural means through which 'colonialism' has been pursued, with 'colonialism' defined as 'the conquest and control of other people's lands and goods'.[12] According to this understanding, the

---

[11] It should be noted that the argument of reason of state could be supported not only through reading Machiavelli and Tacitus but also Cicero. It has been pointed out that there is frequent ambiguity in Cicero's moral and political writings on the relation between *honestas* and *utilitas* and that this ambiguity could be employed to support arguments of *necessitas*. See Peter Miller, *Defining the common good: Empire, religion and philosophy in eighteenth-century Britain* (Cambridge, 1994), ch. 1; Tuck, *Philosophy and government*, p. 7; and Peltonen, *Classical humanism and republicanism in English political thought*, p. 135. This point could be made even more strongly by reference to Cicero's rhetorical works. There are several points in the rhetorical treatises where the orator is provided with instructions on how to argue a case which is expedient but not virtuous. Perhaps most notable of these is the discussion of assumptive justice in forensic rhetoric, particularly comparative assumptive justice, in which the orator defends an action that he concedes was morally wrong. Cicero's *De inventione*, which was studied by every Renaissance schoolboy, provided the standard treatment of this topic; see *De inventione*, trans. H. M. Hubbell (London, 1949), II.71–77; or Thomas Wilson's neo-Ciceronian, *The arte of rhetorique*, ed. Thomas J. Derrick (New York, 1982), pp. 206–8. That rhetoricians should argue in defence of morally wrong actions should cause no surprise if it is remembered that they were often professional lawyers writing for prospective lawyers. The presence of such moral ambiguity in the work of Cicero does not, however, provide grounds with which to review 'the conventional account of the moralism of the early Renaissance' (Tuck, *The rights of war and peace*, p. 10).

[12] Ania Loomba, *Colonialism/postcolonialism* (London, 1998), p. 2. In *Culture and imperialism* (London, 1993), Edward Said suggests that the arguments of his *Orientalism: Western conceptions of the orient* (London, 1978) could be pursued from the foundations of European colonisation. For a critique of this view, see Armitage, 'Literature and empire', p. 101.

central impulse of colonisation is possession – material possession, ideological possession and mimetic possession. The second concern has been with the processes through which colonialism has been resisted by colonised peoples. Numerous studies have presented *The Tempest* as seminal to these two concerns.

It is a central claim of these studies that the play enacts the 'dominant discursive con-texts' of 'English colonialism'.[13] Critics such as Paul Brown have adapted the thought of Edward Said to argue that *The Tempest* is implicated in the exploitation of the inhabitants of the New World.[14] Stephen Greenblatt has emphasised the play's concern with 'linguistic colonialism'. For Greenblatt, as for many post-colonial theorists, the ideology of Prospero is believed to be substantially continuous with that of early modern colonisation.[15] It is central to these interpretations that early modern colonisation is understood in terms of 'colonialism': it is characterised in terms of profit, appropriation and possession.[16] This understanding is not, as we have seen, remote from that of many historians. Critical attention has taken the relationship between Prospero and Caliban to be an axiomatic colonial relationship and has focused upon its ironies and instabilities.

It had, of course, been widely accepted well before the advent of postcolonial theory that when Shakespeare wrote *The Tempest* he employed reports of the Virginia Company.[17] The Jamestown colony was established

---

[13] Francis Barker and Peter Hulme, 'Nymphs and reapers heavily vanish: The discursive con-texts of *The Tempest*', in John Drakakis, ed., *Alternative Shakespeares* (London, 1985), p. 198.

[14] Paul Brown, ' "This thing of darkness I acknowledge mine": *The Tempest* and the discourse of colonialism', in Jonathan Dollimore and Alan Sinfield, eds., *Political Shakespeare: New essays in cultural materialism* (Ithaca, 1985), pp. 48–71. Barbara Fuchs 'Conquering islands: contextualising *The Tempest*', *Shakespeare Quarterly*, 48 (1997), p. 45, has stated that 'It is an axiom of contemporary criticism that *The Tempest* is a play about European colonial experience in America.' On the play enacting colonial ideology, see also Charles Frey, '*The Tempest* and the New World', *Shakespeare Quarterly*, 30, 1 (1979); John Gillies, *Shakespeare and the geography of difference* (Cambridge, 1994); and expressing some caution, Andrew Hadfield, *Literature, travel, and colonial writing in the English Renaissance 1545–1625* (Oxford, 1998), pp. 243–6. Jeffrey Knapp, *An empire nowhere: England, America, and literature from Utopia to The Tempest* (Berkeley, 1992), pp. 220–42 presents the play as an 'antimaterialist' rejection of English 'imperialism', thus conforming to the orthodox view of English colonisation as materialistic.

[15] Stephen Greenblatt, 'Learning to curse: aspects of linguistic colonialism in the sixteenth century', in Fredi Chiappelli, ed., *First images of America: The impact of the New World on the Old*, 2 vols. (Berkeley, 1976) II, pp. 568–71.

[16] A point well made by Meredith Anne Skura, 'Discourse and the individual: the case of colonialism in *The Tempest*', *Shakespeare Quarterly*, 40, 1 (1989), p. 47. The Virginia Company, according to this account, was committed to 'turning a profit'; see Stephen Greenblatt, *Shakespearean negotiations* (Oxford, 1988), p. 148.

[17] The link between *The Tempest* and the literature promoting the Virginia colony was first made in 1808. See William Shakespeare, *The Tempest*, ed. Stephen Orgel (Oxford, 1987), p. 32. This link was most thoroughly explored by Charles Mills Gayley, *Shakespeare and the founders of liberty*

in 1606 and was able to survive only by repeated supply from London. The Company sent a fleet of supply ships in 1609, but the flagship with replacement leaders for the colony was wrecked in a storm upon the Bermudas. Miraculously, everyone on board survived and, after spending a year on the islands, built a small pinnace in which they completed the voyage to Jamestown. There is prolific evidence in the play that Shakespeare employed material from the reports of this wreck. He could have obtained these reports from several sources, including his patron, Henry Wriothesley, the earl of Southampton, one of the leaders of the Company; William Herbert, the earl of Pembroke, a dedicatee of the folio edition of Shakespeare's works, and also a prominent member of the Virginia Company; and Dudley Digges, an active member of the Virginia Council from 1609, linked to Shakespeare through his brother, Leonard.[18]

The reports, and the larger context of New World narratives, clearly suggest aspects of the scene for *The Tempest*, a shipwreck upon an isolated island outside European limits. We cannot mistake the fact that the name Caliban is an anagram of cannibal. The god of Caliban's mother was Patagonian. The play contains an explicit reference to the Bermudas. Both the Bermudas, according to maritime myth, and Prospero's island, were inhabited by spirits. The play frequently draws upon descriptions of nature in the New World.[19] Jonathan Bate has argued that these parallels are superficial when compared with the central themes of *The Tempest*. The play, he argues, is not concerned with the material of New World narratives but with humanist debates on the best form of government.[20] This criticism helps us to focus on the strongest link between the play and the context of Jacobean colonisation. The literature promoting the Virginia Company's colony, like Shakespeare's play, was also profoundly concerned with the nature of the best form of government, for the simple reason that the Company was attempting to establish a new commonwealth (although, as I argue, the

in America (New York, 1917). Gayley attempted to place the play in the context of a patriotic tradition of American history which sought the origins of liberal individualism in early American colonisation. See E. D. Neill, *The English colonisation of America during the seventeenth century* (London, 1871); Alexander Brown, *English politics in early Virginian history* (first published 1901, reissued New York 1968). Cf. Fitzmaurice, 'The civic solution to the crisis of English colonisation, 1609–1625'. There have also been several recent challenges to colonisation as an important context for the play; see, for example, Skura, 'Discourse and the individual'; Jonathan Bate, 'The humanist *Tempest*', in *Shakespeare La Tempête. Etudes critiques*, Actes du colloque de Besançon (1993); Jerry Brotton, ' "This Tunis, sir, was Carthage": contesting colonialism in *The Tempest*', in Ania Loomba and Martin Orkin, eds., *Post-colonial Shakespeares* (London, 1998).

[18] Gayley, *Shakespeare and the founders of liberty*, pp. 22–4; Shakespeare, *The Tempest*, ed. Orgel, p. 32.

[19] See Frank Kermode, introduction to William Shakespeare, *The Tempest* (London, 1954); and Orgel, introduction to Shakespeare, *The Tempest*, pp. 31–6.

[20] See Bate, 'The humanist *Tempest*', p. 6.

play rejected the solution advanced by the Company). Indeed, the Virginia Company pamphlets constitute one of the most vigorous Jacobean discussions of this humanist preoccupation.[21] Rather than this debate being conducted separately from the issue of relations with New World natives, those relations, as we shall see, were believed to be crucial in several ways to the successful foundation and conservation of the new commonwealth.

If the Virginia Company literature is characterised by Ciceronian optimism, *The Tempest* is all Tacitean pessimism. The play is deeply concerned with the Tacitean themes of corruption, with flattery and servility, deceit and dissimulation – the qualities cultivated in the restless and dangerous world of *The Prince*. It is through deceit that Antonio ('he whom next thyself/ Of all the world I lov'd', I.ii.68–9) had seized power from Prospero. Prospero describes Antonio's court in precisely these terms: 'Being once perfected how to grant suits/ How to deny them, who t'advance, and who/ To trash for over-topping' he 'set all hearts i' th' state/ To what tune pleas'd his ear' (I.ii.79–85). Sebastian attempts to exploit Alonso's trust to the same ends (II.i.210–95). And Caliban hopes for advancement through his obsequiousness to Stephano, pleading 'Let me lick thy shoe' (III.ii.22). Prospero's withdrawal into contemplation when he was duke (I.ii.89–92) suggests a Tacitean view that precedes Antonio's betrayal: withdrawal into contemplation was repeatedly stressed by Tacitean writers as the only available response to a corrupt world.

The island commonwealth over which Prospero autocratically rules has the same atmosphere. Caliban plots against Prospero's life. Prospero's favourite, Ariel, longs for freedom. His service to Prospero is secured not by love of his master but through a Machiavellian use of fear: 'If thou more murmur'st, I will rend an oak/ And peg thee in its knotty entrails till/ Thou hast howled away twelve winters' (I.ii.295–7). Both Caliban and Ariel are repeatedly described not merely as Prospero's subjects but as his slaves (for Caliban I.ii.308, 313, 319, 345, 350; for Ariel I.ii.245). Even Prospero's daughter is forced into deceit when she provides Ferdinand with her name (III.i.37–8).

This atmosphere is prefigured early in the play in an exchange concerning the widow Dido which has puzzled critics. Frank Kermode commented that the passage is obscure but could, if understood, 'modify our image of the whole play'.[22] Stephen Orgel has shown that the exchange plays upon

---

[21] See Fitzmaurice, 'The civic solution to the crisis of English colonisation, 1609–1625'; and Andrew Fitzmaurice, 'Classical rhetoric and the promotion of the New World', *Journal of the History of Ideas*, 58 (1997), pp. 121–44.

[22] Shakespeare, *The Tempest*, ed. Kermode, pp. 46–7.

two readings of the myth of Dido that encapsulate 'the play's thematic ambivalence towards human nature'.[23] Dido was the mythical founder of Carthage. According to one account, endorsed by Petrarch, she was a model of chastity who maintained her marriage vows to her murdered husband after fleeing Tyre. Virgil transformed Dido into a fallen woman by introducing Aeneas into the story as her lover. These contrasting images underlie the play's concern with the ethical and the cynical. Orgel's understanding can be further extended. In ch. 17 of *The Prince*, 'Cruelty and mercifulness; and whether it is better to be loved or feared', Machiavelli cites Dido as the primary example of how to consolidate power through deceit and cruelty: 'Virgil makes Dido say, Res dura, et regni novitas me talia cogunt/ moliri, et late fines custode tuere [Harsh necessity and the newness of my kingdom force me to do such things, and to guard all frontiers].'[24] The Machiavellian context for the exchange on Dido in *The Tempest* is cast into greater relief by the contrast with Gonzalo's description, into which it leads, of a utopian commonwealth devoid of the courtly vices of dissimulation. The character of Gonzalo's commonwealth is remote not only from the Milanese and Neapolitan courts but also from Prospero's island (II.i.145–66).[25]

Antonio's cynical version of the Dido myth confirms Prospero's account of his brother's character but, more importantly, reminds us that Prospero, who like Dido is the founder of a new commonwealth, has had to learn how not to be good. Prospero is prepared to use magic of an ambiguous nature to manipulate his subjects.[26] To maintain his state and achieve his ends, he is prepared to cause suffering. He inflicts grief, for example, upon Alonso who weeps for his lost son ('O thou mine heir/ Of Naples and of Milan, what strange fish,/ Hath made his meal on thee?', II.i.109–11), and upon Ferdinand ('I weep: myself am Naples,/ Who with mine eyes, never since at ebb, beheld/ The King my father wrecked', I.ii.435–7). He does not use this suffering merely for revenge; it advances his consolidation of power and facilitates the political marriage of Ferdinand and Miranda: 'It goes on, I see,/ As my soul prompts it' (I.ii.420–1). He is also prepared to use fear, for example, to control Caliban and Ariel, or in hunting Trinculo

---

[23] Shakespeare, *The Tempest*, ed. Orgel, p. 42. The passage has recently also been central to the interpretation of Brotton, ' "This Tunis, sir, was Carthage" ', p. 23.

[24] Machiavelli, *The Prince*, ed. Quentin Skinner and Russell Price (Cambridge, 1988), p. 58.

[25] The contrast is stronger in Florio's 1603 translation of Montaigne's 'Of the Cannibals' from which the passage is drawn. Florio's version concludes: 'The very words that import lying, falsehood, treason, dissimulation, covetousness, envy, detraction, and pardon were never heard of amongst them', cited in Shakespeare, *The Tempest*, ed. Orgel, p. 135.

[26] On the ambiguity of Prospero's magic, see Shakespeare, *The Tempest*, ed. Orgel, pp. 20–2. Cf. Shakespeare, *The Tempest*, ed. Kermode, p. xli.

and Stephano with dogs (Ariel: 'Hark, they roar.' Prospero: 'Let them be hunted soundly', IV.i.263–4.), in each case for political purposes.

We may say that the Virginia Company was also greatly concerned with corruption in its own commonwealth. In characteristic civic fashion, however, the Company diagnosed corruption with an expectation that it should be remedied. In a fashion characteristic of the more pessimistic strain of Tacitism, *The Tempest* offers little hope for moral reform. Antonio and Sebastian, for example, are unrepentant. The Virginia Company frequently appealed to the 'common sort' to embrace virtue and participate in the foundation of the new commonwealth.[27] Even when describing the corruption of colonists, the Company expected them to reform. The commoners Trinculo and Stephano, by contrast, are represented as fit only for being ruled. Ferdinand and Miranda are the next generation of rulers, uniting the divisions of the past and promising hope for the future. But even their love matures into deceit, as Miranda reproaches: 'Sweet lord, you play me false' (V.i).

Perhaps most importantly, we are told that there was a period when Prospero first came to the island in which he treated Caliban with kindness (I.ii.330–75). At this time Prospero and Caliban shared the island; both were at liberty. Caliban abused this trust when he attempted to rape Miranda: 'O ho, O ho! Would't had been done!/ Thou did'st prevent me – I had peopled else/ This isle with Calibans' (I.ii.347–9). He does not, and seemingly cannot, possess civic virtue, as Miranda reminds him: 'Abhorred slave, which any print of goodness wilt not take' (I.ii.353–4). Prospero recognised that he was repeating the mistakes of his rule in Milan. He was too liberal, too trusting. It had been these qualities in his treatment of his brother which provoked his downfall: 'my trust,/ Like a good parent, did beget of him [Antonio]/ A falsehood in its contrary as great/ As my trust was, which had, indeed, no limit' (I.ii.93–6). Caliban raises the issue of possession of the island and claims to hold the just title: 'This island's mine by Sycorax my mother,/ which thou tak'st from me' (I.ii.331–2). Prospero responds 'I have used thee – /filth as thou art – with humane care, and lodged thee/ In mine own cell, till thou didst seek to violate/ The honour of my child' (I.ii.345–8). Caliban's rejection of virtue renders justice a secondary issue. As critics have observed, Prospero makes no further attempt to justify his treatment of Caliban or his usurpation of the island, he simply concludes 'Hag-seed, hence!' (I.ii.365). Enslaving Caliban may not be virtuous but it is the only available response to a world in which

[27] Richard Eburne, *A plaine pathway to plantations* (London, 1624) was devoted to the question of encouraging the 'common sort' to 'adventure'. Although not exclusively concerned with Virginia the tract was derivative of Virginia Company pamphlets.

virtue is scarce. It is the only means by which Prospero can maintain his state.

This understanding of *The Tempest* in terms of Machiavellian and Tacitean thought is not inconsistent with the many readings of Prospero as an 'absolutist' ruler.[28] The description, however, possesses radically different meanings depending upon the context in which it is placed. If the context is the 'discourse of colonialism' and that discourse is an extension of the powers of the European state – an extension of its institutions of appropriation, exploitation and domination – then a Tacitean language would reflect that ideology, both through its language of domination and even in its implied nostalgia for a preceding golden age (or in the unstable characterisations of Prospero and Caliban). This understanding fails to appreciate that the relationship between Prospero and Caliban is in direct opposition to Virginia Company policy. As an act, therefore, the force of the play is precisely opposite to that claimed by critics concerned with the New World context. It is, of course, difficult to view the play purely from the perspective of Prospero. It is possible to sympathise with Caliban and there are doubts about the legitimacy of Prospero's claim to the island. The atmosphere of the play, however, is clearly not the republic of virtue imagined by the Virginia Company. The atmosphere is that of a Tacitean court in which virtue is inadequate for dealing with the realities of a corrupt world.

JOHN SMITH

This contrast between *The Tempest* and the Virginia Company's propaganda is confirmed by the affinities between the Tacitism of the play and those voices in the Virginia enterprise that dissent from the dominant civic ideology of Jacobean colonisation. Most striking, perhaps, is a report entitled *A true declaration of the estate of the colonie in Virginia* published in 1610 and probably written by Dudley Digges. Digges was a prominent gentry member of the Company, parliamentarian, and the author of *Four paradoxes, or politique discourses* in which he was fully conscious of the tensions between Ciceronian and Tacitist perspectives.[29] It has also been suggested that he was a link between Shakespeare and the Virginia Company.[30] One of the

[28] Most recently Hadfield, *Literature, travel, and colonial writing in the English Renaissance*, p. 252, suggests that 'In many ways it can be read as a cynical play, exposing the hollow, absolutist pretensions of Prospero without providing any viable alternative means of government.'

[29] See Dudley Digges, *Four paradoxes, or politique discourses* (London, 1604).

[30] Shakespeare, *The Tempest*, ed. Orgel, p. 32; and Gayley, *Shakespeare and the founders of liberty*, pp. 22–4. In addition to his *Four paradoxes, or politique discourses*, Digges was also the author of an *Art of war*.

central concerns of the *True declaration* is the wreck upon the Bermudas, believed to constitute the immediate context for Shakespeare's play. The tension between what we may call a conventional Ciceronian and a Tacitist perspective is clearly revealed in the report. In defending some apparently dishonest actions of Thomas Gates, who was the captain of the wrecked ship, the author declares 'And thus you see, that Tacitus wisely observed the two great enemies of great actions, "*Ignorantiam veri, et Invidiam*", the ignorance of Truth and the emulation of Virtue.'[31]

This was certainly by no means the first time that expedience had been elevated above honesty in English colonial enterprises. Humphrey Gilbert, the holder of the first patent to colonise in the New World (in 1578), had employed reason of state in the subjection of Ireland. In strongly Machiavellian terms Gilbert had argued: 'no Conquered nacion will ever yelde willinglie their obedience for love but rather for feare'.[32] But while leaving some outline of his colonial ambitions, Gilbert made no systematic statement of reason of state applied to colonial ventures.[33]

Machiavellian themes were to be developed by the most consistently dissenting voice in Jacobean colonisation literature, that of John Smith. Smith had a grammar-school education and significantly, given his Machiavellian perspective, he had occupied himself between his early adventures and his Virginian exploits by reading on the art of war.[34] His Machiavellian attitude

---

[31] *A true declaration of the estate of the colonie in Virginia*, p. 21. Digges was certainly no absolutist in parliamentary debate. Support and opposition for arguments of reason of state are dependent upon context. If he is the author of the *True declaration*, it should be noted that on the whole the report preserves the civic emphasis of the Company. On Digges' political views, see J. P. Sommerville, *Royalists and patriots: Politics and ideology in England 1603–1640* (2nd edn, London, 1999), pp. 97 and 147; and Peltonen, *Classical humanism and republicanism in English political thought*, p. 291. On Digges and the Virginia Company, see Theodore K. Rabb, *Jacobean gentleman* (Princeton, 1988), p. 323.

[32] Humphrey Gilbert, *The voyages and colonising enterprises of Sir Humphrey Gilbert*, ed. David B. Quinn 2 vols. (London, 1940), I, p. 17.

[33] We only have Gilbert's *A discourse of a discovery for a new passage to Cataia* (London, 1586), a treatise concerned with the discovery of a north-western passage to China in which colonisation was a secondary concern. Previous discussions of Machiavellian thought in early modern English colonisation have centred upon Irish rather than Virginian projects. For these cases see Peltonen, *Classical humanism and republicanism in English political thought*, pp. 74–102; Lisa Jardine, 'Mastering the uncouth: Gabriel Harvey, Edmund Spencer and the English experience in Ireland', in John Henry and Sarah Hutton, eds., *New perspectives on Renaissance thought* (London, 1990), including further evidence on Gilbert. Richard Tuck, *The rights of war and peace*, argues that the distinction between conventional humanism and reason of state has been overstated (see n. 11). He accordingly portrays humanists who were nervous about war as 'extremists' (p. 69). Tuck reveals Machiavellian themes in the humanist jurisprudence of Alberico Gentile. He is obliged, however, to minimise Gentile's ambivalence on these themes in his orations *in utramque partem* on the topic of Roman expansion (pp. 17, 69).

[34] 'John Smith' in the *Dictionary of national biography*, eds. Leslie Stephen and Sidney Lee (London, 1917), XVIII, p. 478.

is particularly evident in accounts of his relations with the natives. Almost from the foundation of the colony, Smith was critical of the Company's desire to win favour with the Powhatan confederation. In his first report from colony, Smith was alert to the 'politike salvage'. He frequently described Powhatan, the leader of the Chesapeake confederation, as 'this politician' and observes: 'experience had well taught me to beleeve his friendship, till convenient opportunity suffred him to betray us'.[35] Smith's Machiavellian judgements are by no means limited to relations with the Powhatans. When he feels compelled by critics within the colony to justify an action which appeared intemperate, he replies that 'though some wise men may condemn this too bould attempt of too much indiscretion' yet it was justified by the pursuit of 'matters of worth' and therefore by consideration of 'the publike good'.[36] He does not reject the charge of intemperance, he simply appeals to necessity.

Like Prospero, Smith is between two Tacitean worlds; he can trust neither the 'savages' nor his European rivals for power, each reflects on the other. The atmosphere of the colony is that of a Tacitean court, controlled by envy and with a leader who is threatened by virtuous subordinates:

The President [Christopher Newport] and Councel so much envied his [Smith's] estimation amongst the Salvages...that they wrought it into their understandings, by their great bounty in giving 4 times more for their commodities than he appointed, that their greatnesse and authority, as much exceed his, as their bounty, and liberality.[37]

In a strongly Machiavellian passage, the liberal policy of Newport toward the natives is redescribed as prodigality (a scenario also reminiscent of Prospero awakening ambition in his brother). Newport's liberality provoked deceit in the politic Powhatan who, at the next opportunity, argues:

Captain Newport it is not agreeable with my greatnes in this pedling manner to trade for trifles, and I esteeme you a great werowans, therefore lay me down all your commodities togither, what I like I will take, and in recompence give you that I think fitting their value.[38]

Smith warns Newport that it is Powhatan's 'intent but to cheat us'. Yet Newport agrees to the terms, 'thinking to out brave this Salvage in ostentation

[35] John Smith, *A true relation* (London, 1608), sigs. C4r, D2r and Dv.   [36] *Ibid.*, sig. B3v.
[37] T. Abbay and William Symonds, eds., *The proceedings of the English colonie in Virginia* (Oxford, 1612), p. 17.
[38] Abbay and Symonds, eds., *The proceedings of the English colonie in Virginia*, p. 19.

of greatnes'. Powhatan 'having his desire, valued his corne at such a rate, as I think it better cheape in Spaine'.[39]

The narrative brings these conflicts to a climax:

Powhatan to expresse his love to Newport, when he departed, presented him with 20 Turkies, conditionally to returne him 20 Swords, which immediately were sent him [marginal note: 'An ill example to sell swords to Salvages']; Now after his departure hee presented Captaine Smith with the like luggage, but not finding his humor, obaied in sending him weapons, he caused his people with 20 devises to obtain them, at last by ambuscaodoes at our very ports they would take them perforce, surprise us at work, or any way, which was so long permitted that they became so insolent, there was no rule.[40]

The folly of Newport's liberality is underlined in the symmetry of the twenty swords he traded being used against the colony. This figure of inversion is central to the moral redescription characteristic of Machiavellian thought; it recalls Prospero's lament that 'my trust [in Antonio]... did beget of him/ A falsehood in its contrary as great/ As my trust was'.[41] Apparent virtues such as trust and liberality can breed corresponding vices. Prospero's trust produces falsehood; Newport's liberality produces insolence and rebellion. Thus trust is naivety and liberality is disorder.

The conflict between the Virginia Company's Ciceronian and Smith's Machiavellian understanding of the colony's politics is made explicit in the conclusion of this passage:

... the command from England was so straight not to offend them [the Powhatans], as our authority bearers (keeping their houses) would rather be anything than peace breakers: this charitable humor prevailed, till well it chaunced they meddled with captaine Smith, who without farther deliberation gave them such an encounter, as some he so hunted up and downe the Ile, some he so terrified with whipping, beating and imprisonment...[42]

Here we find that the anxieties we have seen expressed by the Virginia Company about possession and conflict with the natives were not exclusively the stuff of promotional tracts.[43] Through its officers in the colony,

---

[39] *Ibid.*   [40] *Ibid.*, pp. 23–4.

[41] On rhetorical redescription in Renaissance thought, see Quentin Skinner, 'Thomas Hobbes: rhetoric and the construction of morality', in *Proceedings of the British Academy*, 76 (1991), pp. 1–61; and Quentin Skinner, *Reason and rhetoric in the philosophy of Hobbes* (Cambridge, 1996), pp. 138–80.

[42] Abbay and Symonds, *Proceedings of the English colonie in Virginia*, pp. 23–4.

[43] Many historians have expressed scepticism concerning the role of printing in establishing the Jamestown colony, see, for example, David B. Quinn, ed., *New American world: A documentary history of North America to 1612*, 5 vols. (New York, 1979), V, p. 233; and Andrews, *Trade, plunder and settlement*, p. 320. For a reply, see Andrew Fitzmaurice, ' "Every man, that prints, adventures":

the Company attempts to implement precisely these concerns as policy.[44] According to Smith's apologists, the policy is pursued to such an extreme that the colonists are restrained from protecting themselves. For Smith, the policy is out of step with political reality. His response – the use of violence, fear, whipping and hunting – vividly recalls Prospero's use of the same strategies, particularly in the hunting of Caliban and his Machiavellian belief that fear is more productive of obedience than love: 'Thou most lying slave, whom stripes may move, not kindness' (I.ii.345–6).

The Company remained unmoved by Smith's arguments:

> The patient council, that nothing would move to warre with the Salvages, would gladly have wrangled with captaine Smith for his cruelty, yet none was slaine to any mans knowledge but it brought them in such feare and obedience, as his very name wold, sufficiently affright them.[45]

Smith's opposition to the Virginia Company is in seemingly self-conscious Machiavellian language. Cruelty and fear are explicitly endorsed as the only effective means through which to maintain obedience and order, and are justified by their employment to that end. The Company's anxieties about possession and conflict with the natives are rejected as a danger to the continued survival of the colony, a danger to the continued maintenance of the new commonwealth.

The Tacitean element in Smith's analysis of relations with the Powhatans centred upon his perception of the dissimulating power of speech. When trading with Opechancanough, Powhatan's brother, Smith began with the declaration, 'Opechancanough the great love you professe with your tongue seems mere deceit by your actions.'[46] Words cloak true intentions. His scepticism was justified when his company of 16 men were allegedly ambushed by 700 'savages'. In Smith's speech to his men, with their backs literally against a wall, we find the dissimulation of the Powhatans compared with the dissimulation of Smith's 'seeming friends' in the Virginia Company:

> Worthy countrimen were the mischief of my seeming friends, no more than the danger of these enemies, I little cared, were they as many more, if you dare do, but as I. But this is my torment, that if I escape them, our malicious councell with their

---

the rhetoric of the Virginia Company sermons', in Lori Anne Ferrell and Peter McCullough, eds., *The English sermon revised: Religion, Literature and history 1500–1750* (Manchester, 2000).

[44] One of the Company's attempts to legitimise possession was performed through the coronation of Powhatan as James' vassal. Smith was required to assist in the performance of the ceremony but was outspoken in his opposition. This 'more strange coronation', he argued, was a waste of time and energy, Abbay and Symonds, *Proceedings of the English colonie in Virginia*, p. 42.

[45] *Ibid.*, pp. 24–5.   [46] *Ibid.*, p. 65.

open mouthed minions, will make mee such a peace breaker (in their opinions) in England, as wil break my neck; I could wish those here, that make these seem Saints, and me an oppressor.[47]

Seeming friends' were a greater danger than 700 Indians because their open mouthed minions had the rhetorical power to redescribe courage as brutality, treacherous savages as saints, and to redescribe the victim of the 'savages' (Smith) as their oppressor. Again here, Smith reveals that he is fully conscious that his Tacitean analysis of the situation is directly at odds with, and serves as a critique of, the Virginia Company's civic anxieties.

On a separate occasion, under the threat of famine (implicitly an occasion of necessity), Smith set out apparently upon Powhatan's invitation to trade. He was warned by the speech of a friendly werowans of a plot by Powhatan to kill him, but he persisted in his mission. Powhatan 'fained' that he had not sent for Smith, and claimed to have no corn, but he conceded that for forty swords he could procure forty bushels of wheat. Smith reminds Powhatan of his invitation and refuses the terms. Powhatan comments that 'he could eat his corne but not his copper'. 'Seeing the intent of this subtil Savage', Smith makes a speech in which he testifies his love for Powhatan. Powhatan replies with 'flattery' but expresses the fear that Smith has come to conquer. He asks, therefore, that 'To cleare us of this feare, leave abord your weapons, for here they are needless we being friends.' Smith replies that he would require such a course from his enemies not his friends. Powhatan assures his love and promises a steady supply of corn asking only that Smith 'lay downe his armes'. 'To this subtil discourse' Smith complains that Powhatan 'will not rightly conceive of our words.' Powhatan observes that Smith refers to both himself and Captaine Newport as 'father' but 'for all us both, you will do what you list, and wee must seek to content you'. Again here Powhatan points out that the reality of these relationships is the opposite of the appearance and he argues that this is the reason he asks for collateral for Smith's good words. Smith decides that 'This savage but trifled the time to cut his throat' and so falsely promises 'to content you tomorrow I will leave my armes and trust your promise'.[48] Smith resolved that his survival demanded the adoption of the Tacitean exploitation of language to deceive and flatter that he perceived in his opponents. Prospero claims to have been the victim of similar lies and deceits from Caliban and similarly faces a treacherous plot against his life. Both Smith and Prospero resemble Tacitus's Octavian, a man with virtues, who consolidated his authority

[47] *Ibid.*, pp. 67–8.　　[48] *Ibid.*, pp. 58–65.

through the exploitation of trickery; but in a corrupt world, according to Tacitus, such methods were the only real choice.

It will, of course, be objected that a man of Smith's humble origin and pragmatic outlook would not have corrupted his mind with Cicero, Tacitus and Machiavelli. It could be concluded that he is being dragooned here into the humanists' ranks. In reply, it must first be remembered that Smith had a grammar-school education and that most students armed with this education in Elizabethan England would have been conversant with a broad range of classical and humanist texts. Numerous studies of Shakespeare's grammar-school education have underlined this fact.[49] Moreover, this education was believed to provide the necessary tools for an active life. It is also important in responding to the charge of dragooning to note that not only did Smith, as we have seen, consciously appeal to conventional distinctions between Machiavellian and Ciceronian thought, he also explicitly acknowledged that he had read Machiavelli. Indeed, he did not merely read Machiavelli, he devoted himself for a period, by his own account, to the study of Machiavelli and Marcus Aurelius to the exclusion of all the comforts of life. We find an account of this period, when he was in his twenties, in his *True travels* published in 1629:

he retired himselfe into a little wooddie pasture, a good way from any towne, invironed with many hundred Acres of other woods: Here by a faire brook he built a Pavillion of boughes, where only in his cloaths he lay. His studie was *Machiavells Art of warre*, and *Marcus Aurelius*; his exercise a good horse, with his lance and Ring; his food was thought to be more of venison than any thing else; what he wanted, his man brought him.

The 'countrey', we are told, were 'wondering at such an Hermite'.[50] They may have been wondering at Smith's determination to take to a quixotic extreme the commonplace humanist occupation of retirement into contemplation in preparation for the active life. Smith's reading of Marcus Aurelius was probably the translation by Antonio de Guevara, entitled *The dial of princes*, one of the most popular books of the sixteenth century.[51] It

---

[49] Most notably T. W. Baldwin, *William Shakepere's small Latine and lesse Greeke*, 2 vols. (Urbana, 1944). See also Donald L. Clark, *John Milton at St Paul's School: A study of ancient rhetoric in English Renaissance education* (New York, 1948).

[50] John Smith, *The true travels and adventures of Captain John Smith* (London, 1629), reprinted in Edward Arber, *Captain John Smith, Works* (Birmingham, 1884), p. 823.

[51] On Smith's use of Guevara's edition, see Philip L. Barbour, *The three worlds of Captain John Smith* (London, 1964), p. 14. On Guevara, see Skinner, *Foundations of modern political thought*, I, pp. 214–15.

was a useful work for an ambitious young man as it was read as a handbook for the courtier in the same mould as Baldassare Castiglione's *Book of the courtier* and Thomas Elyot's *Book named the governor*. Machiavelli's *Art of war* was, of course, no mere military manual; it pursued many of the themes which were to be developed in *The prince* and *The discourses*. In book IV of the *Art of war* we find, for example, Machiavelli's characteristic analysis of the use of terror in order to produce compliance; a theme, as we have seen, which was also thoroughly explored by Smith in his dealings with the Powhatans.

We are probably saved from considering the narratives of Smith's adventures as a source for *The Tempest* by the fact that they were published as *A Map of Virginia* and *The proceedings of the English colonie in Virginia* in 1612, the year after the first performance of the play. It is true that these accounts may have first circulated in manuscript and we have seen that there was also a suggestion of these themes in Smith's *Relation* of 1608. The more significant point, however, is that the parallel between the views of Smith and the atmosphere of *The Tempest* reveals the degree to which Tacitism and Machiavellism were the natural idioms for critiquing discussions of colonisation when those discussions were deeply permeated by civic languages. Notably, it has been claimed that the publication of the narratives in Oxford, and not with the Virginia Company's usual London printers, reflected Company hostility to Smith.[52]

This conclusion is consistent with recent historiography that has shown that New World experience shaped Old World ideology.[53] The experiences of Smith and Prospero fit that understanding. Both entered a colonial context with an ideological armoury that proved inadequate to political realities (although it is important to remember that the Company's civic ideology had also been forged by experience). Smith was expected to conduct his relations with 'savages' through an ideology of civic virtue, central to which were concerns about corruption arising from conquest and colonial profit and possession. According to Smith, he is instead confronted by a people whose political behaviour is not unlike that of the Jacobean court. He inhabits a world in which, if he is virtuous, he will perish. This realisation forced his shift from Ciceronian to Tacitean policy: that is, to a policy of necessity and expedience. It is important to stress that Smith's move was innovative in the realm of colonial policy, but that it was also a

---

[52] John Parker, *Books to build an empire* (Amsterdam, 1965), p. 208.

[53] Anthony Pagden, *European encounters with the New World: From Renaissance to Romanticism* (New Haven, 1993); Karen Kupperman, *Providence island 1630–1641: The other puritan colony* (Cambridge, 1993).

resort to a prevailing critique of civic thought. Smith shows, however, that the experience of early modern colonisation contributed to the growing interest in reason of state.

In the light of this intellectual innovation we must reassess Smith's role in early modern colonisation. From Alexander Brown to Philip Barbour and Alden T. Vaughan, the study of Smith's writings has focused upon the veracity of his accounts.[54] Those, such as Brown, who diminished the importance of his role, question his truthfulness. Historians, such as Barbour, who have granted Smith importance in early modern colonisation have sought to prove his honesty through corroborating his accounts. When we assess Smith's place in intellectual history, however, the problem of his honesty is incidental (except in so far as lies and manipulation of the record constitute part of the Machiavellian tradition). From the perspective of intellectual history we find support for those who have argued that Smith was an important figure in the history of colonisation. And yet, Smith has been neglected as a figure in intellectual history, just as the intellectual history of early modern colonisation has itself been neglected. His contribution, I would argue, to the history of colonial possession was as important, if not more important, as his contribution in any other area of colonisation.

The larger conclusion to be drawn from the conflict between *The Tempest* and its context concerns the history of colonial possession. Critics have been correct to observe that Prospero is unapologetic in his possession of the island, but perceiving this act to be continuous with the play's colonial context (that is, failing to see the conflict between the play and its ideological context), these critics have failed to give due credit to a central ideological innovation in the play. Historians have similarly emphasised the humanist concern with glory in colonisation. Against that background, Smith's arguments also appear less dramatic. It has been assumed that, from its outset, English colonisation embodied an ideology of colonial possession, even when it is acknowledged that that ideology was incoherent. Early English colonisers were comfortable with claims for possession only as a last resort, and, even in that instance, they were still vitally concerned to justify the act of possession. What Smith and (while *The Tempest* may be equivocal) Prospero introduced for the first time into English colonial thought – that is, what reason of state introduced for the first time into colonial narratives – was an unequivocal claim to possession which pushed anxieties about justice

---

[54] Alexander Brown, *The genesis of the United States*, 2 vols. (Boston, 1890, reprinted New York, 1968), II, pp. 1006–10; Barbour, *The three worlds of Captain John Smith*, pp. ix–x; Alden T. Vaughan, *American genesis: Captain John Smith and the founding of Virginia* (Boston, 1975).

into the background. The language of reason of state was used to show that such anxieties were vanities that endanger the survival of the enterprise – self-preservation was elevated above virtue. Possession was made possible not by a coherent justification of colonisation but by the rejection of precisely that anxiety. It was from this moment, when reason of state entered into English colonisation, that the ideological assertion of English colonial possession joined with the history of English colonisation.

CHAPTER 7

Conclusion

The early period of English interest in New World colonisation is better understood from the perspective of the preceding centuries of the European Renaissance than from the following centuries of British empire. In the projects of the sixteenth and early seventeenth centuries we do not find a platform for the empire of commerce. It was a Renaissance preoccupation with the pursuit of glory that motivated colonisers and a concern with corruption that lent their designs a distinctive nervousness and that inspired their opponents.

The nervousness of colonisation was both outward and inward looking: outward in the concern with just conduct toward colonised peoples; inward in a concern with the corruption of the metropolis. Against the outward-looking concern we may say that the nervousness of dispossession did not stop humanist inspired colonies from dispossessing native Americans. To speak of colonisation separated from dispossession would appear to be oxymoronic, particularly when we look at what English colonisation, for example, became. But we must be careful again not to argue from consequences. The fact of dispossession did not prevent English would be colonisers' ambivalence on the question. Nor did it prevent them from frequently protesting that dispossession was not their desire. Francis Bacon's well-known discomfort on the matter was supported by a foundation of corresponding sentiment on the part of colonial promoters. Sometimes the ambivalence of promoters was genuine. Clearly at other times it was disingenuous. The very need to be artful on these questions revealed that there was no clear ideological mandate for unapologetic conquest.[1]

It is true, of course, that whether genuine or not this ambivalence masked practices in colonisation that were clearly at odds with the ideology of the projects. Colonisers were violent toward indigenous people and were

[1] Cf. Francis Jennings, *The invasion of America* (1975, Chapel Hill); Robert A. Williams, *The American Indian in western legal thought: The discourses of conquest* (New York, 1990).

appropriating their lands. Humanism did, however, have an impact upon relations between colonisers and native Americans. The violence of the colonisers was justified by the humanist pursuit of glory. The humanist concern with how to achieve greatness supported the glorification of war and conquest. Moreover, colonisers were not always bent on the path of dispossession and violence. The other side of glory, the humanist concern about corruption, was evident in the presentation of justice as a matter of delicacy. In its first years, prior to the 1621 massacre, the Virginia Company, for example, clearly tried to appease the Powhatan confederation (even if not consistently). It was, of course, greatly motivated by the dependence of the colony upon the good will of the Powhatans, both for security and food.[2] But it chose to understand its situation through the humanist language of virtue and corruption. Certainly, the policy of appeasement was not shared by all. John Smith, the most outspoken of the critics, responded to the Company with a Machiavellian contempt for the delicacies of justice. This debate reflected the deepest division within northern humanism: namely, a conventional Ciceronianism against the rising language of reason of state.[3]

The rise of a Machiavellian language of dispossession did not entirely erase neo-Roman discomfort with the enslavement of subject peoples.[4] The expression of these neo-classical fears persists through to the eighteenth century. At that time, native Americans were still portrayed by authors such as Cadwallader Colden as possessing the martial virtues by contrast with the luxury and effeminacy of Britain.[5] We have seen that that tradition of uncertainty finds its origins in an extensive early modern discussion of the moral dangers of colonisation. The distinguishing feature of this early modern discourse is its scope and depth and a consequent impression that a

---

[2] See Karen Kupperman, *Settling with the Indians* (London, 1980); Karen Kupperman, *Indians and English: Facing off in early America* (Ithaca, 2000).

[3] See Richard Tuck, *Philosophy and government, 1572–1651* (Cambridge, 1993); Maurizio Viroli, *From politics to reason of state: The acquisition and transformation of the language of politics 1250–1600* (Cambridge, 1992).

[4] While 'slavery' may not be the commonly used term here, we must remember that for humanists, as for Romans, dependence was slavery. Note Tacitus' observation on the subjection of the Britons through colonisation: they 'gave the name of culture to this aspect of their slavery [*servitus*]' (Tacitus, *Agricola*, trans. M. Ogilvie (Cambridge, Mass., 1970), 21). See also Quentin Skinner, *Liberty before liberalism* (Cambridge, 1998); and Chaim Wirszubski, *Libertas as a political idea at Rome during the Late Republic and Early Principate* (Cambridge, 1950).

[5] Cadwallader Colden, *The history of the five Indian nations of Canada* (London, 1747), pp. 2–19, is the best known of these accounts. See also James Axtell, *The invasion within: The contest of cultures in colonial North America* (Oxford, 1981); Robert F. Berkhofer, Jr, *The white man's Indian: Images of the American Indian from Columbus to the present* (New York, 1978); James Tully, 'Placing the *Two Treatises*', in Nicholas Phillipson and Quentin Skinner, eds., *Political discourse in early modern Britain* (Cambridge, 1993), pp. 279–80.

judgement about the justice of dispossession is in the balance. By contrast, the later debate reflects the nostalgia of a culture that perceives itself to be further advanced in the progress of history. Colonial promoters in the sixteenth and seventeenth centuries did not coherently subscribe to this progressive understanding of history. They were equally, as I have argued, attached to a cyclical model of history in which the English could appear corrupt and in which native Americans were in virtuous ascendance.

Concerns about the justice of dispossession were only a secondary source for anxiety about colonies. The more pressing danger was inward looking – the possibility that colonies could corrupt the coloniser. The Roman experience showed that empire posed a threat to liberty. Sallust is clear on this point, as is Cicero. Even when Cicero was lamenting the unjust treatment of subject peoples as a violation of the fellowship of humanity, he nominated Sulla and Caesar as those most responsible.[6] Thus he linked the violation of other peoples to the men he held responsible for the violation of Roman liberty. Empire presents the dangers of excessive ambition, wealth and luxury. More concerned by their own liberty than that of native Americans, the promoters repeatedly warned against elevating profit to be the highest priority of the enterprises.

Again, the rise of commerce over the course of the seventeenth century did not entirely expunge neo-Roman ambivalence about empire. Anxiety about empire would reappear in English republican thought, particularly in criticism of Thomas Cromwell's Western Design of 1654–5. John Milton, Marchamont Nedham and James Harrington compared Cromwell with Sulla.[7] The republicans confronted the problem using Machiavelli's *Discorsi*. Machiavelli's response to Sallust (and Cicero) in this case was that it was better to have loved and lost than never to have loved at all: republics that expand lose their liberty but acquire greatness in the process, whereas those which do not expand lose their liberty anyway.[8] These neo-Roman fears of 'Asiatic' luxury extended well into the nineteenth century with regard to Britain's south Asian empire.[9] The foundations of that

---

[6] Cicero, *On duties* trans. and ed. M. T. Griffin and E. M. Atkins (Cambridge, 1991), II, 26–9.

[7] David Armitage, *The ideological origins of the British empire* (Cambridge, 2000), ch. 5; David Armitage, 'The Cromwellian Protectorate and the languages of empire', *The Historical Journal*, 35 (1992); Blair Worden, 'Milton and Marchamont Nedham', in David Armitage, Armand Himy and Quentin Skinner, eds., *Milton and republicanism* (Cambridge, 1995).

[8] Niccolo Machiavelli, *The discourses*, trans. Leslie J. Walker, SJ, and ed. Bernard Crick (Harmondsworth, 1970), II, 3–4; and Armitage, *The ideological origins of the British empire*, p. 130.

[9] P. J. Marshall, '*A free though conquering people*': Britain and Asia in the eighteenth century, Inaugural Lecture, King's College London, 5 March 1981; cf. Miles Taylor, 'Imperium et Libertas? Rethinking the radical critique of imperialism during the nineteenth century', *Journal of Imperial and Commonwealth History*, 19 (1991), pp. 1–23.

nervous tradition of expansion are in the sixteenth- and early seventeenth-century discussions of colonisation that we have examined here. In these later episodes, however, concerns about imperial corruption sit beneath a greater cultural confidence in the desirability of expansion and the fact of imperial success. By contrast, in the early period of colonisation these anxieties are in balance with the pursuit of glory. This early prominence of colonial ambivalence complemented the failure of colonial designs at the same time as it contributed to holding the English back from colonising.

The colonial projects of the sixteenth and early seventeenth centuries attempted to reconcile expansion with liberty in which the models were Thomas More and Cicero more than Machiavelli. For this reason Thomas Smith could boast 'have I not set forth to you another Eutopia', and Lawrence Keymis could write of 'the persuasion and hope of a new found Utopia'.[10] If colonies were to be established they had to be established as commonwealths and be governed according to the principles of a good commonwealth.[11] Only in this way could the corruption generated by empire be avoided. Indeed, the term 'empire' was notably absent from these plans.[12] More's commonwealth was not a colony, but it was a model of a commonwealth in the New World in which the citizens were vigilant against the corrupting vices of luxury. Cicero gave one of the strongest warnings that those who build empire should not allow greatness of spirit to slip into 'excessive desire of pre-eminence', the love of riches and the unjust treatment of subject peoples.[13] The early modern promoters of colonies argued that if these principles were scrupulously followed England would not be corrupted and injustice would not be visited upon native Americans. In echoing this argument several generations later, Harrington can be seen to be at the end of a strong Ciceronian discussion of English colonisation.[14]

---

[10] [Thomas Smith], *A letter sent by I.B. gentleman unto his very frende Master R.C. esquire, wherin is conteined a large discourse of the peopling & inhabiting the cuntrie called the Ardes* (London, 1572), sig. Eir; Lawrence Keymis, *A relation of the second voyage to Guiana* (London, 1596), sig. A4v.

[11] Andrew Fitzmaurice, 'Classical rhetoric and the promotion of the New World', *Journal of the History of Ideas*, 58 (1997); David Armitage, 'Greater Britain: a useful category of historical analysis?', *American Historical Review*, April (1999), p. 440.

[12] David Armitage, 'Literature and empire', Nicholas Canny, ed., *The origins of empire*, vol. 1 of *The Oxford history of the British empire*, ed. Wm Roger Louis (Oxford, 1998).

[13] Cicero, *On duties*, I, 64–8 and II, 26–9.

[14] When we consider that Petty was almost already moving in a new direction, Harrington's contribution may in this sense be reactionary rather than innovative; Armitage, *The ideological origins of the British Empire*, ch. 5. See also Steven Pincus, 'Neither Machiavellian moment nor possessive individualism: commercial society and the defenders of the English Commonwealth', *American Historical Review*, June (1998); and cf. Jonathan Scott, *England's troubles: seventeenth century English political instability in European context* (Cambridge, 2000), p. 291.

This civic thought, as we have seen, was the language of government in early modern England. It was used both by 'Commonwealthmen' to justify limited self-government, and by apologists for absolutism who were more concerned with the public service of their subjects than with self-government (the corollary of that service). In the case of the New World, the language of the *vita activa* was believed to be necessary to establish colonies. There was a need, therefore, for a deeper commitment to civic thought in colonisation than in England, where it was possible to defend the *vita contemplativa*, and where retirement offered an alternative to the restrictions of court life. Indeed, pursuing the active life in the New World was an alternative to the limits on political participation in England and thus an alternative to retirement. But there was a further and related reason for the deeper commitment to civic thought in the New World context. Given that colonies presented their own peculiar threat to liberty, they therefore demanded greater vigilance and civic participation on that account. The colonies were portrayed as the foundation of new political communities and the 'Oriental' dangers to those communities demanded greater civic commitment than was required in the metropolis.

Does this point us to a deeper tradition of American liberty? In a rhetorical sense, certainly: the civic character of early colonisation facilitated the revolutionary claim to a continuous tradition of colonial liberty. Moreover, Jefferson's classical republicanism evolved from the early modern humanist mentality that we have explored here.[15] He certainly would have found much that was familiar in the writings of the first colonial promoters. There were also important differences, however, between the republicanism of Jefferson's generation and the civic disposition of early colonisation. The republicanism of the founders was a synthesis of the classical republican tradition and the language of rights from which modern liberalism would develop.[16] The early colonisers did not use the language of rights to claim liberty or to describe their actions (although they did use natural law arguments to dispossess aboriginal peoples). They perceived their 'citizenship', as Robert Gordon would have it, or their liberty as subjects, in terms of the paradox of ancient liberty: namely, liberty as slavery to the common good.

---

[15] J. G. A. Pocock, *The Machiavellian moment. Florentine political thought and the Atlantic republican tradition* (Cambridge, 1975); Paul A. Rahe, *Republics ancient and modern*, 3 vols. (Chapel Hill, 1994, first published 1992); Gordon S. Wood, *The radicalism of the American revolution* (New York, 1992).

[16] Rahe, *Republics ancient and modern*; Joyce Appleby, *Liberalism and republicanism in the historical imagination* (Cambridge, Mass., 1992); Wood, *The radicalism of the American revolution*; Michael Leinesch, *New order of the ages* (Princeton, 1988); Lance Banning, *The Jeffersonian persuasion* (Chapel Hill, 1980); J. G. A. Pocock, 'Between Gog and Magog: the republican thesis and *Ideologia Americana*', *Journal of the History of Ideas*, 48, 2 (1987).

Their concern was with duty and service, with political participation, and not with the negative freedom, or rights, of modern political language.[17] In this respect their writing can also be contrasted with the republicanism of the post-civil war period in England in which the language of duties was again mixed with that of rights.[18]

By the late nineteenth century the ideological character of the early writing on colonies was clearly misunderstood. While late nineteenth- and early twentieth-century patriotic historians claimed to have discovered the principles of liberty in Jacobean colonisation, the liberty they recognised was alien to sixteenth- and early seventeenth-century Europeans: it was Lockean and liberal, based upon rights rather than duties.[19] The character of this early colonisation has remained obscured behind the ideologies of subsequent generations of historians. While the views of the patriotic historians were overturned, early colonisation came to be seen as part of the foundation of capitalism and commerce. Early colonisation, according to historians from S. M. Kingsbury to Jack Greene, was economically motivated and politically disinterested.[20]

It is true that just as the colonial promoters frequently disclaimed the intention to dispossess and then proceeded to do precisely that, so they disclaimed avarice but showed little compunction about exploiting colonists. Would be colonisers were seemingly happy to exploit the personnel employed in their enterprises and justify that exploitation in the name of not pursuing profit. The repeated rebellion of ships' crews employed by humanist promoters of colonies, from Rastell to Gilbert, underlines the

[17] On the contrast between ancient and modern liberty, see Benjamin Constant, 'The liberty of the ancients compared with that of the moderns', in Constant, *Political writings*, ed. Biancamaria Fontana (Cambridge, 1988); Isaiah Berlin, 'Two concepts of liberty', in Berlin, *Four essays on liberty* (Oxford, 1969); Quentin Skinner, 'The republican idea of political liberty', in Gisela Bock, Quentin Skinner and Maurizio Viroli, eds., *Machiavelli and republicanism* (Cambridge, 1990); Philip Pettit, *Republicanism: A theory of freedom and government* (Oxford, 1997); Skinner, *Liberty before liberalism*.

[18] Skinner, *Liberty before liberalism*, p. 18; Scott, *England's troubles*, p. 288.

[19] Alexander Brown, *English politics in early Virginian history* (first published 1901, reissued New York, 1968), pp. 11–13; E. D. Neill, *The English colonisation of America during the seventeenth century* (London, 1871); Charles Mills Gayley, *Shakespeare and the founders of liberty in America* (New York, 1917). See Michael Sandel, *Democracy's discontent* (Cambridge, Mass., 1996) on the survival of republican values into the early twentieth century.

[20] S. M. Kingsbury, ed., *The records of the Virginia Company of London*, 4 vols. (Washington, 1906–35), I, pp. 12–15; Wesley F. Craven, *The dissolution of the Virginia Company* (Oxford, 1932), p. 24; Herbert L. Osgood, *The American colonies in the seventeenth century*, 3 vols. (first published 1904, reissued New York, 1930); Edmund S. Morgan, *American slavery/American freedom* (New York, 1975), pp. 44–5, 95, 118; Kenneth R. Andrews, *Trade, plunder and settlement: Maritime enterprise and the genesis of the British empire* (Cambridge, 1984), p. 5; Jack P. Greene, *Pursuits of happiness* (Chapel Hill, 1988), p. 8; Jack P. Greene, *Peripheries and center: Constitutional development in the extended polities of the British empire and the United States 1607–1788* (Athens, Ga., 1986).

point. Later, the Virginia Company were content to employ indentured labour while promoting civic commitment. Ideology and reality also appear out of step when at times it appears that the Virginia Company's concern over greed was motivated precisely by the perception that colonists were avaricious. But this does not mean that humanist ideology was merely the wallpaper over colonisation. The first impact of humanism upon English colonisation may be that humanist anxieties contributed to the inaction of the English in America in the sixteenth century. It was hard for those who initiated colonising projects to gain support for their enterprises. Their choice to persuade the audience on points of moral philosophy indicates an awareness of a humanist opposition, and we get glimpses of that opposition in satire from Alexander Barclay to Joseph Hall. Secondly, the disavowal of profit clearly aided the Virginia Company in maintaining public support for twenty years for an unprofitable project. The public service, the virtues of courage and temperance demanded by the company, assisted in gaining the self-sacrifice needed to establish a permanent colony. Most profoundly, as I have argued, ideology defined the scope within which actions had to be legitimised or criticised.

What, then, tipped the balance and submerged the neo-classical colonising queasiness? As David Armitage has recently argued, eighteenth-century political economy attempted to square the circle of empire and liberty.[21] Expanding commerce forced a reconsideration of the nature of wealth and luxury.[22] The former vices were now seen to be positive social forces. When the common good could be understood in terms of commerce it was possible also to understand empire as a contributor to that good.

In the writing of John Smith and Shakespeare we have found another, earlier, solution to the problems foreign possession presented for liberty. At this time, Ciceronian anxieties about the corrupting influences of imperial wealth found a rival in the rising language of interest.[23] Machiavellian and Tacitean ideas of interest were not eighteenth-century political economy, but they do mark a turning point in the understanding of colonisation. In the eighteenth century self-interest began to emerge as positive.[24] In the

---

[21] Armitage, *The ideological origins of the British empire*, ch. 6.
[22] See, for example, Bernard Mandeville, *The fable of the bees: or, private vices, public benefits*, ed. F. B. Kaye, 2 vols. (Oxford, 1924). See also I. Hont and M. Ignatieff, eds., *Wealth and virtue: The shaping of political economy in the Scottish Enlightenment* (Cambridge, 1983). On Mandeville, see M. M. Goldsmith, 'Liberty, luxury and the pursuit of happiness', in Anthony Pagden, *The languages of political theory in early-modern Europe* (Cambridge, 1987), pp. 225–51.
[23] Tuck, *Philosophy and government 1572–1651*.
[24] Albert O. Hirschman, *The passions and the interests: Political arguments for capitalism before its triumph* (Princeton, 1977; reissued 1997 with a foreword by Amartya Sen).

sixteenth and seventeenth centuries, self-interest continued to have a bad name but could be defended in terms of survival or necessity: survival for the subject, necessity for the state.[25] Just as dispossession could be represented as necessary, so colonists' behaviour in general could be represented in terms of interest, rather than in terms of honour. That defence rested on the claim that the political world was a dangerous place, in which the prince's subjects were guided more by survival than concern for the common good. In this environment virtue simply ceased to be a central concern; it was an impediment, or no concern at all. For the first time, when colonisation was unfettered by such anxieties, expedience, including profit, could be elevated above honour and virtue as the motive for colonising. John Smith argued for this new colonial ideology in 1624 as the Virginia Company was receiving its last rites. As an epitaph to the *Utopia* in which Thomas More had banished greed, Smith declared: 'I am not so simple to thinke that ever any other motive then wealth will ever erect there a commonwealth.'[26]

---

[25] Tuck, *Philosophy and government 1572–1651*; Miller, *Defining the common good*; Maurizio Viroli, *From politics to reason of state: The acquisition and transformation of the language of politics 1250 – 1600* (Cambridge, 1992).

[26] John Smith, *The Generall History of Virginia, New England, and the Summer Isles* (London, 1624), p. 219.

Bibliography

PRIMARY SOURCES

Abbay, T., and William Symonds, eds., *The proceedings of the English colonie in Virginia* (Oxford, 1612).

Alexander, William, *An encouragement to colonies* (London, 1624).

Aristotle, *'Art' of rhetoric*, trans. J. H. Freese (London, 1926).

Bacon, Francis, *The essayes or counsels, civill and morall*, ed. Michael Kiernan (Oxford, 1985).

Barbour, Philip L., ed., *The Jamestown voyages under the first charter, 1606–1609*, 2 vols. (Cambridge, 1969).

Barclay, Alexander, *The ship of fools*, ed. T. H. Jamieson, 2 vols. (Edinburgh, 1874, reprinted New York, 1966).

Boccalini, Trajano, *The new-found politicke* (London, 1626).

Bradford, William, and Edward Winslow, *A relation of Plymouth* (London, 1624).

C., T. [Thomas Cary?], *A short discourse of the Newfoundland* (Dublin, 1623), reprinted in Gillian T. Cell, ed., *Newfoundland discovered* (London, 1982).

Chapman, George, Ben Jonson and John Marston, *Eastward ho*, ed. R. W. Van Fossen (Manchester, 1979).

Churchyard, Thomas, *A prayse and reporte of Maister Martyne Forboishers voyage to meta incognita* (London, 1578).

Cicero, *De officiis*, trans. Walter Miller (Cambridge, Mass., 1913).

Brutus, trans. G. L. Hendrickson (Cambridge, Mass., 1939).

Orator, trans. H. M. Hubbell (Cambridge, Mass., 1939).

De oratore, trans. E. W. Sutton and H. Rackham, 2 vols. (London, 1942).

De inventione, trans. H. M. Hubbell (London, 1949).

On duties, trans. and ed. M. T. Griffin and E. M. Atkins (Cambridge, 1991).

Clément, Pierre, *Lettres, instructions et mémoires de Colbert* (Paris, Imprimerie Impériale, 1865).

Colden, Cadwallader, *The history of the five Indian nations of Canada* (London, 1747).

Constant, Benjamin, 'The liberty of the ancients compared with that of the moderns', in Benjamin Constant, *Political writings*, ed. Biancamaria Fontana (Cambridge, 1988).

Copland, Robert, *Virginia's God be thanked* (London, 1622).

Coryat, Thomas, *Thomas Coriat traveller for the English wits* (London, 1616).

Crakanthorpe, Richard, *A sermon at the inauguration of King James* (London, 1609).

Crashaw, William, *A sermon preached before the right honourable the Lord Lawarre* (London, 1610).

Crashaw, William, ed., *A plaine description of the Bermudas, now called the Sommer Ilands* (London, 1613).

Crosse, Henry, *Vertues common-wealth: or the high-way to honour* (London, 1603).

Cushman, Robert, *A sermon preached at Plimmoth* (London, 1622).

A declaration of the state of colonie and affaires in Virginia (London, 1620).

Dee, John, *General and rare memorials pertayning to the perfect arte of navigation* (London, 1577).

Digges, Dudley, *Four paradoxes, or politique discourses* (London, 1604).

Donne, John, *A sermon...preach'd to the honourable company of the Virginian plantation* (London, 1622).

Eburne, Richard, *A plaine pathway to plantations* [London, 1624], ed. Louis B. Wright (Ithaca, 1962).

Eden, Richard, *A treatyse of the newe India* (London, 1553) reprinted in Edward Arber, ed., *The first three English books on America* (Birmingham, 1885).

  The decades of the newe worlde or west India (London, 1555) reprinted in Edward Arber, ed., *The first three English books on America* (Birmingham, 1885).

  A history of travayle in the West and East Indies, ed. Richard Willes (London, 1577).

Erasmus, Desiderius, *Collected works of Erasmus*, ed. Craig R. Thompson, (Toronto, 1978–).

[Ferrar, Nicholas], *Sir Thomas Smith's misgovernment of the Virginia Company*, ed. D. R. Ransome (Cambridge, 1990).

Gilbert, Humphrey, *The voyages and colonising enterprises of Sir Humphrey Gilbert*, ed. David B. Quinn, 2 vols. (Cambridge, 1940).

  A discourse of a discovery for a new passage to Cataia (London, 1586).

[Gilbert, Humphrey], 'The erection of an achademy in London for educacion of her Majesties Wardes' [c.1570], in F. J. Furnivall, ed., *Queene Elizabethes achademy, a booke of precedence, &c.* (London, 1869).

Gordon, Robert, *Encouragements* (Edinburgh, 1625).

Gorges, Ferdinando, *A brief relation of the discovery and plantation of New England* (London, 1622), in *Sir Ferdinando Gorges and his province of Maine*, ed. J. P. Baxter (New York, 1967).

Gray, Robert, *A good speed to Virginia* (London, 1609).

Edward Haies, *A report of the voyage*, in Richard Hakluyt, *The principal navigations, voiages and discoveries of the English nation* (London, 1589); reprinted in *The voyages and colonising enterprises of Sir Humphrey Gilbert*, ed. David B. Quinn, 2 vols. (Cambridge, 1940), II.

Hakluyt, Richard, *The principal navigations, voiages and discoveries of the English nation* (London, 1589).

Hakluyt, Richard, ed., *Divers voyages touching the discovery of America* (London, 1582).

Hakluyt, Richard, the Elder and Richard Hakluyt, *The original writings and corre-spondence of the two Richard Hakluyts*, ed. E. G. R. Taylor, 2 vols. (London, 1935).

Hall, Joseph, *The discovery of a new world: mundus alter et idem* (London, 1609). *Quo vadis? A just censure of travell* (London, 1617).

Hamor, Ralph, *A true discourse of the present estate of Virginia* (London, 1615).

Harriot, Thomas, *A brief and true report of the new found land of Virginia* (London, 1588).

A brief and true report of the new found land of Virginia, ed. Theodore de Bry (Frankfurt, 1590).

Hayman, Robert, *Quodlibets, lately come over from New Britaniola, Old Newfound-land* (London, 1628).

Hughes, Lewis, *A letter, sent into England from the Summer Ilands* (London, 1615).

A plaine and true relation of the goodness of God towards the Summer Iles (London, 1621).

Jobson, Richard, *The Golden trade: or, a discovery of the River Gambra, and the golden trade of the Aethiopians* (London, 1623).

Johnson, Robert, *Nova Britannia* (London, 1609). *The new life of Virginea* (London, 1612).

Jourdain, Sylvester, *A discovery of the Bermudas* (London, 1610).

Keymis, Lawrence, *A relation of the second voyage to Guiana* (London, 1596).

Kingsbury, S. M., ed., *The records of the Virginia Company of London*, 4 vols. (Washington, 1906–35).

Machiavelli, Niccolo, *The discourses*, trans. Leslie J. Walker, SJ and ed. Bernard Crick (Harmondsworth, 1970).

The Prince, ed. Quentin Skinner and Russell Price, (Cambridge, 1988).

Malcolm, Noel, ed., *The origins of English nonsense* (London, 1998).

Mandeville, Bernard, *The fable of the bees: or, private vices, public benefits*, ed. F. B. Kaye, 2 vols. (Oxford, 1924).

Mason, John, *A brief discourse of the new-found-land* (London, 1622), reprinted in Gillian T. Cell, ed., *Newfoundland discovered* (London, 1982).

More, Thomas, *Utopia*, ed. George M. Logan and Robert M. Adams (Cambridge, 1989).

A note of the shipping, men, and provisions, sent to Virginia (London, 1619).

A note of the shipping, men, and provisions, sent and provided for Virginia (London, 1620).

Parmenius, Stephen, *The new found land of Stephen Parmenius*, ed. David B. Quinn (Toronto, 1972).

Peacham, Henry, *Garden of eloquence* (London, 1577).

Peckham, George, *A true report of the late discoveries . . . by Sir Humphrey Gilbert*, reprinted in Richard Hakluyt, *The principal navigations, voiages and discoveries of the English nation* (London, 1589), and in Humphrey Gilbert, *The voyages and colonising enterprises of Sir Humphrey Gilbert*, ed. David B. Quinn, 2 vols. (Cambridge, 1940).

Percy, George, *A true relacyon of the procedeings and occurrentes of momente which have hapned in Virginia* (c.1625), in *Virginia: Four personal narratives*, Research library of colonial Americana (New York, 1972).

Plutarch, *The lives of the noble Grecians and Romans*, trans. Thomas North (Oxford, 1928).

Price, Daniel, *Sauls prohibition staide* (London, 1609).

Purchas, Samuel, *The kings towre* (London, 1623).

    Hakluytus posthumus or Purchas his pilgrimes, 4 vols. (London, 1625).

Quinn, David Beers, ed., *New American world: A documentary history of North America to 1612*, 5 vols. (London, 1979).

Quintilian, *Institutio oratoria*, trans. H. E. Butler, 4 vols. (London, 1920–22).

Ralegh, Walter, *The discoverie of the large, rich and bewtiful empyre of Guiana* (London, 1596), reprinted in ed. Neil L. Whitehead (Manchester, 1997).

Rastell, John, *A new interlude and mery of the nature of the four elements*, in *Three Rastell plays*, ed. Richard Axton (Cambridge, 1979).

Rhetorica ad Herennium, trans. and ed. Henry Caplan (London, 1954).

Rich, Richard, *Newes from Virginia* (London, 1610).

Rolfe, John, *Relation of the state of Virginia* in *Virginia: Four personal narratives* [1616], Research Library of Colonial Americana (New York, 1972).

Sallust, *Sallust* trans. J. C. Rolfe (London, 1921).

Shakespeare, William, *The Tempest*, ed. Frank Kermode (London, 1958).

    The Tempest, ed. Stephen Orgel (Oxford, 1987).

Sherley, Anthony, *Sir Antony Sherley his relation of his travels into Persia* (London, 1613).

Smith, John, *A true relation* (London, 1608).

    A map of Virginia (Oxford, 1612).

    The generall history of Virginia, New England, and the Summer Isles (London, 1624).

    The true travels and adventures of Captain John Smith (London, 1629), reprinted in Edward Arber, *Captain John Smith, Works* (Birmingham, 1884).

Smith, Thomas, *A discourse of the commonweal of this realm of England* [London, 1581], ed. Mary Dewar (Charlottesville, 1969).

    The commonwealth of England [De republica Anglorum], [London, 1583], ed. L. Alston (Cambridge, 1906).

[Smith, Thomas], *A letter sent by I.B. gentleman unto his very frende Master R.C. esquire, wherin is conteined a large discourse of the peopling & inhabiting the cuntrie called the Ardes* (London, 1572).

Strachey, William, *The historie of travell into Virginia Britannia* [1609–1612], eds. Louis B. Wright and Virginia Freund (London, 1953).

    A true reportory of the wracke and redemption of Sir Thomas Gates, in Samuel Purchas, *Hakluytus posthumus or Purchas his pilgrimes*, 4 vols. (London, 1625).

Symonds, William, *Virginia* (London, 1609).

Tacitus, *Agricola*, trans. M. Ogilvie (Cambridge, Mass., 1970).

    A dialogue on oratory (Cambridge, Mass., 1970).

    Germania, trans. M. Hutton (Cambridge, Mass., 1970).

A true declaration of the estate of the colonie in Virginia (London, 1610).

A true and sincere declaration of the purpose and ends of the plantation begun in Virginia (London, 1610).

Tynley, Robert, *Two learned sermons* (London, 1609).

Vaughan, William, *The golden fleece* (London, 1626).

Vitoria, Francisco de, *Political writings*, eds. Anthony Pagden and Jeremy Lawrance (Cambridge, 1991).

Whitaker, Alexander, *Good newes from Virginia* (London, 1613).

Whitbourne, Richard, *A discovery and discourse of Newfoundland* (London, 1622).

White, John, *The American drawings of John White 1577–1590*, eds. Paul Hulton and David B. Quinn, 2 vols. (London, 1964).

Wilson, Thomas, *The arte of rhetorique*, ed. Thomas J. Derrick (New York, 1982).

The art of rhetoric, ed. Peter E. Medine (Pennsylvania, 1994), p. 79.

Woudhuysen, H. R., ed., *The Penguin book of Renaissance verse*, selected and introduced by David Norbrook (London, 1992).

SECONDARY SOURCES

Adams, Robert P., *The better part of valor: More, Erasmus, Colet, and Vives, on humanism, war, and peace, 1496–1535* (Seattle, 1962).

Adams, S. L., 'Foreign policy and the parliaments of 1621 and 1624', in Kevin Sharpe, *Faction and parliament: Essays on early Stuart history* (Oxford, 1978).

Alford, Stephen, *The early Elizabethan polity: William Cecil and the British succession crisis 1558–1569* (Cambridge, 1998).

Andrews, Charles M., *The colonial period of American history* (New Haven, 1934).

Andrews, Kenneth R., *Trade, plunder and settlement: Maritime enterprise and the genesis of the British empire* (Cambridge, 1984).

Anglo, Sidney, 'A Machiavellian solution to the Irish problem: Richard Beacon's *Solon his follie* (1594)', in Edward Chancey and Peter Mack, eds., *England and the continental Renaissance: Essays in honour of J. B. Trapp* (Woodbridge, 1990).

Appleby, Joyce, *Liberalism and republicanism in the historical imagination* (Cambridge, Mass., 1992).

Arber, Edward, ed., *The first three English books on America* (Birmingham, 1885).

Archer, Ian, *The pursuit of stability: Social relations in Elizabethan London* (Cambridge, 1991).

Armitage, David, 'The Cromwellian Protectorate and the languages of empire', *The Historical Journal*, 35 (1992)

'The New World and British historical thought', in Karen Kupperman, ed., *America in European consciousness 1493–1750* (Chapel Hill, 1995).

'Making the empire British: Scotland in the Atlantic world 1542–1707', *Past and Present*, 155 (May 1997).

'Literature and empire', in Nicholas Canny, ed., *The origins of empire*, vol. I in *The Oxford history of the British empire*, ed. Wm Roger Louis (Oxford, 1998).

'Greater Britain: a useful category of historical analysis?', *American Historical Review* (April 1999).

The ideological origins of the British empire (Cambridge, 2000).

Axtell, James, *The invasion within: The contest of cultures in colonial North America* (Oxford, 1981).

Baldwin, T. W., *William Shakespere's small Latine and lesse Greeke*, 2 vols. (Urbana, 1944).

Banning, Lance, *The Jeffersonian persuasion* (Chapel Hill, 1980).

Barbour, Philip L., *The three worlds of Captain John Smith* (London, 1964).

Barker, Francis, and Peter Hulme, 'Nymphs and reapers heavily vanish: the discursive con-texts of *The Tempest*', in John Drakakis, ed., *Alternative Shakespeares* (London, 1985).

Barry, Jonathan, 'Literacy and literature in popular culture: reading and writing in historical perspective', in Tim Harris, ed., *Popular culture in England, c.1500–1850* (London, 1995).

Bate, Jonathan, 'The humanist *Tempest*', in *Shakespeare La Tempête: Etudes critiques*, Actes du colloque de Besançon (1993).

Bateson, F. W., ed., *The Cambridge bibliography of English literature* (Cambridge, 1969).

Berkhofer, Robert, Jr, *The white man's Indian: Images of the American Indian from Columbus to the present* (New York, 1978).

Berlin, Isaiah, *Four essays on liberty* (Oxford, 1969).

Billings, Warren M., 'The transfer of English law to Virginia 1606–1650', in K. R. Andrews, N. Canny and P. E. H. Hair, eds., *The westward enterprise: English activities in Ireland, the Atlantic, and America 1480–1650* (Liverpool, 1978).

Bitzer, Lloyd, 'Aristotle's Enthymeme revisited', in Keith V. Erickson, ed., *Aristotle: The classical heritage of rhetoric* (Metuchen, 1974).

Brenner, Robert, *Merchants and revolution: Commercial change, political conflict, and London's overseas traders, 1550–1653* (Cambridge, 1993).

Brotton, Jerry, ' "This Tunis, sir, was Carthage": contesting colonialism in *The Tempest*', in Ania Loomba and Martin Orkin, eds., *Post-colonial Shakespeares* (London, 1998).

Brown, Alexander, *English politics in early Virginian history* (first published 1901, reissued New York, 1968).

The genesis of the United States, 2 vols. (reprinted New York, 1964).

Brown, Paul, ' "This thing of darkness I acknowledge mine": *The Tempest* and the discourse of colonialism', in Jonathan Dollimore and Alan Sinfield, eds., *Political Shakespeare: New essays in cultural materialism* (Ithaca, 1985).

Burckhardt, Jacob, *The civilisation of the Renaissance in Italy*, 2 vols. (New York, 1958).

Burke, Peter, 'Tacitism', in T. A. Dorey, ed., *Tacitus* (London, 1969).

Popular culture in early modern Europe (London, 1978).

'Tacitism, scepticism and reason of state', in *The Cambridge history of political thought 1450–1700*, eds. J. H. Burns and Mark Goldie (Cambridge, 1991).

'America and the rewriting of world history', in Karen Kupperman, ed., *America in European consciousness 1493–1750* (Chapel Hill, 1995).

Canny, Nicholas, 'The ideology of English colonisation: from Ireland to America', *The William and Mary Quarterly*, 30 (1973).

The Elizabethan conquest of Ireland: A pattern established, 1565–76 (London, 1976).

'The permissive frontier: the problem of social control in English settlements in Ireland and Virginia', in K. R. Andrews, N. Canny, P. E. H. Hair, eds., *The westward enterprise: English activities in Ireland, the Atlantic, and America 1480–1650* (Liverpool, 1979).

'The origins of empire: an introduction', in Nicholas Canny ed., *The origins of empire*, vol. I of *The Oxford history of the British empire*, ed.Wm Roger Louis (Oxford, 1998).

Cardin, Allen, 'The communal ideal in puritan New England, 1630–1700', *Fides et historia*, 17 (1984).

Cell, Gillian T., ed., *Newfoundland discovered* (London, 1982).

Clark, Donald L., *John Milton at St Paul's School: A study of ancient rhetoric in English Renaissance education* (New York, 1948).

Clifford, James, *The predicament of culture* (Cambridge, Mass., 1988).

Collinson, Patrick, 'The monarchical republic of Queen Elizabeth I', *Bulletin of the John Rylands University Library of Manchester*, 69 (1987).

De republica Anglorum: or, history with the politics put back. Inaugural lecture delivered 9 November (Cambridge University Press, 1989).

Condren, Conal, *The language of politics in seventeenth century England* (London, 1994).

'Liberty of office and its defence in seventeenth-century political argument', *History of Political Thought*, 3 (1997).

Cormack, Lesley B., *Charting an empire: Geography at the English universities, 1580–1620* (Chicago, 1997).

Craven, Wesley F., *The dissolution of the Virginia Company* (Oxford, 1932).

Croll, Morris, *'Attic' and Baroque prose style: Essays by Morris Croll*, ed. Max Patrick and Robert O. Evans (Princeton, 1966).

Curtis, Mark H., *Oxford and Cambridge in transition 1558–1642* (Oxford, 1959).

Daston, Lorraine, and Katherine Park, *Wonders and the order of nature, 1150–1750* (New York, 1998).

Earle, Carville V., 'Environment, disease, and mortality in early Virginia', in Thad W. Tate and David L. Ammerman, eds., *The Chesapeake in the seventeenth century* (Chapel Hill, 1979).

Earle, Peter, *The making of the English middle class* (London, 1989).

Elliott, J. H., *The Old World and the New* (Cambridge, 1970).

Ferro, Marc, *Colonisation: A global history*, trans. K. D. Prithipaul (London, 1997).

Fitzmaurice, Andrew, 'Classical rhetoric and the promotion of the New World', *Journal of the History of Ideas*, 58 (1997).

'The civic solution to the crisis of English colonisation, 1609–1625', *The Historical Journal*, 42, 1 (1999).

' "Every man, that prints, adventures": the rhetoric of the Virginia Company sermons', in Lori Anne Ferrell and Peter McCullough, eds., *The English sermon revised: Religion, literature and history 1500–1750* (Manchester, 2000).

Foster, Stephen, *Their solitary way: The puritan social ethic in the first century of settlement in New England* (New Haven, 1971).

Franklin, Julian H., *Jean Bodin and the sixteenth-century revolution in the methodology of law and history* (New York, 1963).

Franklin, Wayne, *Discoverers, explorers, settlers: The diligent writers of early America* (Chicago, 1979).

Frey, Charles, '*The Tempest* and the New World', *Shakespeare Quarterly*, 30, 1 (1979).

Fuchs, Barbara, 'Conquering islands: contextualising *The Tempest*', *Shakespeare Quarterly*, 48 (1997).

Fuller, Mary, 'Ralegh's fugitive gold', in *New World encounters*, ed. Stephen Greenblatt (Berkeley, 1993).

Voyages in print: English travel to America 1576–1624 (Cambridge, 1995).

Fumaroli, Marc, 'Rhetoric, politics, and society: from Italian Ciceronianism to French classicism', in James J. Murphy, ed., *Renaissance eloquence* (Berkeley, 1983).

Gayley, Charles Mills, *Shakespeare and the founders of liberty in America* (New York, 1917).

Gillies, John, *Shakespeare and the geography of difference* (Cambridge, 1994).

Gerbi, Antonello, *Nature in the New World*, trans. Jeremy Moyle (Pittsburgh, 1985).

Ginsburg, Carlo, *The cheese and the worms: The cosmos of a sixteenth century miller*, trans. John and Anne Tedeschi (London, 1980).

Goldie, Mark, 'The unacknowledged republic: officeholding in early modern England', in Tim Harris, ed., *The politics of the excluded, c.1500–1850* (London, 2001).

Goldsmith, M. M., 'Liberty, luxury and the pursuit of happiness', in Anthony Pagden, *The languages of political theory in early modern Europe* (Cambridge, 1987).

Grafton, Anthony, *New worlds, ancient texts: The power of tradition and the shock of discovery* (Cambridge, Mass 1992).

Grafton, Anthony, and Lisa Jardine, ' "Studied for action": How Gabriel Harvey read his Livy', *Past and Present*, 129 (1990).

Green, L. C., and Olive P. Dickason, *The law of nations and the New World* (Edmonton, 1989).

Greenblatt, Stephen J., 'Learning to curse: aspects of linguistic colonialism in the sixteenth century', in Fredi Chiappelli, ed., *First images of America: The impact of the New World on the old*, 2 vols. (Berkeley, 1976).

Marvellous possessions (Oxford, 1988).

Shakespearean negotiations (Oxford, 1988).

Greenblatt, Stephen, ed., *New World encounters* (Berkeley, 1993).

Greene, Jack P., *Peripheries and center: Constitutional development in the extended polities of the British empire and the United States 1607–1788* (Athens, Ga., 1986).

Pursuits of happiness (Chapel Hill, 1988).

Hadfield, Andrew, *Literature, travel, and colonial writing in the English Renaissance 1545–1625* (Oxford, 1998).

Harris, Tim, 'Problematising popular culture', in Tim Harris, ed., *Popular culture in England, c.1500–1850* (London, 1995).

Harris, Tim, ed., *The politics of the excluded, c.1500–1850* (London, 2001).

Hay, Milicent V., *The life of Robert Sidney* (Washington, 1984).

Hendrickson, G. L., 'The origin and meaning of the ancient characters of style', *American Journal of Philology*, 26 (1905).

Hirschman, Albert O., *The passions and the interests: Political arguments for capitalism before its triumph* (Princeton, 1977, reissued 1977 with a foreword by Amartya Sen).

Hont I., and M. Ignatieff, eds., *Wealth and virtue: The shaping of political economy in the Scottish Enlightenment* (Cambridge, 1983).

Howell, Wilbur Samuel, *Logic and rhetoric in England, 1500–1700* (Princeton, 1956).

Jardine, Lisa, 'Mastering the uncouth: Gabriel Harvey, Edmund Spenser and the English experience in Ireland', in John Henry and Sarah Hutton, eds., *New perspectives on Renaissance thought* (London, 1990).

Erasmus, man of letters (Princeton, 1993).

Jennings, Francis, *The invasion of America: Indians, colonialism, and the cant of conquest* (New York, 1975).

Jones, Howard Mumford, 'Origins of the English colonial idea in England', *Proceedings of the American Philosophical Society*, 85 (1942).

Juricek, John T., 'English claims in North America to 1660: a study in legal and constitutional history' (Ph.D., University of Chicago, 1970).

'English territorial claims in North America under Elizabeth and the Early Stuarts', *Terræ Incognitæ*, 7 (1975).

Kelley, Donald, *The foundations of modern historical scholarship* (New York, 1970).

Kishlansky, Mark, *Parliamentary selection: Social and political choice in early modern England* (Cambridge, 1986).

Knapp, Jeffrey, *An empire nowhere: England, America, and literature from Utopia to The Tempest* (Berkeley, 1992).

Konig, David Thomas, 'Colonization and the common law in Ireland and Virginia, 1569 –1634', in James A. Henretta, Michael Kammen and Stanley N. Katz, eds., *The transformation of early American history* (New York, 1991).

Kristeller, Paul Oskar, *Renaissance thought and its sources*, ed. Michael Mooney (New York, 1979).

Kupperman, Karen, *Settling with the Indians* (London, 1980).

Providence island 1630–1641: The other puritan colony (Cambridge, 1993).

Indians and English: Facing off in early America (Ithaca, 2000).

Kupperman, Karen Ordahl, 'Definitions of liberty on the eve of civil war: Lord Saye and Sele, Lord Brooke, and the American puritan colonies', *The historical journal*, 32, 1 (1989).

Leinesch, Michael, *New order of the ages* (Princeton, 1988).

Lestringant, Frank, *Le Huguenot et le Sauvage. l'Amérique et la controverse coloniale en France au temps des guerres de religion, 1555–1589* (Paris, 1990).

Loomba, Ania, *Colonialism/postcolonialism*, (London, 1998).

Louis, Wm Roger, foreword to *The origins of empire*, ed. Nicholas Canny, vol. I of *The Oxford history of the British empire*, ed. Wm. Roger Louis (Oxford, 1998).

McCabe, Richard, *Joseph Hall. A study in satire and meditation* (Oxford, 1982).

McCann, Franklin T., *English discovery of America to 1585* (New York, 1952).

McConica, James B., 'Humanism and Aristotle in Tudor Oxford', *English Historical Review*, 94 (1979).

Malcolm, Noel, 'Hobbes, Sandys, and the Virginia Company', *The Historical Journal*, 24 (1981).

Marshall, P. J., *'A free though conquering people': Britain and Asia in the eighteenth century*, inaugural lecture, King's College London, 5 March 1981.

Marx, Leo, *The machine in the garden: Technology and the pastoral ideal in America* (London, 1964).

Miller, Perry, *The New England mind: The seventeenth century* (New York, 1939).

Miller, Peter, *Defining the common good: Empire, religion and philosophy in eighteenth-century Britain* (Cambridge, 1994).

Montrose, Louis, 'The work of gender in the discourse of discovery', in Stephen Greenblatt, ed., *New World encounters* (Berkeley, 1993).

Morgan, Edmund S., *American slavery, American freedom* (New York, 1975).

Neill, E. D., *The English colonisation of America during the seventeenth century* (London, 1871).

Norbrook, David, 'Lucan, Thomas May, and the creation of a republican literary culture', in Kevin Sharpe and Peter Lake, eds., *Culture and politics in early Stuart England* (London, 1994).

  Writing the English republic: Poetry, rhetoric and politics, 1627–1660 (Cambridge, 1999).

O'Malley, John W., 'Content and rhetorical forms in sixteenth century preaching', in James J. Murphy, ed., *Renaissance eloquence* (Berkeley, 1983).

Ong, Walter J., *Ramus, method, and the decay of dialogue* (Cambridge, Mass., 1958).

Onuf, Peter S., 'Reflections on the founding: constitutional historiography in bicentennial perspective', *William and Mary Quarterly*, 46 (1989).

Osgood, Herbert L,. *The American colonies in the seventeenth century*, 3 vols. (first published 1904, reissued New York, 1930).

Pagden, Anthony, *The fall of natural man: The American Indian and the origins of comparative ethnology* 2nd edn, (Cambridge, 1986).

  European encounters with the New World: From Renaissance to Romanticism (New Haven, 1993).

  Lords of all the world: Ideologies of empire in Spain, Britain and France c.1500–c.1800 (New Haven, 1995).

Parker, John, *Books to build an empire* (Amsterdam, 1965).

Parks, George Bruner, *Richard Hakluyt and the English voyages* (New York, 1961).

Parry, G. J. R., 'Some early reactions to the three voyages of Martin Frobisher', *Parergon*, new ser., 6 (1988).

Patterson, Annabel, 'John Donne, kingsman?', in Linda Levy Peck, ed., *The mental world of the Jacobean court* (Cambridge, 1991).

Pearl, Valerie, *London and the outbreak of the Puritan revolution* (Oxford, 1961).

Peltonen, Markku, *Classical humanism and republicanism in English political thought, 1570–1640* (Cambridge, 1995).

Pettit, Philip, *Republicanism: A theory of freedom and government* (Oxford, 1997).

Pincus, Steven, 'Neither Machiavellian moment nor possessive individualism: commercial society and the defenders of the English Commonwealth', *American Historical Review*, June 1998.

Pocock, J. G. A., *The Machiavellian moment: Florentine political thought and the Atlantic republican tradition* (Princeton, 1975).

Virtue, commerce and history: Essays on political thought and history, chiefly in the eighteenth century (Cambridge, 1985).

'Between Gog and Magog: the republican thesis and *Ideologia Americana*', *Journal of the History of Ideas*, 48, 2 (1987).

Porter, H. C., *The inconstant savage: England and the North American Indian 1500–1660* (London, 1979).

Prouty, C. T., *George Gascoigne: Elizabethan courtier, soldier and poet* (New York, 1942).

Quinn, David B., *England and the discovery of America 1481–1620* (London, 1974).

'Renaissance influences in English colonisation', *Transactions of the Royal Historical Society*, 5th ser., 26 (1976).

'The colonial venture of Sir Thomas Smith in Ulster, 1571–1575', *The Historical Journal*, 28 (1985).

Quinn, David Beers, 'Sir Thomas Smith (1513–1517) and the beginnings of English colonial theory', *Proceedings of the American Philosophical Society*, 4 (1945).

Rabb, Theodore K., *Enterprise and empire: Merchant and gentry investment in the expansion of England, 1575–1630* (Cambridge, Mass., 1967).

Jacobean gentleman: Sir Edwin Sandys, 1561–1629 (Princeton, 1998).

Rahe, Paul A., *Republics ancient and modern*, 3 vols. (Chapel Hill, 1994, first published 1992).

Reed, A. W., *Early Tudor drama* (London, 1926).

Reid, John G., 'Sir William Alexander and North American colonisation: a reappraisal', a lecture delivered at the university of Edinburgh, published by the Centre for Canadian Studies (Edinburgh, 1990).

Reinhard, Wolfgang, ed., *Humanismus und Neue Welt* (Bonn, 1987).

Ryan, Lawrence V., 'Richard Hakluyt's voyage into Aristotle', *Sixteenth Century Journal*, 12 (1981).

Said, Edward, *Orientalism: Western conceptions of the Orient* (London, 1978).

Salmon, J. H. M., 'Seneca and Tacitus in Jacobean England', in Linda Levy Peck, ed., *The mental world of the Jacobean court* (Cambridge, 1991).

Sandel, Michael, *Democracy's discontent* (Cambridge, Mass., 1996).

Schmitt, Charles B., *John Case and Aristotelianism in Renaissance England* (Kingston, Ont., 1983).

Scott, Jonathan, *England's troubles: Seventeenth century English political instability in European context* (Cambridge, 2000).

Seed, Patricia, *Ceremonies of possession in Europe's conquest of the New World 1492–1640* (Cambridge, 1995).

Seigel, Jerold E., *Rhetoric and philosophy in Renaissance humanism* (Princeton, 1968).

Sherman, William H., *John Dee: The politics of reading and writing in the Renaissance* (Amherst, Mass., 1995).

Sherwin-White, A. N., *Racial prejudice in imperial Rome* (Cambridge, 1967).

Shuger, Debora, *Sacred rhetoric: The Christian grand style in the English Renaissance* (Princeton, 1988).

Skinner, Quentin, *The foundations of modern political thought*, 2 vols. (Cambridge, 1978).

'Political philosophy', in *The Cambridge history of renaissance philosophy*, eds. C. B. Schmitt and Quentin Skinner (Cambridge, 1988).

'The republican ideal of political liberty', in Gisela Bock, Quentin Skinner and Maurizio Viroli, eds., *Machiavelli and republicanism* (Cambridge, 1990).

'Thomas Hobbes: rhetoric and the construction of morality', in *Proceedings of the British Academy*, 76 (1991).

Reason and rhetoric in the philosophy of Hobbes (Cambridge, 1996).

Liberty before liberalism (Cambridge, 1998).

Skura, Meredith Anne, 'Discourse and the individual: the case of colonialism in *The Tempest*', *Shakespeare Quarterly*, 40, 1 (1989).

Sommerville, J. P., *Politics and ideology in England 1603–1640* (London, 1986; 2nd edn. entitled *Royalists and patriots: Politics and ideology in England 1603–1640*, London, 1999).

Stephen, Leslie, and Sidney Lee, eds., *Dictionary of national biography* (Oxford, 1917).

Struever, Nancy S., *The language of history in the Renaissance* (Princeton, 1970).

Stump, Eleonore, 'Dialectic and Aristotle's *Topics*', in *Boethius's De topicis differentiis*, ed. Eleonore Stump (Ithaca, 1978).

'Topics' in *The Cambridge history of later medieval philosophy*, eds. Norman Kretzmann, Anthony Kenny and Jan Pinborg (Cambridge, 1982).

Taylor, E. G. R., ed., *Tudor geography, 1485–1583* (London, 1930).

Taylor, Miles, 'Imperium et Libertas? Rethinking the radical critique of imperialism during the nineteenth century', *Journal of Imperial and Commonwealth History*, 19 (1991).

Thomas, Nicholas, *Entangled objects* (Cambridge, Mass., 1991).

Todorov, Tzvetan, *The conquest of America: The question of the Other*, trans. Richard Howard (New York, 1984).

Tomlins, Christopher, 'The legal cartography of colonization, the legal polyphony of settlement: English intrusions on the American mainland in the 17th century', *Law and Social Inquiry*, 26, 2 (2001).

Tuck, Richard, *Philosophy and government 1572–1651* (Cambridge, 1993).

The rights of war and peace: Political thought and the international order from Grotius to Kant (Oxford, 1999).

Tully, James, *An approach to political philosophy: Locke in contexts* (Cambridge, 1993).

'Placing the *Two Treatises*', in Nicholas Phillipson and Quentin Skinner, eds., *Political discourse in early modern Britain* (Cambridge, 1993).

Vaughan, Alden T., *American genesis: Captain John Smith and the founding of Virginia* (Boston, 1975).

'From white man to red skin: changing Anglo-American perceptions of the American Indian', *American Historical Review*, 87 (1982).

Vickers, Brian, 'Some reflections on the rhetorical textbook', in Peter Mack, ed., *Renaissance rhetoric* (London, 1994).

Vetterli, Richard, and Gary Bryner, *In search of the Republic: Public virtue and the roots of American government* (Totowa, 1987).

Viroli, Maurizio, *From politics to reason of state: The acquisition and transformation of the language of politics 1250–1600* (Cambridge, 1992).

Wallace, W. A., 'John White, Thomas Harriot and Walter Ralegh in Ireland', Durham Thomas Harriot seminar occasional papers (Durham, 1985).

White, Richard, *The middle ground: Indians, empires and republics in the Great Lakes region, 1650–1815* (Cambridge, 1991).

Williams, Robert A., *The American Indian in western legal thought: The discourses of conquest* (New York, 1990).

Wirszubski, Chaim, *Libertas as a political idea at Rome during the Late Republic and Early Principate* (Cambridge, 1950).

Wittgenstein, Ludwig, *On certainty*, tr. G. E. M. Anscombe and G. H. von Wright (Oxford, 1974).

Wood, Gordon S., *The radicalism of the American revolution* (New York, 1992).

Worden, Blair, 'English republicanism', in J. H. Burns and Mark Goldie, eds., *The Cambridge history of political thought, 1450–1700* (Cambridge, 1991).

'Ben Jonson among the historians', in Kevin Sharpe and Peter Lake, eds., *Culture and politics in early Stuart England* (Basingstoke, 1994).

'Milton and Marchamont Nedham', in David Armitage, Armand Himy and Quentin Skinner, eds., *Milton and republicanism* (Cambridge, 1995).

Wright, Louis B., *Religion and empire: The alliance between piety and commerce in English expansion, 1558–1625* (New York, 1965).

Wrightson, Keith, *English society 1580–1680* (London, 1980).

Index

IDEAS IN CONTEXT

Edited by QUENTIN SKINNER (*General Editor*),
LORRAINE DASTON, DOROTHY ROSS and JAMES TULLY